A CULTURAL HISTORY
OF THEATRE

VOLUME 3

A Cultural History of Theatre
General Editors: Christopher B. Balme and Tracy C. Davis

Volume 1
A Cultural History of Theatre in Antiquity
Edited by Martin Revermann

Volume 2
A Cultural History of Theatre in the Middle Ages
Edited by Jody Enders

Volume 3
A Cultural History of Theatre in the Early Modern Age
Edited by Robert Henke

Volume 4
A Cultural History of Theatre in the Age of Enlightenment
Edited by Mechele Leon

Volume 5
A Cultural History of Theatre in the Age of Empire
Edited by Peter W. Marx

Volume 6
A Cultural History of Theatre in the Modern Age
Edited by Kim Solga

A CULTURAL HISTORY
OF THEATRE

IN THE EARLY MODERN AGE
VOLUME 3

Edited by Robert Henke

BLOOMSBURY ACADEMIC
LONDON • NEW YORK • OXFORD • NEW DELHI • SYDNEY

BLOOMSBURY ACADEMIC
Bloomsbury Publishing Plc
50 Bedford Square, London, WC1B 3DP, UK
1385 Broadway, New York, NY 10018, USA
29 Earlsfort Terrace, Dublin 2, Ireland

BLOOMSBURY, BLOOMSBURY ACADEMIC and the Diana logo are trademarks
of Bloomsbury Publishing Plc

First published in hardback in 2017
Reprinted 2019
This paperback edition published 2022

Copyright © Robert Henke and contributors, 2017, 2022

Robert Henke has asserted his right under the Copyright, Designs and Patents Act, 1988,
to be identified as Editor of this work.

Cover image: Peeter Baltens, *Peasant Kermis* with the *'Clucht van plaijerwater'*
(Farce of the Phony-Water), ca. 1560. Rijksmuseum, Amsterdam.
Courtesy Rijksmuseum Photo Service

All rights reserved. No part of this publication may be reproduced or transmitted in
any form or by any means, electronic or mechanical, including photocopying,
recording, or any information storage or retrieval system, without prior
permission in writing from the publishers.

Bloomsbury Publishing Plc does not have any control over, or responsibility for, any
third-party websites referred to or in this book. All internet addresses given in this
book were correct at the time of going to press. The author and publisher regret any
inconvenience caused if addresses have changed or sites have ceased to exist,
but can accept no responsibility for any such changes.

A catalogue record for this book is available from the British Library.

A catalog record for this book is available from the Library of Congress.

ISBN:	HB:	978-1-4725-8574-5
	HB Set:	978-1-4725-8584-4
	PB:	978-1-3502-7769-4
	PB Set:	978-1-3502-7782-3
	ePDF:	978-1-3501-3538-3
	eBook:	978-1-3501-3537-6

Series: Cultural Histories

Typeset by RefineCatch Limited, Bungay, Suffolk
Printed and bound in Great Britain

To find out more about our authors and books visit www.bloomsbury.com
and sign up for our newsletters.

for Tom Postlewait,
maestro di color che sanno

CONTENTS

LIST OF ILLUSTRATIONS	ix
NOTES ON CONTRIBUTORS	xii
SERIES PREFACE	xv
EDITOR'S ACKNOWLEDGEMENTS	xvi

Introduction: Culture, Cultural History and Early Modern Theatre   1
Robert Henke

1   Institutional Frameworks for Theatre, 1400–1650: Mapping
Theatrical Resources   15
Tom Bishop and Robert Henke

2   Social Functions: Audience Participation, Efficacious Entertainment   35
Erika T. Lin

3   Sexuality and Gender: The Early Modern Theatrical Body   51
Eric Nicholson

4   The Environment of Theatre: Urbanization and Theatre
Building in Early Modern Europe   71
Karen Newman

5   Circulation: Aristocratic, Commercial, Religious and
Artistic Networks   93
Pavel Drábek

viii

6   Interpretations: Antitheatrical Thinking and the Rise of 'Theatre'   109
Stefan Hulfeld

7   Communities of Production: Lives In and Out of the Theatre   127
William N. West

8   Repertoire and Genres: Culture and Society   147
Friedemann Kreuder

9   Technologies of Performance: From Mystery Plays to the
Italian Order   161
Blair Hoxby

10 Knowledge Transmission: Theatre at the Crossroads of Concept,
Medium and Practice   183
Ellen MacKay

NOTES   205
BIBLIOGRAPHY   223
INDEX   245

LIST OF ILLUSTRATIONS

CHAPTER ONE

1.1	Map of theatrical resources.	18
1.2	Woodcut of Elizabethan clown Will Kemp (1560–1603), dressed as a traditional morris dancer.	19
1.3	Representation of a ballet before Henri III and his court, in the Gallery of the Louvre.	24
1.4	*Skomorokhi* in a Russian village.	26
1.5	Restored, surviving *corral* playhouse in Almagro, Spain.	29

CHAPTER TWO

2.1	Iconoclasm during the reign of Edward VI of England.	42
2.2	Venetian procession around St Mark's Square.	44
2.3	Native dancers from the Caribbean island of Hispaniola.	46
2.4	Tumblers and rope-dancers.	46

CHAPTER THREE

3.1	GianLorenzo Bernini, *The Ecstasy of St. Teresa*, 1647–52.	52
3.2	Frontispiece to *The Roaring Girle, or Moll Cut-purse*, 1611, by Thomas Middleton and Thomas Dekker.	59
3.3	Venetian courtesan with blind Cupid, *c.* 1588.	61
3.4	Venetian courtesan with 'raised skirt' (flap of paper). Engraving by Pietro Bertelli, from *Diversarum nationum habitus* (1591).	62

x

3.5 Anonymous, detail of Izumo No Okuni performing in hybrid
samurai and European costume, *c.* 1610.   68

CHAPTER FOUR

4.1 Théâtre de Tabarin, 1620s.   74
4.2 French and Italian characters from the *commedia dell'arte*
with Molière, 1670.   76
4.3 *View of an Ideal City*, attributed to Luciano Laurana, fifteenth
century.   77
4.4 Perspective view of Florence with the Palazzo Vecchio and
Brunelleschi's dome of Santa Maria del Fiore, circa 1570.   78
4.5 Tragic scene: theatrical scene design by Sebastiano Serlio,
1545.   80
4.6 Comic scene: theatrical scene design by Sebastiano Serlio,
1545.   80
4.7 Interior of Teatro Olimpico, Vicenza, Veneto, Italy.   82
4.8 Charles Hulpeau, *Le Jeu royal de la paume*, 1632.   86
4.9 Detail, Claes Jansz Visscher, view of London.   88

CHAPTER SIX

6.1 A sketch of Hans Holbein the Younger in Desiderius Erasmus'
personal copy of the 1515 edition of his *The Praise of Folly*, Basel. 112
6.2 Title page of a codex held by the Bibliothèque de l'Arsenal in
Paris as Ms. 664.   118
6.3 Frontispiece of the 'scherzo carnevalesco' entitled *Scola di
Pulcinelli*, printed in Roncilione in 1676.   123

CHAPTER SEVEN

7.1 The Seven Ages of Life. From Jean Corbichon, *Des propriétés
des choses* (1486).   129
7.2 Harlequin with a family of Harlequins. From Tristano Martinelli,
Compositions de rhétorique de Mr. Don Arlequin (1601).   132
7.3 Scene from Commedia dell'arte, *Two Ages* (second half of sixteenth
century).   134
7.4 Jan Steen, *The Rhetoricians* (*c.* 1655).   138
7.5 Hans Sachs, who identified himself as 'Shoemaker, and also
Poet', at age 80.   145

CHAPTER NINE

9.1 Hypothetical reconstruction of the *ingegni* designed by Filippo Bruneleschi for Santa Annunziata, 1439. — 162

9.2 Apparatus for a Forty Hours' Devotion at the Chiesa del Gesù on 6 April 1646, designed by Niccolò Menghini. — 163

9.3 Diagram for a performance of *The Castle of Perseverance* (*c.* 1400–25). — 166

9.4 Baldassare Peruzzi. Theatrical perspective with the symbolic monuments of Rome, A291. — 167

9.5 Hypothetical reconstruction of the stage with sun machine erected in the courtyard of the Palazzo Medici in Florence in 1539. — 169

9.6 Scheme of *periaktoi* in Joseph Furtenbach's *Architectura recreationis* (1640). — 171

9.7 Scene featuring an entrance upon clouds. San Salvatore, Venice, 1670s. — 174

9.8 The machinery behind the entrance upon clouds shown in Figure 9.7. — 175

9.9 Jean Berain, design for the appearance of demons among flames. — 176

9.10 Jean Berain, finale of Philippe Quinault and Jean-Baptiste Lully's *tragédie en musique Armide*, 1686. — 177

9.11 Farnese Theatre of the National Gallery in the Pilotta Palace, originally designed by Giovanni Battista Aleotti for Runuccio I Farnese, Duke of Parma, in 1618 and inaugurated in 1628. — 180

CHAPTER TEN

10.1 Gros Guillaume, street performer of the Pont Neuf and actor in the *Troupe Royale*. — 185

10.2 Turlupin, street performer of the Pont Neuf and actor in the *Troupe Royale*. — 186

10.3 Gautier Garguille, street performer of the Pont Neuf and actor in the *Troupe Royale*. — 187

10.4 A velvet chopine designed to elevate and encumber a woman of quality or means. — 191

10.5 A page from Edward Alleyn's part of Orlando in Robert Greene's play *Orlando Furioso* (approximately 1591). — 193

10.6 Benedictine monks toppling an idol in Haiti during Columbus's second voyage. From *Nova Typis Transacta Navigatio* [*A New Account of the Navigation*] by Caspar Plautius, writing pseudonymously as Honorio Philopono, engravings by Wolfgang Kilian, 1621. — 200

NOTES ON CONTRIBUTORS

Tom Bishop is Professor and Head of English at the University of Auckland, New Zealand. He is the author of *Shakespeare and the Theatre of Wonder* (1996), the translator of Ovid's *Amores* (2003), editor of Shakespeare's *Pericles, Prince of Tyre* for the Internet Shakespeare, and a general editor of *The Shakespearean International Yearbook*. He has published articles on Elizabethan music, Shakespeare, Jonson, Australian literature and other topics, and is currently writing a book on Shakespeare's Theatre Games.

Pavel Drábek is Professor of Drama and Theatre Practice at the University of Hull. His research interests are in Shakespeare, early modern European theatre, drama translation, and theatre theory. He has published on translations of Shakespeare in *České pokusy o Shakespeara* (translated as *Czech Attempts at Shakespeare*, 2012), on John Fletcher (*Fletcherian Dramatic Achievement: The Mature Plays of John Fletcher*, 2010), on seventeenth-century English comedy in Germany, on early modern puppet theatre, and on theatre structuralism (collaborating with the StruG Project, Masaryk University). He is an opera librettist, playwright and translator. From 2003 to 2015 he was Artistic Director of the Ensemble Opera Diversa, a professional music and modern opera company based in Brno, Czech Republic.

Robert Henke is Professor of Drama and Comparative Literature at Washington University in St. Louis. He is the author of *Pastoral Transformations: Italian Tragicomedy and Shakespeare's Late Plays* (1997), *Performance and Literature in the Commedia dell'Arte* (2002), and *Poverty and Charity in Early Modern Theater and Performance* (2015). With Eric Nicholson, he has co-edited two essay collections produced by the Theater Without Borders research group: *Transnational Exchange in Early Modern Theater* (2008) and *Transnational*

Mobilities in Early Modern Theater (2014). He is now writing a book on Shakespeare and Italian early modern theatre. Since 2014, he has been the Co-director of the Washington University Prison Education Project.

Blair Hoxby is Professor of English at Stanford University. His most recent publications are *What Was Tragedy? Theory and the Early Modern Canon* (2015), honourable mention for the Renaissance Society of America's Phyllis Goodhart Gordon Book Prize and, as co-editor, *Milton in the Long Restoration* (2016). He is currently writing a monograph on allegorical drama and editing three collections: *Darkness Visible: Tragedy in the Enlightenment*; *Trans-Atlantic Tragedy: Theatre, Enlightenment, and Revolution*; and *Opera and Tragedy: From Absolutism to Enlightenment*. He has published essays on tragedy, opera, allegorical drama, Jesuit school theater, early modern acting, and the writings of Milton and Dryden.

Stefan Hulfeld is Professor of Theatre Studies at the University of Vienna. He was born and educated in Switzerland, graduating in Theatre Studies and German Literature from the University of Berne in 1996. His doctoral thesis in the field of eighteenth-century theatre history, entitled *Zähmung der Masken, Wahrung der Gesichter*, was published in 2000. His second book, *Theatergeschichtsschreibung als kulturelle Praxis*, published in 2007, is a study in theatre historiography from the sixteenth to the twentieth century. Further publications include the chapter 'Modernist Theatre' in the *Cambridge Companion to Theatre History* (edited by David Wiles and Christine Dymkowski in 2013) and an edition of the 'Scenari Corsiniani', published in 2014 under the title *Scenari più scelti d'istrioni*.

Friedemann Kreuder is Professor for Theatre Studies at the Johannes Gutenberg University Mainz. He has published books about the theatre of the German director Klaus Michael Grüber (*Formen des Erinnerns im Theater Klaus Michael Grübers*, 2002) and the bourgeois theatre of the eighteenth century (*Spielräume der Identität in Theaterformen des 18. Jahrhunderts*, Tübingen 2010), and articles about the theatre of Richard Wagner and medieval passion plays. He is currently running a research project on 'Theatre between reproduction and transgression of body-based distinction'.

Erika T. Lin is an Associate Professor in the PhD Program in Theatre at The Graduate Center, The City University of New York. She is the author of *Shakespeare and the Materiality of Performance*, which won the 2013 David Bevington Award for Best New Book in Early Drama Studies. Her essays have appeared in *Theatre Journal*, *New Theatre Quarterly*, and various edited collections. She is currently writing a book on seasonal festivities and early modern commercial theatre, a project supported by an Andrew W. Mellon Long-Term Fellowship at the Folger Shakespeare Library.

Ellen MacKay is Associate Professor of English at the University of Chicago. She was director of the Institute for Digital Arts and Humanities at Indiana University. She is the author of *Persecution, Plague and Fire: Fugitive Histories of the Stage in Early Modern England* (2011), and numerous chapters and articles on theatre history and the things that imperfectly preserve it, including forgeries, tchotchkes, and heritage environments. She is currently completing a study of the audience as a crypto-equatic collectivity in early modern England.

Karen Newman is Owen Walker '33 Professor of Humanities and Professor of Comparative Literature and English at Brown University. She has written widely on early modern English and continental letters and culture and on Shakespeare and Renaissance drama. Her books include *Fashioning Femininity and English Renaissance Drama* (1991); *Fetal Positions: Individualism, Science, Visuality* (1997); *Cultural Capitals: Early Modern London and Paris* (2007) and *Essaying Shakespeare* (2009). Recent collections include *Early Modern Cultures of Translation,* co-edited with Jane Tylus (2015), and *This Distracted Globe: Worldmaking in Early Modern Literature,* edited with Jonathan Goldberg and Marcie Frank (2016). She is currently working on early modern translation and on the reception of Shakespeare in Europe.

Eric Nicholson teaches at New York University, Florence, and at Syracuse University in Florence. He is also an active member of the international research group 'Theater Without Borders'. Focusing on sexuality, gender, and female theatrical performers, he has published widely in the field of early modern theatre studies. With Robert Henke, he has edited the volumes *Transnational Exchange in Early Modern Theater* (2008), and *Transnational Mobilities in Early Modern Theater* (2014). At NYU and elsewhere, he has directed full-scale productions of plays by Shakespeare, Molière, Pirandello and others. A professional actor and voice artist, he has appeared several times on stage in Italy, and has worked on several audio guides and animated cartoons.

William N. West is Associate Professor of English, Classics, and Comparative Literary Studies at Northwestern University. He has written *Theatres and Encyclopedias in Early Modern Europe* (2002) and *As If: Essays in As You Like It* (2016). He edits the journal *Renaissance Drama* (with Jeffrey Masten) and has also edited (with Helen Higbee) Robert Weimann's *Author's Pen and Actor's Voice: Writing and Playing in Shakespeare's Theatre* (2000) and (with Bryan Reynolds) *Rematerializing Shakespeare: Authority and Representation on the Early Modern Stage* (2005). He has recently published articles on playing in and out of context; baitings, dances, and contests in playhouses; *Romeo and Juliet*'s understudies, and Ophelia's intertheatricality (with Gina Bloom and Anston Bosman). His current work focuses on understanding and confusion in the Elizabethan playhouses.

SERIES PREFACE

A Cultural History of Theatre is a six-volume series examining a cultural practice that emerged in antiquity and today encompasses practically the whole globe. Theatre is generally acknowledged to be the most social of artistic practices, requiring collectives to both produce and consume it. Theatrical performance's ability to organize and cohere markers of cultural belonging, difference, and dissonance are the hallmarks of social life. Its production and reception have, however, altered significantly over the past two and a half thousand years. Despite these changes the same chapter headings structure all six volumes: institutional frameworks, social functions, sexuality and gender, environment, circulation, interpretations, communities of production, repertoire and genres, technologies of performance and knowledge transmission. These headings represent significant cultural approaches as opposed to purely regional, national, aesthetic or generic categories. This allows for comparative readings of key cultural questions affecting theatre both diachronically and synchronically. The six volumes divide the history of theatre as follows:

Volume 1: A Cultural History of Theatre in Antiquity (500 BC–1000 AD)
Volume 2: A Cultural History of Theatre in the Middle Ages (1000–1400)
Volume 3: A Cultural History of Theatre in the Early Modern Age
    (1400–1650)
Volume 4: A Cultural History of Theatre in the Age of Enlightenment
    (1650–1800)
Volume 5: A Cultural History of Theatre in the Age of Empire (1800–1920)
Volume 6: A Cultural History of Theatre in the Modern Age (1920–2000+)

Christopher B. Balme and Tracy C. Davis, General Editors

EDITOR'S ACKNOWLEDGEMENTS

If cultural history accords particular importance to the social production of knowledge, this book is the result of many people thinking together. Thanks to Mark Dudgeon at Bloomsbury for a large-scale vision that did not preclude attention to the smallest details, and to Emily Hockley and Susan Furber for their quick assistance with logistical and technical issues, especially regarding images. Tracy Davis and Chris Balme were magisterial general editors, providing the volume editors with a thoughtful and sensible chapter grid, reading each and every one of the abstracts and draft chapters and offering acute and supportive comments, and helpful advice and encouragement at each stage of the process. Thanks to my fellow editor Jody Enders for moral support and good humor. Corinne Zeman provided expert and timely help in getting the typescript put together in its final stages, and gave me some much-needed advice with some technical issues.

Most of the contributors to this volume are part of the Theater Without Borders research group, to which thanks is generally owed even to group members who did not contribute to this volume. For permissions and production of images, I wish to thank Getty Images, ArtResource, the Bibliothèque Nationale de France, the British Museum, Dulwich College, the Bata Shoe Museum in Toronto, the Folger Shakespeare Library, the Basil Kunstmuseum, the Biblioteca Casanatense in Rome, the Rijksmuseum in Amsterdam, the Metropolitan Museum of Art, the Kyoto National Museum, the Gabinetto Fotografico delle Gallerie degli Uffizi, Paola Ventrone, the Città Metropolitana di Firenze, Houghton Library at Harvard University, The Lilly Library at Indiana University and the Centre Historique des Archives Nationales in Paris. I would like to thank my superb group of authors for their hard work, conscientiousness, patience, brilliance, good communication and forbearance with my many emails. Finally, I would like to thank my wife Suzanne Loui for her enthusiasm, intellectual companionship and support throughout this project, and our children Gwyneth, Marina and Nick.

Introduction

Culture, Cultural History and Early Modern Theatre

ROBERT HENKE

Early modern theatre provides particularly fruitful arenas of inquiry for a cultural history of the theatre. The socio-economically heterodox nature of theatre and performance between 1400 and 1650 causes us to interrogate the complex concept of 'culture' in both its wide, Gramscian meaning of the ordinary, everyday process of finding shared meaning and values[1] and the alternative meaning of the creative work of discovery in artistic and intellectual endeavours.[2] Despite the fact that studies devoted to the early modern period have crucially shaped the field of cultural history from the nineteenth century to the present, from Burckhardt's sweeping study of Renaissance Italy[3] to Carlo Ginzburg's microhistory of a sixteenth-century miller,[4] theatre histories of the early modern period have generally been slow to incorporate the insights of cultural history.[5] It is true that studies of early modern theatre associated with new historicism have amply drawn from cultural history and the general 'anthropological turn' in studies of culture, but the work of such scholars as Stephen Greenblatt, Steven Mullaney, Louis Montrose and others has mostly focused on English early modern theatre. To be sure, our understanding of the transvestite boy actor in England has been completely transformed by new historicism and cultural historical studies of sexuality and gender. But any serious inquiry into the ten cultural questions framing the chapters of this and the other five volumes of *A Cultural History of Theatre* must be transnational. As Eric Nicholson does in Chapter 3, the English boy actor should be studied alongside one of the great theatrical events of the day, the emergence of international *commedia dell'arte* diva-actresses such as Isabella Andreini, and the vexed but productive actresses in Spain and France. Transnational theatre history must examine both social and cultural phenomena that do not respect borders, such as the spike in poverty and the massive changes wrought by the printing press, even as it contrasts crucial differences between theatres of various geo-linguistic areas: both those of emerging nations (England, Spain, France) and those of pre-national regions such as Italy and Germany. As Stefan Hulfeld demonstrates in his chapter on 'Ideology' in the present volume and as the Paris-based research group La Haine du Théâtre[6] has been demonstrating, attacks and defences on the theatre ran in remarkably parallel directions across early modern Europe: parallels all the more interesting for emphasizing differences as well. What we offer in these pages is a *transnational* cultural analysis of early modern European theatre through the cultural prisms of institutional frameworks, social functions, sexuality and gender, the environment of theatre, circulation, ideology, communities of production, genres and repertoires, technology, and knowledge transmission.

In examining the quintessentially *social* cultural production and consumption of the 'art' of theatre, we find particularly useful the approach of the British Marxist critic Raymond Williams. Williams' emphasis on the social dimension of 'culture' and the concept's capacity to embrace both creative works of art and ordinary ways of viewing and experiencing the world provides a particularly fruitful approach to early modern theatre and performance.[7] As Robert Henke and Tom Bishop show in their discussion of 'Institutional Frameworks', early modern theatre combined the elite culture of humanism, the academy, and the court with the ordinary culture of piazza performance, seasonal ritual, and public performance: it included the piazza mountebank and the royal entry, the paratheatrical and the theatrical. As a 'cultural materialist', Williams firmly grounds his concept of culture in tangible material and social life. At the same time, in his view, culture is not simplistically determined by economic substructure, but is the product of free human agency and creativity: a freedom that occurs on the social as well as individual level.[8]

As an alternative to the deterministically connoted term 'ideology', Williams prefers 'structures of feeling' in order to account for the process-oriented, dynamic, changing, and flexible nature of social postures and practices.[9] He ascribes particular importance to 'residual' and 'emergent' attitudes, beliefs, tonalities that complicate 'dominant' societal attitudes and postures – particularly important for examining phenomena, as we will do in this volume, of *longue durée*.[10] Theatre between 1400 and 1650 absorbed, questioned, complicated, and anticipated residual, dominant and emergent social structures of feeling. It could be residually neo-feudal even as bourgeois, capitalist forms and attitudes emerged. Strong absolutist patronage did not prevent the rebellious Earl of Leicester from enlisting the Lord Chamberlain's Men to stage Shakespeare's *Richard II*, including the deposition scene. Ideological supporters of draconian

INTRODUCTION

new poor laws designed to discipline the poor could momentarily feel and imagine, in the two hours' traffic of the stage, that they perhaps had 'ta'en too little care' of the ravages of economic inequality. In the fractious post-Reformation era, theatre could complicate and challenge ostensible confessional loyalties, as residually Catholic ideas – such as the domain of purgatory – could be evoked in image and feeling. Early modern theatre represented both dominant ideologies and the 'hints and half-guesses' of the vestigial past and the anticipatory future. As Henke and Bishop demonstrate in Chapter 1 and Karen Newman in Chapter 4, the institutional frameworks and playing spaces of theatre itself in the early modern period were characterized both by innovation and *longue durée*: the age saw both the emergence of purpose-built theatres across Europe, as Newman shows, and the dogged persistence of religious drama and its urban, processional staging. Certainly what counted as legitimate knowledge of the theatre worthy of being passed on from one generation to the next was sharply contested so that vestigial and dominant could even become relative terms, as Ellen MacKay demonstrates in her discussion of the *Querelle du Cid* and other topics in Chapter 10.

Williams' social approach parallels the work of *Annales*-based French cultural history that emphasizes collective 'mentalities' or discourses in periods of history. Just as anthropologists ask in their objects of study, a history of *mentalités* examines the collective comportments, sensibilities, imaginations, gestures, beliefs and habits of mind that produce symbolic webs of meaning for the culture that both creates and consumes them.[11] In considering how theatre was perceived, conceived and used in the period, a cultural history of the theatre can consider the 'mental equipment' ('*l'outillage mental*', in Lucien Febvre's words[12]) that filtered theatrical and performance-conceived experience and discourse. How were ideas, absorbed through theatre and performance, 'good to think with' for the people of the time? Ideas of the 'scene', the 'player', the 'tragic and 'comic', etc. pervade the cultural imagination of the period, and not just among the elite: the world as a stage, theatrical self-fashioning, the existential ramifications of fertility-generating comedy and death-terminating tragedy, the ethical and even ontological questions posed by fictional representation that were addressed by both antitheatricalists and defenders of the theatre. In a theatrical period that witnessed the first professional actress in Italy, the emergence of the transvestite boy player as a powerful cultural force, and the intermittent licensing and prohibition of female players in Spain, changing ideas about gender and sexual personae were crucially mediated on the stage. (See Nicholson in Chapter 3.) Early modern theatre and performance interrogated culture as much as they reflected it. Just as Erika Lin in Chapter 2 explores the ways that early modern theatre spectators felt and thought, and William West in Chapter 7 explores what it meant to produce theatre at different stages in one's life, we may generally ask what did early modern theatre mean – and *how* did it mean – for the people who both consumed and produced it.

If the ancient and medieval volumes in this series have certainly shown how irrevocably social the production and consumption of theatre was in the period preceding ours, our temporal purview will see new social conditions and economic means of production coming to bear. The age generated new urban, early-capitalistic modes of production and organization that made sustained, organized professional theatre possible for the first time in Western history. Italy was both the birthplace of Western capitalism and the crucible of the professional actor (even as the early modern professional actor, across Europe, oddly straddled neo-feudal and proto-capitalist modes). Architects, entrepreneurs and actors created new kinds of purpose-built playing spaces, some of which accommodated distinctly mixed-class audiences (the English amphitheatres, the Spanish *corrales*). At the same time, the sixteenth century witnessed both the birth of the national state and new absolutist ideologies spanning both states and petty duchies. For the first time we can talk about the 'drama of a nation' in England and Spain.[13] The social conditions of theatre were being reconceived and reworked at the bottom, middle and top. The dominant socio-economic crisis of the period – the sharp spike in poverty and territorial displacement – generated the very ordinary and thoroughly social performance posture of the early modern beggar: a performance that could take place anywhere and any time.[14]

Producers and consumers of theatre in the early modern period viewed art as social, not individual production. No nineteenth-century notion of the 'aesthetic' as a distinct sphere governed the 'artistic' productions of our period: the works wrought by early modern playwrights, actors, set designers, theatre architects, costume-makers, accessory fabricators (many of whom were female)[15], theatre musicians, and piazza/street performers, and even the new entrepreneurs like Philip Henslowe, were no more considered immaterial objects of aesthetic production (a product reserved for the 'inner life of man') than the gold-work issuing from Benvenuto Cellini's workshop.[16] The great *commedia dell'arte* actor-writer Pier Maria Cecchini, who wrote the first extended actor's handbook in Western theatre history, advocated that the new professional Italian troupes be socially and economically modelled after the venerable Florentine 'Arti' or craft-guilds.[17]

Despite the looming presence of Shakespeare, who is still difficult to disentangle from the myth of the solitary Bard, early modern playwriting was a *social* process: over half the plays written in the Elizabethan–Jacobean era were the product of at least two hands, and the on-stage 'compositions' (as they were called) of the improvising *commedia dell'arte* troupes were obviously social products of art. (Shakespeare surely was a social writer himself, co-writing several plays and conceiving plots, dialogue, scene and speech with his fellow

INTRODUCTION

actors in mind.) As Friedemann Kreuder demonstrates in his discussion of 'Repertoire and Genres' in Chapter 8, the forms and repertoires of early modern theatre were thoroughly social and collaborative, whether performed from script or scenario. Any significant history of early modern theatre will have to illuminate the 'constitutive social processes' (Williams) that created and sustained 'Renaissance theatre': an example of mass theatrical culture even surpassing in scale and cultural influence the popular, urban Corpus Christi cycles (in fact, the greater part of this 'late medieval' phenomenon took place within the historical parameters of our period rather than the previous one, and emerged from similar urban developments that would in turn make the theatres of Hamlet and Arlecchino possible). In short, the present study cannot be a history of great individuals (Shakespeare, Lope de Vega, Corneille) or great theatrical events (the construction of James Burbage's The Theatre in 1576) but must primarily dwell on social, collective practices of mostly *longue durée*: residual, dominant, and emergent.

If we are taking the social realm seriously, we must extend our purview to the kinds of plays and performances produced by those of modest or low means and destined for those ranging from the middling to the destitute. In this respect, the actor-based Italian professional theatre, which emerged adjacent to the piazza mountebank and despite some notable court success never became completely divorced from this figure, provides just as important a model as the theatres of Shakespeare and Lope. During our period, European cities were flooded with new immigrants, whether forced by changes and pressures in agricultural economies or drawn by new opportunities, and the burgeoning early modern city became a site of continual performance: beggars performing their destitution, mountebanks, ballad singer-sellers, hand-to-mouth performers of infinite variety, mongers of cheap print, merchandise hawkers, street criers, prostitutes on display, prostitutes publicly shamed by carting rituals, public executions, Lord Mayor's shows, royal entries and progressions, and much, much more. As Clifford Geertz asked of a Balinese cock fight[18] and Robert Darnton of an eighteenth-century cat massacre,[19] we need to ask what strange public performances that are opaque to us today (e.g., bear baitings) meant to those experiencing, thinking, and feeling them at the time.

Any theatre history that hopes to consider what theatrical performance meant to the mass of actual people of the time must also consider the sustained importance, in the post-Reformation age, of religious theatre, which continued unabated despite the triumphs of Shakespeare's and Lope's predominantly secular theatres. Considered transnationally, Corpus Christi cycles and Passion plays flourish more in our historical period than in that of the previous volume. The Spanish *auto sacramental* does not gain sustained institutional traction until the early sixteenth century. The fulminous anti-theatricality of English puritans tends to obscure from our view the fact that continental religious reformers, including Melanthon and even Luther, were no enemies of theatre, which was quickly engaged for ideological purposes. Positively dwarfing the international influence of Shakespeare within our temporal confines was the 1539 neo-Latin play *Hecastus* by the Dutch Humanist Macropedius. This Everyman-type play that was late-medieval in theme but classical in structure was translated into German, Danish, and Swedish, and performed in Nurnberg, Konigsberg, Basel, Prague, Danzig, Nordlingen and Munich between 1549 and 1609 – *Weltliteratur* for the day, and largely because of its religious appeal.[20] Shakespeare was barely known outside of England.

On the other hand, the early modern period poses interesting complexities that tilt us back to a notion of culture that includes the products of 'art and intellect'. In their attack on what they perceived as the narrowness of scholastic inquiry, humanists such as Petrarch and Erasmus elevated the importance of ancient literary works relative to the scholastic domains of logic, theology, and metaphysical philosophy. If perhaps below epic in the hierarchy of genres, the dialogic and social nature of drama generally appealed in humanist circles promoting the conversational style and the capacity, whether in speech or writing, to mix stylistic registers. Erasmus championed Terence to what seems to us today an inordinate degree – he argued that Terence was good to think with, as well as to write with and to talk with – and devoted much time and attention to translating Euripides into Latin. The prestige and influence (radiating from Italy) of Horace's *Ars Poetica* and Aristotle's *Poetics* placed the classical genres of tragedy and comedy front-and-centre in the new field of literary theory. The dazzling innovations in technology and architecture discussed by Blair Hoxby in Chapter 9 were largely avant-garde, humanist inventions: only a transnational approach such as the one Hoxby takes can demonstrate both Italy's importance as an innovatory source and the transmission of Italian ideas across geo-linguistic boundaries. Drama acquired a pride of place in the avant-garde Italian literary theory of the 1540s and afterwards that is difficult to imagine in the era of post-structuralism, which has rarely chosen drama for its representative theoretical cases. Theatre could lead the way, from a humanist perspective, in restoring the lustre of classical civilization that had allegedly been so obscured by medieval ignorance. The terms 'tragedy' and 'comedy', with added value from their classical origins lent them by humanist elites, joined the classical term 'theatre', which had garnered added sheen from Poggio Bracciolini's 1414 rediscovery of Vitruvius' *De architectura* in a Swiss monastery and the ensuing humanist dissemination of Vitruvian ideas about 'theatre' as an architectural structure rather than a place of playing. James Burbage's 1576 christening of his new, purpose-built theatrical structure in the Shoreditch district of London as 'The Theatre' was meant to confer elite cultural value. Contemporaries lauded 'Marlowe's mighty line' and his heroic overreachers for finally restoring, after two millennia, the tragic buskin to the stage. When Ben Jonson and John Webster complain

INTRODUCTION

of the ignorant 'understanders' and garlic-reeking ignoramuses that couldn't understand their lofty, classically formed works of 'comedy' and 'tragedy', they are asserting, in the humanist tradition, normative ideals of cultural value and hierarchy. They are also implying, in the humanist project launched by Petrarch, that after the dark chasm of the 'middle ages' they are advancing something like 'civilization' and 'culture' (although these are later terms) by disinterring and restoring the glories of the ancient past. For, like Petrarch, humanist playwrights and stage 'composers' (the improvising Italian actors were steeped in the humanist tradition as well) identified themselves with a particular moment in history. They passionately believed that they were doing something new, and this awareness constituted a genuine historical shift even by itself. The cultural and historiographical self-consciousness of the university wits, Du Bellay and other Pleiade theorists as they resurrected ancient dramatic ideas, the apologists for the *commedia dell'arte* actor (and actress) who deemed him (her) the new Roscius of the day – all of these beliefs and postures were meant to mark a moment of historical difference.

Especially in the realm of theatre, humanism helped foster across Europe a common, transnational language – and one that reached beyond the elite circles to which humanist literature was normally confined. Just as humanism reached a relatively wider socio-economic ambit (though not without its exclusions) through the school manuals and literary texts disseminated through the printing press, humanist ideas about theatre could move from elite discussions between Italian and German scholars about comic theory to the production of classical comedies to audiences that could include the middle class. Humanism rendered late-fifteenth-century German dramatic theorists comprehensible to Dutch university professors interested in both understanding drama and staging classical plays, and those plays were not only performed before academic audiences. In the early humanist period of the fifteenth century (the beginning of our historical purview), exciting rediscoveries were made of Plautine, Terentian, and Vitruvian texts, and the still common vehicle of Latin enabled the development of a transnational cultural language of theatre that moved from humanist elite to groundlings at London amphitheatres, Spanish *corrales*, and the French *parterre*.

Moreover, despite the predictable presence of idealist conservatives such as Giason Denores, who argued that the forms of tragedy, comedy, and pastoral were as inviolable and unchanging as Platonic forms, many humanists interested in theatre – such as Denores' antagonist Battista Guarini in the debate over the non-classical form of tragicomedy – approached dramatic forms as Vico viewed history itself: something made by humans beings for other human beings, and historically conditioned. For Guarini, the generic concepts of tragedy and comedy were not fixed forms but plastic materials, like the stuff of a painter's palette, matter to be mixed, combined, rearranged, deconstructed in the process of composition and reception.[21] Polonius's 'tragical-comical-historical-pastoral' bespeaks the same early modern penchant, whether practised by the dramatist in a script or the improvising actor from a scenario, of playing with genre, and theatrical matter in general. Although the elite courtier-academician-professor Guarini wanted to safeguard this combinatory process from the rabble, his essentially social and cultural view of theatre and dramatic genre irrevocably let the cat out of the bag, just as his Platonic opponent Denores feared: no one better executed his theory that dramatic genre and theatrical language (as with any other kind of cultural language) was something shaped by human beings for other human beings than the professional actors whom he despised: the actor-composers of the *commedia dell'arte*. What Guarini theorized and the *commedia dell'arte* performed was very like what Bakhtin discussed in his Rabelais book for a much wider socio-economic swath than that viewed from Guarini's academy:[22] not the *langue* of an disinterested, asocial system but the *parole* of active, social beings crowded together in the marketplace: the dialogic speech-genres[23] that animate the pages of Rabelais, the fifteenth-century farces that he loved, and the popular culture of carnival, charivari, and the Renaissance fair. As a social and historical creation, the language of early modern theatre – the webs of symbolic meaning spun from the material of theatrical production – may be seen as a 'system' but one that was fluid, changing, diachronic and flexible. It was when humanist theatrical ideas found deep socio-economic soil – when the new, otherwise 'elite' ideas could be fused with popular, oral life, as in the case of the *commedia dell'arte* and the theatres of Shakespeare and Lope – that early modern theatre became a powerful and socially consequent cultural phenomenon. Don Quixote found Sancho Panza.

* * *

The field of cultural history has been closely intertwined with Renaissance and early modern studies. Furthermore, debates about culture and the nature of cultural historiography have significant implications for the cultural analysis of early modern theatre and performance. Williams has shown how the concept of 'civilization' emerged in the eighteenth century to mean an 'achieved state' contrasted with 'barbarism' but also extended to signify a rational, achieved state of development implying 'historical process and progress'.[24] Insofar as such an 'achieved state' in the eighteenth and nineteenth centuries quickly became associated with the urban civilizations of England and France, and external qualities such as those of politeness and luxury, the term unsurprisingly encountered resistance, whether from Rousseauian quarters on the basis of a perceived 'natural' ethic or from Marxist ranks by virtue of politico-economic analysis. In the nineteenth century, the notion of 'culture' emerged in

INTRODUCTION

counterpoint to 'civilization', designating an 'inner' or 'spiritual' as opposed to 'external' development. In contrast to the 'externalities' of 'civilization', 'culture' came to encompass religion, art, and even the family and personal life, referring to the domain of the 'inner life': individuality, subjectivity, and generating certain 'quasi-metaphysical forms' such as 'the imagination', 'creativity', 'inspiration' and the 'aesthetic'.[25] The problem, of course, was that the domains of art, intellectual life, and religion were fundamentally social, not individual. For Williams, although he stresses that the implications of Marx for cultural history have been insufficiently realized, Marx provided a salutary corrective to the over-subjectivization of 'culture', restoring the sense, fundamental and already present in Vico, that culture as well as history is that which human beings make.

One of the founding figures of cultural history, or *Kulturgeschichte*, as an alternative to political history (which sometimes carried with it an implied celebration of the State) was Jacob Burckhardt, whose *The Civilization of the Renaissance in Italy* (1860) remains required reading today for early modern scholars. In Burckhardt's very title, the original 'Kultur' (*Die Kultur der Renaissance in Italien*) that was translated into 'civilization' may be seen to reflect the paradoxes Williams discusses. And this raises the perennial historiographical question of whether early modern culture – and early modern theatre and performance by extension – should be seen as a teleological, and more-or-less linear advance. (In the domain of theatre studies, the teleological view should be considered as more than easily dismissible, for it is still tempting and in fact not completely erroneous for historians to tell the story of ragtag piazza culture culminating in the splendid troupes of the Italian *commedia dell'arte*, itinerant household players reaching the rationalized prosperity of the Lord Chamberlain's men, and Lope de Rueda's theatre-from-a-trunk giving way to Lope de Vega.) Certainly Burckhardt, like the Renaissance humanists themselves, saw major cultural advances in the achievements of the Renaissance in the realm of painting, architecture, and literature, while his political analysis of Renaissance despots was less sanguine. Even in regard to 'culture', Burckhardt retained some ambivalence, particularly when considering the individualism that he, famously, regarded as the kernel of cultural development in the age. And in his later *Reflections on History*,[26] he explicitly rejected Hegelian progressivism or any other variant of 'philosophy of history'.

If Burckhardt himself was ambivalent about 'Renaissance culture', the field of early modern theatre studies has always negotiated, on the one hand, the optimism and sense of teleological completion implicit in the term 'Renaissance Drama' and, on the other hand, the sober resonance in theatrical representation of the incipient slavery, patriarchy, suppressive absolutism, early colonialism and nationalist-abetted racism of the age. In his early work on the self-fashioning of the individual, Stephen Greenblatt can be said to follow both Burckhardt's positive and negative assessments of Renaissance individuality; and studies of race, colonialism, gender and absolutism in early modern theatre have severely checked both optimism and teleology.

An approach to cultural studies that tended to emphasize continuity rather than change, associated with the French *Annales* school, was the study of 'mentalities'. Many *Annales*-based works were devoted to the medieval and early modern period.[27] Consonant with Foucault's later articulation of the 'episteme' – a system of discourse with implicit rules about what can and cannot be spoken – *Annales* cultural historians such as the medievalist Marc Bloch and the early modern scholar Lucien Febvre studied patterns of thought and discourse of *longue durée*. Works like Febvre's on the persistence of religious belief in the century of François Rabelais tended to complicate teleology by identifying long-view patterns of thought and practice of ordinary as well as elite people.[28] Drawing from the approaches of anthropology and psychology, Febvre introduced the metaphor of the 'mental toolbox' (*outillage mental*), investigating the mental habits, frames of perception, conceptual horizons, vocabularies and grammars of a given age.[29] The study of mentalities could consider myths, beliefs and symbols, but unlike the disembodied and short-lived 'history of ideas' approach of Arthur Lovejoy[30] (and congruent with Raymond Williams' cultural materialism) it did not divorce ideas from the material conditions that shaped them: an approach that bodes well for early modern theatre. Like Robert Darnton in his study of the mirth produced by killing cats by eighteenth-century French apprentices, many *mentalité* scholars tend not to begin with familiar but with weird, uncanny events, beliefs and practices, using them as cruxes to discover something new and important about the given culture, seen not as universal and transparent but as strange and alien.[31] In this vein (whether or not explicitly influenced by the *mentalité* approach) can be seen several studies of the strange practice of the boy actor in English professional theatre, most notably Stephen Orgel's *Impersonations*, which begins with the question 'Why did the English take boys for women?'[32] Also emanating from the *Annales* school was the rigorous, materially based grand opus of Fernand Braudel, which examines collective structures of economic life centred on market and exchange.[33] Although interested in phenomena – but in his case practices rather than ideas – of *longue durée*, Braudel extends both the temporal and geographic span of the 'early modern' in ways that the authors of this volume have found fruitful. For those scholars of early modern theatre (like the present authors) wishing to go beyond national boundaries, Braudel's big-picture, structural analysis of Mediterranean material culture (and other similar studies that have followed in Braudel's wake) have been relatively untapped, but could prove enormously useful in the future, especially as enhanced by big data digital analysis. Braudel's analysis of roads, sea routes, river passages, and canal networks linking the 'Mediterranean

INTRODUCTION

world' provides the kind of material substructure without which a comprehensive study of English, Italian, German, Spanish, French, Danish, Dutch, and Czech travelling actors (not isolated by the geo-linguistic region usually corresponding to the origin of the scholar herself, but informed by a pan-European picture) would be impossible. If early modern theatre can be seen as a flexible and active system of transnational exchanges, Braudel's work on the material and social transactions of early modern Mediterranean commerce can illuminate the *conditions* of early modern theatrical production: not as a crudely 'Marxist' substructure rigidly dictating cultural production, but in Williams' sense (derived from a close reading of Marx's original German text) of 'determination' as the 'setting of limits and parameters'.[34]

Of central concern in cultural history, and a major topic in works of cultural history directed to the early modern period, has been the serious investigation of popular culture implicit in Williams' social understanding of 'culture', whether its relationship to learned, print culture is stressed or whether its relative independence is explored. Bakhtin's study of Rabelais, mentioned above, in which the learned culture of the Erasmian Rabelais may not be sufficiently emphasized, still holds fruitful possibilities for early modern theatre studies, especially when we consider how close Rabelais himself was to the paratheatrical world of farce. No figure has been more important in this domain than Peter Burke, who has also provided significant methodological reflections on the field of cultural history itself.[35] Burke's examinations, in *Popular Culture in Early Modern Europe*,[36] of the linguistic cant of rogues and the talismanic function of written fragments in a still-largely oral culture relate closely to the dynamics of early modern performance, if not organized theatre as well.

Probably the greatest impact of cultural history on early modern theatre studies has come through the work of new historicism, which was distinctly influenced by both anthropology and the discourse analysis of Michel Foucault. Thirty years ago, new historicism fruitfully began to look at early modern theatre and performance as collective, social practices deeply integrated into other types of cultural signification. Stephen Greenblatt, Louis Montrose, Steven Mullaney, and other new historicist critics juxtaposed privileged dramatic texts with colonialists' reports, gynecological treatises, exorcism tracts, witch trials, and much more. Greenblatt's preferred term for the new approach, in fact, was 'cultural poetics'. Greenblatt's emphasis on social negotiations and processes in Shakespeare can be seen to follow Williams' line of cultural history. New historicism drew on anthropologists like Clifford Geertz who read culture like a language; on post-structuralist philosophers like Michel Foucault, who examined collective discourse as a system of rules and exclusions; and on social historians such as Carlo Ginzburg, who recovered the voices of popular culture by reading what official documents both said and left unsaid. Montrose and other new historicists have been especially insightful in identifying, à la Williams' emphasis on 'residual' structures of feeling not extirpated by dominant culture, the vestigial presence, via secularization, of religious ritual in early modern theatre. In this respect Montrose is congruent with British culture studies in the vein of Keith Thomas's *Religion and the Decline of Magic: Studies in Popular Beliefs in Sixteenth- and Seventeenth-Century England* (1971).

But while new historicism showed, and continues to show, how illuminating to the study of early modern theatre anthropological, cultural and socio-historical approaches can be, its insights have been largely confined to early modern English theatre, and increasingly (in a strange turn) focused on the single figure of Shakespeare. This volume attempts both to extend its purview to the continent of Europe and the New World (with regrettably, only scattered references to non-Western theatres), and to attempt, as no new historicist study has ever done, a cultural-historical theatre history of the early modern age. While no theatre history can claim to be 'comprehensive', the aim in these pages is to extend the geographical and socio-economic range of early modern theatre history as far as possible while remaining focused on the same ten cultural questions that guide the chapters of each of this series' six volumes.

The ten rubrics framing the chapters pose cultural questions that do not respect geo-linguistic, national boundaries; indeed, any serious reckoning with these matters *requires* transnational triangulation. Similarities conditioned by the historical parameters provide a fulcrum that can clarify salient differences. We are committed to a transnational approach that examines not just the 'big four' theatres of early modern England, Spain, France, and Italy, but also theatre and performance in the German-speaking regions, the Low Countries, Scandinavia, Eastern Europe, and the New World. Although most explicitly addressed by Pavel Drábek in Chapter 5, 'Circulation', many elements of theatre and performance travelled across geo-linguistic boundaries in the early modern period: travelling actors, printed and manuscript scripts and scenarios, short stories (*novelle*) ransacked for dramatic ideas and theatrical pranks, actors' gags, character types and configurations, plot modules, costumes, designs and ideas about theatre architecture and scenic technology, nuggets of dramatic theory, costumes, dynastic marriage partners who were patrons of the theatre (e.g., Catherine de' Medici), etc. Although no one would deny transnational mobility to the ancient or medieval periods, the new commercial circulations abetted by early capitalism, the pan-European humanist movement that disseminated so many texts and ideas about theatre from the early fifteenth century on, and the religious crises of the sixteenth century – both Reformation and Counter-Reformation engaging theatre for its own ideological purposes – all tended to increase by both rate and quantity the international circulation of theatrical ideas and practices.

INTRODUCTION

Transnational mobility, moreover, is not just a quaint characteristic of early modern theatre; it constitutes a generating principle in its own right, in which (as per Williams) the 'artistic' and the 'social' were altogether enmeshed. The first organized professional theatre, which begins to appear in the 1540s and expands in the 1560s, was the pan-Italian *commedia dell'arte*, always already 'transnational' if we consider that the troupes made very early forays to the German-speaking lands. It soon established Paris as a regular venue, and from the beginning had to negotiate the borders between the duchies, republics and petty states of pre-national Italy. The cross-fertilization generated by Italian troupes travelling into France was fundamental to the growth of French theatre, especially when, after the decline of the northern Italian courts that patronized the professional actors, the Italian actors gradually established a pied-à-terre at the Parisian Comédie-Italienne. Transplanted actors like Domenico Biancolelli (the second great Arlecchino/Harlequin) and Tiberio Fiorillo, in arte Scaramouche, increasingly began to perform in French,[37] just as the English actors touring the German states and the Low Countries began to perform in German in a surprisingly short time. The international entrepôt of Venice was replete with Greek, Albanian, Croatian, German, and other districts, and collected Bergamasks and other peoples from the hinterlands of its empire.[38] There, it can be argued, the 'theatre of dialect' that issued into the polylingual *commedia dell'arte* was born. The stage macaronic language of Tristano Martinelli, who mixed Spanish, Latin, French, and Italian in his verbal productions, and the shards of Babel performed by the English actor John Posset on the continent are not far away. Transnational mobility – and we can understand it in the most concrete and material terms – quite literally generated 'aesthetic' invention: the maschera of Arlecchino/Harlequin was invented on the road, by a Mantuan actor sharing a Parisian stage with French farceurs, and Pickelhering was developed by English itinerant actors on Dutch and German soil.[39] The international networks of itinerant actors were constituted by a meld of the material and the immaterial: no actor travelled where a road, or sea route, or canal passage wasn't established or constructed; but letters mattered more than mules when the many hindrances to extended travel and border crossing obtained: long routes, poorly maintained roads, bad weather, surly customs agents, and geo-political protectionism. As Stephen Greenblatt argues in *Cultural Mobility: A Manifesto*,[40] 'mobility studies' should address the resistance to border crossing as well as transnational passages (moderating our post-1989 elation at fallen walls with the sober realization of identity resurgence, especially in the year 2016, on regional and national levels). In addition to the obstacles mentioned just above, we can examine the cultural impediments to transnational exchange, such as the English antipathy to the practice of having actual women play female roles, and thus the surprising absence of Italian professional companies in London between 1577 and the Restoration, with only minor exceptions. To know how actors' bodies, costumes, accessories, plots, scripts, scenarios, theatregrams, gags, architectural ideas and stage technologies could not overcome geo-linguistic borders quickens our understanding of how they could.

If early modern theatre was transnationally mobile, this volume practises 'mobility' in its scholarly approach as well, as we propose a genuinely transnational cultural history of early modern theatre.

CHAPTER ONE

Institutional Frameworks for Theatre, 1400–1650

Mapping Theatrical Resources

TOM BISHOP AND ROBERT HENKE

As with the histories of most complex cultural phenomena, no single or linear narrative adequately charts the institutional frameworks regulating, ideologically forming, and financially supporting theatre and performance from 1400 to 1650 in Europe. This is especially the case if one considers the matter transnationally, and even beyond the four most prominent early modern theatres of England, Spain, France and Italy. The patchwork of institutions and the temporality of change were uneven, and the most secure generalization that can be made is that institutional frameworks underwriting theatre and performance in this period were socially and economically hybrid, reflecting the age's uneven transition from feudal to capitalist modes of production and organization. Complicating the situation even more is the fact that paratheatrical and diverse performative practices (whether perceived as involving 'performance' or not) positively thrived in a period when increased urban growth and the rise of the courts both generated conspicuous public stages. The age abounds with myriad forms of street and piazza theatre, carnival, charivari, public executions, public shaming rituals, royal entries, urban pageants, succession ceremonies, and much, much more. In considering early modern forms of theatre and performance, cultural history in the Marxist tradition of Gramsci and Raymond Williams can closely attend to economic 'sub-structure' while also acknowledging the independent agency and mobility of cultural forces.[1] An understanding of the larger currents of political and economic change can clarify some of the parameters of artistic production, and also illuminate the social 'structures of feeling' that, in Williams's view, constitute culture.[2] Residual and emergent, as well as dominant cultural ideas, postures, attitudes and assumptions should be examined in order to gain as full a picture as possible.

Between 1400 and 1650, broadly speaking, developments in economic and political realms pulled in contrary but dialectically related directions. On the one hand, a generally freer circulation of money, commodities, labour and land compounded a fraying of tighter feudal relations with the emergence and expansion of mercantile commercialism and capitalist modes of production in European towns and cities.[3] Urban corporations and those who controlled them sought and increasingly gained a measure of independence from local feudal lords and seigneurs. Their success in these endeavours underwrote the creation of a Europe-wide network of increasingly wealthy traders, merchants and bankers, and tapped at large into national and international networks of trade and, especially in the case of extra-European activity, plunder. It is out of this widening network that the central economic drivers and institutions of the future – industrialization, the corporation and the bank – appear at the end of our period. On the other hand, such wrenching conflicts as the Wars of the Roses, the Castilian and Catalonian Civil Wars and the Conquest of Granada, and the Hundred Years' War eventually enabled and resulted in a drive to consolidate political and military power under strong national or imperial leaders: Henry VII in England, Ferdinand and Isabella in Spain, Louis XI in France, Maximilian I in the Holy Roman Empire. The rule of these monarchs was increasingly conceived and expressed in 'absolutist' terms, as the king or emperor or duke became in effect a transferred and enlarged 'apparatus of feudal domination' whose chief task was to suborn or dominate the remnants of feudalism itself.[4]

Capitalism and absolutism thus grew up together, but were also checked and limited in various ways, including by each other. Emergent capitalism was retarded in its drive to value extraction and market efficiency by the persistence of feudal habits of organization and production, particularly in outlying and remoter areas, and by its need to rely on monarchical power, for instance for the protection afforded by monopolies and military force. Absolutism, meanwhile, was checked both by ongoing struggle against surviving feudal magnates in times of weakness (as during the Fronde in France), and by its recurrent need to rely directly on the financial backing of capital to fight its wars and promulgate its glories.[5] In the longer view, Perry Anderson argues, absolutism was a *transitional* structure – though it cannot, of course, have seemed like one at the time – which sought to absorb from the feudal aristocracy its local jurisdiction in law and violence, but it was shot through with contradictions at every point, most especially in its ever-increasing dependence on capital markets, and never more clearly than in the case of Habsburg Philip II's eventually disastrous imperial overreach in both the New World and in northern and central Europe.

The implications of these large-scale pressures and changes for theatrical activity across Europe are sketched below. In broad terms, we argue, the parallel growth of absolutist patronage and expanded urban markets drove innovation in theatrical institutions. The claim that theatrical and theatre-supporting institutions were particularly tied, even in their non-homogeneity, to larger economic and social patterns of organization, depends in turn upon recognizing theatre as a cultural form that requires a concentration of material, temporal and human resources that some other forms comparatively do not. Though substantial training may be required to become a poet, and substantial patronage of one kind or another to sustain poetry as a livelihood, the corresponding requirements for theatrical enterprise are, for the most part, even more exigent. Local and punctuated theatrical activity, of the kind tied, say, to a calendrical cycle, may be able to survive, and even flourish, on the intermittent commitment of available resources by patrons or community. The largest and most important theatrical development of the period in question, however – the emergence of regular, secular, commercial, urban and professional playing that could provide sustained presentation and livelihood – depended on fundamental changes in the concentration, organization and flow of resources across societies as a whole that were deeply related to the entwined emergence of capitalism and absolutism. These changes made possible new ways of directing resources to theatre, and new reasons for doing so, even while older ways persisted, sometimes right alongside and even within the new.

To clarify these relations, we offer a systematic taxonomy or 'map' that may provide general orientation on how and when and with what concentrations of resources theatrical activity was organized across the period at large. Diachronic changes can, in this way, be observed in relation to a large matrix that continues to register areas where change lags. This is important since many cultural and social practices that continued to inform early modern modes of performance and reception were of *longue durée*, extending on both sides of the period in question, even though one can observe a broad transformative shift from festival-based occasional theatre to more or less quotidian professional theatre primarily based on the market and drawing resources and strategies from emergent capitalist modes of production and absolutist lines of patronage.

For the purposes of this taxonomy then, we identify two intersecting axes along which to locate theatrical activity. One axis charts the *level* of resources in material, time, remuneration and other support, from low to high, exiguous to lavish. The other axis charts the *continuity* of resource support that potential performers have access to, from strictly limited in time to an access regular enough to function as sustaining (Figure 1.1).

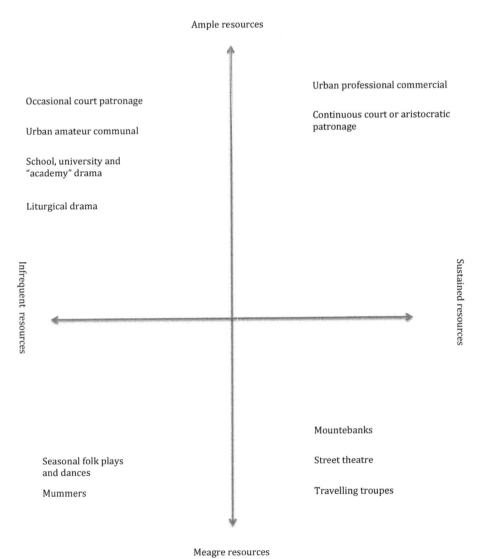

FIGURE 1.1: Map of theatrical resources.

I

In one corner of the resulting 'map' (lower left) are the various performances with access to resources both poor and discontinuous. Where access is constrained by geography or lack of mobility in an area that cannot or will not generate continuous support even at a low level, sustained livelihood activity for theatre is impossible. But this does not mean there is no performance. Here we find such theatrical enterprises as rural mummings, folk plays, and other performances associated with religious rites or other festivals, drawing on local skills and aptitudes and in general mobilized from the ordinary surrounding world of work (Figure 1.2).

This small-scale but almost ubiquitous and highly durable institutional framework both pre-dates and post-dates our period. Everywhere longstanding village folk dramas treating heroes such as Robin Hood, hero combats, wooing, gender reversals, the battle between winter and summer or between Lent and Carnival, and issues or rituals of fertility were keyed to important annual festivals or local observances. In England, principal occasions included Christmas, Epiphany, Shrove Tuesday/Carnival, Hock Tuesday, Easter, Plough Monday, Pentecost, May Day, Midsummer Watch and All Souls. The community festivities of such days created a sense of cohesiveness and connection with the past, and possibly helped to mediate between local feudal lords and peasantry. Though partly threatened by the retreat of feudalism and partly frowned on by religious reformist zeal for their patent, if often tempered, pagan elements, these performances survived long and late, and increasingly catered to an emerging early modern nostalgia for a feudal past.

The Church remained the chief institutional sponsor of these activities, which were often produced by groups of villagers organized somewhat like a guild. They provided an income source – a form of charity – for churches, even after they had first paid off the amateur performers themselves. Whereas England tended to bifurcate its festivity between the indoor games and entertainments of the Christmas season and the outdoor entertainments focused around May Day, Corpus Christi Day, and Midsummer, the warmer countries of southern Europe made the earlier Carnival period itself – and especially the few days culminating in Mardi Gras – the time of intense outdoor theatrical activity. In the countryside of Italy and other continental countries, carnival plays, produced by churches and townspeople in the manner of the English

FIGURE 1.2: Woodcut of Elizabethan clown Will Kemp (1560–1603), dressed as a traditional morris dancer. From Kemp's *Nine Day's Wonder* (1600). (Photo by Time Life Pictures/Mansell/The LIFE Images Collection/Getty Images.)

village plays, often involved the figure of Carnival himself being tried, convicted, reading his last will and testament, then executed, and lamented.

Such traditional forms of folk performance do not get frequent mention in early modern theatre histories (except in regard to Shakespeare). However, from a cultural historical perspective that asks, across the socio-economic spectrum, (1) who made theatre, (2) how it mattered to the people who produced and consumed it, and (3) how emergent forms of theatre in the period were put together, such traditional forms are fundamental.

II

Discontinuous, intermittent or irregular performance at the *high* end of the resource axis (upper left) is already well established at the beginning of our period. Large civic and religious institutions had been sponsoring occasional or festival drama on a lavish scale for a considerable time. Liturgical drama in monasteries, civic presentations of Passion plays and Corpus Christi cycles and large-scale carnival theatricalities in both urban and rural areas show sponsorship variously centralized or parcelled out. In some ways, these are simply big-budget versions of the smaller village festivals – they serve the same local function of celebrating community and continuity under God and Time. But their impact and organizational requirements are also qualitatively different, and they adopt some specific strategies, such as outsourcing the creation of scripts to a literate cadre, as the surviving English cycle-play manuscripts suggest. Generally, the framework of reliable if intermittent support based in alliances between church and community declines across the period, as disruptive changes in religious life and institutions have a considerable impact. But these changes can bolster as much as decimate. The English religious plays cease, for reasons economic and political. But the Spanish *autos sacramentales* begin only in the sixteenth century, shadowing the consolidation of Catholicism as Spanish national policy, and revived Catholicism in Habsburg central Europe also promoted religious drama, though such religious institutional support as continued into the Reformation/Counter-Reformation era – for example in German Reform churches, and among the Jesuits – was often significantly less opulent either than previous large-scale presentations or than the magnificent performances sponsored by contemporary courts to be discussed shortly.

The socio-economic framework informing such large-scale calendrical theatricality as a *regular* occurrence – a critical mass of population, wealth, literacy, education, and labour organization (guilds) – did not really develop until the late medieval period. The first references to the York mystery cycles come from the late fourteenth century. The Corpus Christi-based Spanish *auto sacramental*, although it may draw from fifteenth-century traditions, was not codified until the early sixteenth century, was inflected by the

INSTITUTIONAL FRAMEWORKS

Counter-Reformation, and flourished in the seventeenth-century drama of Lope and Calderón. Records of mystery plays in the Czech Lands, Hungary, and Dalmatia date back to the fourteenth and fifteenth centuries, but it was only the sixteenth century that saw a flowering of the mystery play in Poland and Croatia-Dalmatia, where a certain critical level of civic wealth had now been reached.[6] Aside from devotional feeling, what mattered particularly in such processions and theatrical stagings was displaying and celebrating the structure of the social order. For the most part, these calendrical events were produced by 'amateur' performers, producers, designers and builders, if we understand the word to designate not 'the unskilled' but those for whom theatre did not provide a primary livelihood.

In urban centres that prospered from commerce and economic growth, pre-Lent theatrical activity also grew. In Nuremberg, for one, the *Fastnachtspiele* (Shrovetide plays), most famous as written by the shoemaker-poet and Mastersinger, Hans Sachs (1494–1576), were produced at the city Carnival or *Schembartlauf* (until it was banned in 1539).[7] After permission was granted by the city fathers to perform the plays (not all of Sachs' plays were approved), tradesmen-actors performed these farcical and satirical pieces in halls, squares and church courtyards. Processions with floats, usually constructed by confraternities or guilds, filled the streets, where costumes and masks allowed for some flouting of normal social and sexual constrictions, and the line between performer and spectator was blurred.

In such an environment, it is not surprising that social groups who wished to assert or reinforce their standing often sought to do so by public theatrical activity. A particularly important focus of such organization throughout the period can be found in groups of young men of various classes, from informal groups in small towns and villages that organized the charivari or 'rough music' to larger and more organized groupings with access to more prestige and resources. Such youth companies mounting theatrical revelries can be found very widely: the Inns of Court (London), the Abbaye des Conards (Rouen), Compagnie de la Mere Folle (Dijon), or Compagnie della Calza (Venice).

France was especially productive of such theatricalizing youths. The battle between Carnival and Lent, vividly depicted in the Peter Brueghel the Elder painting of 1559, was dramatically enacted in a fifteenth-century French text, 'The Battle of Saint Pensard'.[8] The play was written to be produced and performed in Tours in 1485 by a group of educated young men who formed a 'society of fools'. In Paris, public secular theatre from the second quarter of the fifteenth century to the mid-sixteenth was dominated by the Clercs de la Basoche, a literary society of law clerks numbering as many as ten thousand by 1500.[9] This was a bourgeois phenomenon, drawn from a class of magistrates and clerics created by the king to check the power of feudal lords. Mirroring the lawyers' own professional societies, the clerks formed a counterpart group, and from writing and staging *causes grasses*, or burlesque trials to be staged during Carnival, to short farcical plays for public entertainment, the road was not far. By 1442, the Confrérie de la Passion, which controlled religious performances in Paris, was allowing the Basochiens to perform their farces in between the days of their *mystères*, first at the Hôpital de la Trinité and then at the Hôtel de Bourgogne (their monopoly theatre in Paris). In effect, the Basochiens inserted themselves in the interstices of the liturgical calendar in order to perform their secular, realistic farces set in a bourgeois milieu. The farce of *Maitre Pierre Pathelin* is only the most famous. Performing up to the mid-sixteenth century, the Basochiens skirt the border of professionalism, and no doubt there were members involved whose devotion to theatre at least matched their trade affiliation. Increasing royal censorship and the rise of truly professional playing in the later sixteenth century caused their demise.

Comparable to the Basoche societies in their support for theatre were the four English Inns of Court, which admitted young men to study law, usually the sons of gentry or above, or occasionally, like John Webster, the sons of prosperous citizens. Their self-funded production of plays, as well as masques, orations and dancing, occurred mostly during the festive Christmas season, under the guidance of a Master of the Revels, or, occasionally, a Lord of Misrule. Up until the late 1560s, theatrical performance was mostly undertaken by amateurs, but later, professional players were often hired to contribute to the revels, as with the Lord Chamberlain's Men's performance of Shakespeare's *Twelfth Night* at the Middle Temple on 2 February 1602.

Even the learned and aristocratic humanist academies of France and Italy might be included under this rubric, though both their means and their memberships were a great deal more sophisticated. Italian academies such as the Olympic Academy, responsible for the erection of the Teatro Olimpico (1585), became increasingly important producers of theatre as the entrepreneurial sway of northern courts like Mantua and Florence began to wane after the 1620s. Somewhat like the English Inns of Court, the Italian academies provided a site where professional and amateur theatre producers worked together, with the academy occasionally providing a cover against antitheatrical attacks on those who performed theatre for sordid money.

A significant counterpart can also be found in the *Rederijkerskamer* (Chambers of Rhetoric) of the Netherlands, although as an institutional phenomenon, these organizations vex both a 'medieval–Renaissance' and a 'sacred–secular' division. Originating as secular devotional brotherhoods assisting clergy in religious processions, these were amateur membership groups, but underwritten by both aristocratic patrons sponsoring each chamber and by the municipal festivals in which they participated. They emerge and prosper exactly within the temporal reach of the present volume, with about sixty created in the course of the fifteenth century and some one hundred and twenty more in the sixteenth.

Central players in the public life of thriving Dutch towns, they put on *tableaux vivants* for church feast days (Palm Sunday, Easter, Corpus Christi, Pentecost) but also produced original poetry and drama, and provided pageant wagons and triumphal arches for secular occasions such as royal entries. The sheer numbers of these Chambers demonstrate their wide reach into bourgeois social and cultural life, and their adaptability to a range of audiences and genres renders these amateur theatrical groups a vital phenomenon for a cultural history of early modern theatre. They played a key role in the Dutch 'public sphere' and are thus comparable at once to the English trade-guilds of the mystery cycles, but without the craft affiliation, and to the Italian academies, but without the class exclusivity: theirs was predominantly a distinctively civic and republican character.

However, the institutions best resourced and most keen to advertise themselves by theatrical means were the royal courts. These latter, also sponsors of discrete high-resource events, expanded enormously across our period. Though court entertainments such as royal entries, court mummings, and festive revels are well attested in the fifteenth century, such court-based and court-backed events are driven throughout the sixteenth and into the seventeenth century by massive new aggregations of resources formed in particular under the emerging absolutist orders of France, Spain and England – and on a regional scale in the duchies and city-states of Italy, Germany, the Czech Lands and elsewhere. By 1600, courts as institutions both sponsored regular, staggeringly expensive, and elaborate forms of theatrical performance, and also promoted extravagant forms of theatricality on a day-to-day basis (Figure 1.3).

Self-aggrandizing court magnificence seized on theatre as an especially effective medium. As part of this movement of co-optation, courts not only sponsored their own events, drawing on whatever expertise they needed – for masques, entertainments, entries, processions, coronations, anniversaries, funerals, etc. – but they frequently extended their protection and patronage to professional theatre-makers under attack by municipal and ecclesiastical opponents, operating not merely as their intermittent direct financial backers but also as established political sponsors. In Italy, for instance, the patronage of *commedia dell'arte* companies by Mantuan, Florentine and Savoian courts provided the players with the economic security and cultural capital also to play in 'public' theatres such as the Teatro di Baldracca in Florence.[10] In England and France, professional players eventually came under the direct political patronage and protection of the royal family. But such co-optations could be complex, and often policed theatrical activity as much as they promoted it. In England, the 1572 law by which professional players had to be at least nominally attached as 'retainers' to reputable sponsors was precisely an attempt (not entirely successful) to contain professional playing in limited hands from a

FIGURE 1.3: Representation of a ballet before Henri III and his court, in the Gallery of the Louvre. Re-engraving from an original on copper in the *Ballet comique de la Royne* by Balthazar de Beaujoyeulx (Paris: Ballard, 1582). (Photo by: Universal History Archive/UIG via Getty Images.)

more dispersed and unregulated field. As a corollary to this protection, governments often also developed machineries of vetting and censorship as, again in England, through the Office of the Revels. The relation of these developments to other nascent practices of governmental regulation and oversight being instituted by the monarchies is notable.

The extension of royal and other aristocratic court patronage to the learned also had the effect of sponsoring drama as a by-product – especially from the new humanist intellectuals for whom drama was a high-status classical form. Gil Vicente (*c*. 1465–*c*. 1536) wrote principally, in both Spanish and Portuguese, for court performance. Juan del Encina (1468–*c*. 1530), a priest and musician, composed pastorals and comedies at the court of the second Duke of Alba. In England, Henry Medwall was patronized by Cardinal Morton, and John Skelton tutored the young future Henry VIII.

One group or location of cultural authority that did *not* notably sponsor theatrical activity in the period was what we might now be tempted to call 'the government'. At one level this absence merely reflects the fact that, in the period in question, 'government' barely existed in our sense of an organized bureaucratic apparatus administering concerted and centrally determined policies through a

INSTITUTIONAL FRAMEWORKS

variety of means. But this claim at once admits of two important exceptions that indicate significant developments. In England, Thomas Cromwell's 'government' reforms, as they can only be called given their scope and purpose, included the remarkable innovation of briefly supporting a company of touring players to disseminate plays of Protestant theology commissioned from the polemicist ex-Carmelite John Bale (1495–1563).[11] The project itself suggests the radicality of Cromwell's programme of reform.[12]

The other instance of 'government theatre' is located far away, in Spanish Mexico, where the early colonial governmental and religious authorities (in practice hardly separate) supervised missionary theatre under the auspices at first of the Franciscans, and later also of the Jesuits. From 1533, large-scale custombuilt theatrical spectacles in both Spanish and indigenous languages on subjects such as *The Conquest of Rhodes* (Mexico City, 1539, in Nahuatl), and *The Conquest of Jerusalem* (Tlaxcala, 1539) were mounted in response to news of a supposed impending Catholic crusade in Europe. The *Rhodes* play was probably performed during Carnival and had substantial feasting, processions and other typical celebratory forms associated with it. It was sponsored under the joint auspices of the city and the Franciscans, and Cortés himself may even have played the Christian general attacking Rhodes. The Tlaxcala *Conquest* (1539) was, according to Las Casas's report, entirely staffed, arranged and performed by Indians in indigenous languages. With participants estimated at 1,500, it was performed on Corpus Christi and integrated directly into the end of that festival's religious procession. It was only one of a series of regular Christian-inspired pageants and performances, lavish and on a grand scale: Las Casas reported witnessing one with an audience of 'more than eighty thousand people'.[13]

The humanist educational movement, discussed at more length below, was particularly active in drama through its investment in the rhetorical and poetic imitation of antiquity. But we should note that humanism was not an institution per se; rather, it was a set of ideologies and cultural practices brought into contact with a variety of institutions in different ways: the court or academy, as with Ariosto and the Este court in Ferrara; the guildhall, as with the Dutch rhetoric chambers; the school, as with Udall at Eton or in the Jesuit orders. In the case of the companies of English boy players, humanist educational drama even crossed over from a curricular instrument sometimes also displayed as court entertainment to become a sustained, if controversial, professional enterprise, especially for its managers. And with this last instance, we may pass over from predominantly amateur to professional *livelihood* performance.

III

In the third quadrant of the 'map' (lower right) we locate forms of theatre where comparative poverty of resources was offset by continuous access to them, especially by a strategy combining mobility with a sufficient geographical density of resources tapped 'in series', even if only in a hand-to-mouth manner. On the street, at the fair, in the marketplace, or even in a local hall, such itinerant theatrical activity comprises both solo and small company performances of music, animal acts, sleight-of-hand tricks, acrobatics, mountebankery, even some kinds of begging, as well as plays. Geographically, the mode extends right across Europe, from the retinues of itinerant *fili* in traditional Ireland to the disreputable *skomorokhi* – wandering satiric minstrels – in Russia (Figure 1.4).

In the earlier part of our period, itinerant performance provides one antecedent of more settled theatrical enterprise, and continues to intersect or alternate with it, and to provide a ready fallback, as when English companies of the late-sixteenth century resorted to touring in difficult times. Shakespeare's *Hamlet* and Munday's *Sir Thomas More* both include depictions of troupes in this mode – in effect the forebears of the very men playing them. In France, the recourse was even more common: the *Comediens du roi* regularly had to retrench to provincial touring in the early seventeenth century, and after the 1645 collapse of the *Illustre Théâtre*, Molière wandered for years as leader of an itinerant troupe that eventually resumed residency and at last morphed into the Comédie-Française. The companies of 'English comedians' that toured cities, towns and courts in Germany and further east, especially those under the

FIGURE 1.4: *Skomorokhi* in a Russian village. François Nicholas Riss (1804–86).

INSTITUTIONAL FRAMEWORKS

indefatigable Robert Browne for thirty years after 1593, were the first in those areas 'to create an awareness of theatre in its own right, not just as a diversion at holiday festivities or as a means of religious instruction'.[14] Though the records of these travelling troupes tend to be thin and fragmentary, this mode probably constitutes the most widespread institutional model of professional or semi-professional performance across these years.

Perhaps the most interesting case of comparative scarcity combined with more-or-less continuous access, and one which also may be seen as a transitional stage to the next quadrant, is the mobile, itinerant, Italian professional theatre, dubbed 'commedia dell'arte' by Goldoni and posterity. Not only were mountebanks associated with *commedia dell'arte*, but the piazza entertainer who earns his living from performance all year round may be seen to mark a transition from occasional to continuous, professional theatre. Generally, the *commedia dell'arte* oscillated between neo-feudal and proto-bourgeois business arrangements. Agreements were secured between, on the one hand, the ducal agents, or sometimes the duke himself, of northern Italian courts such as Mantua and Florence and, on the other, the *capocomico*, or head of the Arte company, with the fiction that the actor was the sovereign's 'servant'. Secure performance arrangements at court frequently allowed the companies to perform also in *stanze*, or halls, of a more popular caste, such as the Florence 'Baldracca' theatre mentioned above. In one urban sojourn, therefore, the professional actors could play both the court and the market. In the face of antitheatrical attacks, actor-writer Pier Maria Cecchini advocated for theatre as a mercantile 'arte', whose technical standards matched those of any urban trade. At the same time, and contrasting with these neo-feudal arrangements, we also find new bourgeois models developed by Venetian entrepreneurs after 1580.

IV

It is in the final quadrant of the grid-map (upper right), where high-resource production combines with continuous access, that we find the most important addition to the network of institutional frameworks for drama in the period. At the beginning of our period, this quadrant is essentially empty. Its occupation by full-time, established, professional companies earning their livelihoods in large urban centres by 1650 is the period's truly lasting innovation. These companies emerge in major cities in Italy, England, Spain, and elsewhere over approximately the period of the 1540s to the 1570s. A crucial factor is the increasing size of the host cities, as this enabled the frequent, often daily, attraction of sufficiently concentrated funds to underwrite drama by direct aggregation at the performance itself, without the need either for institutional sponsors (though courts often also supported these companies in various ways, as noted) or for movement to a new site while demand replenished at the abandoned one.

These companies could sustain themselves *in situ* for as long as sufficient resources could be attracted. When inhibited from doing so, by plague, political upheaval, economic disaster or limited-duration licensing (as in Madrid), they tended to revert to the older model of itinerant performance. So when, in the first decade of the seventeenth century, Valleran le Conte's *Comédiens du roi* leased the Hôtel de Bourgogne theatre from its monopolists, the Confraternité de la Passion, they repeatedly struggled to attract a sustainable audience, despite holding the patronage of the French king and offering both expert current-affairs-based clowning and the latest in modern humanist plays by Alexandre Hardy. Disappointed and fractious, the troupe returned to touring the provinces, where they found if not a more fervent at least a more renewable welcome.[15]

Resident professional troupes in urban centres were both innovative and flexible. They tended both to cultivate novel forms of organization, such as the outsourcing of script-production to humanist-educated writers, and to absorb within themselves key elements of earlier performance frameworks – such as independent clowns (Tarlton, Zan Ganassa, Lope de Rueda, Valleran le Conte), older spectacular effects (the hell-mouth in *Doctor Faustus*), and the figurative resonances of festive occasions (*Twelfth Night*, *Bartholomew Fair*, etc.). While the general conditions of economic and social change had some broad similarities, professional companies were also organized internally in various ways across geo-linguistic boundaries, from *capocomico*-style leader-management in Italy to 'joint stock' partnership in England. Spain and England both developed professional theatres in this period, but their respective national contexts and cultures resulted in quite different 'attachment points' of the companies to the social networks of emergent capitalism they inhabited.

Although urban growth and its concentration of resources was the necessary condition of the professional playing troupes, the latter integrated with their national urban economics in various ways. Across Europe, the dissolution of the feudal system 'freed' the serf, in Marx's words, to work for wages, often necessitating travelling to the city 'where he found his master waiting for him'. Such workers provided much of the resource-income that enabled professional playing. But, at the same time, many of these would-be urban workers quickly became beggars instead, depending on emergent forms of urban charity. Along with the demographic and economic rise of major cities came the emergence of a new urban underclass amply represented in Spanish picaresque literature, as well as in the Italian figure of the destitute zanni of the *commedia dell'arte*, and in the English cony-catching pamphlets and German rogue books. In Spain, the necessities of this newly miserable group, which presented a serious problem of public order as well as a challenge to the consciences of their neighbours, were addressed by a network of new *confradías*, or religious brotherhoods, established in the reign of Philip II. In the latter part of the century, these organizations began to lease out the courtyards, or *corrales*, of facilities owned by them or under their jurisdiction to professional acting companies, with a portion of the receipts – explicitly labelled 'alms' – going to the confraternity (Figure 1.5). Professional theatre in Spain was thus indirectly linked to the rise of new poverty as well as new wealth. As theatre became a major income source for charity, in Valladolid and Granada as well as Madrid, the tide of Spanish ecclesiastical attacks on the theatre also eased. Even if the production of plays was considered immoral, it was ingeniously argued that it was acceptable to turn the profits of immortality to charitable purposes.[16] Furthermore, professional playwrights and actors dependent on this nexus could then be, and were, enlisted to write and perform *autos sacramentales* during the feast of Corpus Christi.

The major playing companies of London expertly managed the double recourse to aristocratic patronage and urban consumer markets for financial support in a different way, drawing for their internal organizational framework both on emergent capitalist practices and older models of guild culture.[17] Internally, the tripartite division of the late-century English professional acting company into sharers, hired men, and apprentices resembled in general terms the hierarchy of English guilds, even though the actors lacked a central organization that could oversee their profession, such as Spanish actors obtained in 1631 in the Cofradía de la Novena. Yet the only part of the English model

FIGURE 1.5: Restored, surviving *corral* playhouse in Almagro, Spain. (Photo: Antonio Leyva.)

directly borrowed from the guild system was the practice of apprenticeship, and this because guilds were the only organizations through which apprentices could be enrolled.[18] Hired men, on the other hand, remained precisely that – hired to play for a limited term. They were not, as in the guild system, journeymen members of a legal organization, though they might aspire to, and sometimes did, become sharers. The existence of sharing and of the joint-stock model of the company, meanwhile, was a highly innovative borrowing from a form of corporate association previously known only in mercantile adventuring and mining.[19] Its adaptation to theatre-making is in fact quite remarkable, a possible outgrowth of the 1583 creation of the Queen's Men by government fiat through cherry-picking the leading players of the day – with the result that no single member could easily be appointed its leader. Even more suggestively, the number of the original Queen's Men, twelve, matches the standard number of sharers in the capitalist joint-stock venture, which was almost always a multiple of twelve.[20]

If the internal structure of English companies took elements from both older guild and newer capitalist institutions, the matrix of external institutional regulation and support was similarly hybrid. Legislative regulation by the English state, ever concerned for managing public order, led to a gradual confinement of players within an increasingly stringent requirement for official patronage and license by appropriate members of the state, extending variously from gentry up to the monarch.[21] This requirement built on a link to feudal ideas of 'retainership', but also evinced the growing digestion of playing within the developing routines of central government, as also did the parallel imposition of various routines of censorship and vetting via the Master of the Revels and others. If playing was to be an industry, it was to be a regulated one, in the country as in the city.

In London, the epicentre of innovation, we can also track the involvement of the playing companies with various machineries of early modern business: landholding, leasing, moneylending, and, inevitably, litigation. The majority of the professional actors in London were hired men, who worked for weekly wages, received no share of company profits, and were more vulnerable than the sharers to persistent negative prejudices against actors as vagabonds. Sharers, on the other hand, collectively owned the 'stock' of the company (including its scripts, costumes and licenses), and were paid a percentage of the daily profits. Their livelihoods could be fairly secure and, in some cases, as with Alleyn or Shakespeare, handsome, as long as their companies prospered. Other companies were more marginal affairs, and could come to be 'managed' and even exploited by landlord-financiers such as Philip Henslowe or, later, Christopher Beeston. Most companies did not own the theatre building in which they performed, but paid rent with a percentage of their per-performance income. Shakespeare's company, the Lord Chamberlain's/King's Men, were

INSTITUTIONAL FRAMEWORKS

unusual after 1599 in owning not just the outdoor Globe theatre and the lease for the land on which it stood, but, as of 1608, the indoor venue in the Blackfriars as well. Court (and other private) performances, for which the company was paid, were another important source of income and, just as important, of prestige that offered protection from hostile city regulators. London theatre was economically, as John Lyly called its plays, a 'mingle-mangle', but so were those of the other great urban centres, in different ways.

V

A further word needs to be said about 'humanism', that plastic set of ideologies and rhetorical practices that spread and adapted itself across the cultural landscape of Europe throughout this period, finding a home for its devotees and disseminators variously in republics, monarchies, civil services, metropolises, colonies, grammar schools, universities, and churches both Roman and Reformed. Humanism in regard to drama, beginning in Italy and spreading across Europe, drove the rediscovery, editing, annotating, translating and theorizing of ancient dramatic texts, especially Latin ones, their imitation in new compositions, and their performance, beginning with Giovanni Sulpizio da Veroli's landmark staging of Seneca in 1468 in an open-air Vitruvian amphitheatre on the Campo dei Fiori in Rome. Even after its exponents turned from Latin to the vernacular, the movement remained a resolutely transnational affair, creating across wide distances striking homologies in learned theatrical cultures and in their uptake by vernacular performers.

However, humanism per se tended not to be, as it were, 'independently wealthy'. For it to underwrite theatre materially, it needed to be attached to some other institution: a court, university, school, academy, confraternity, seminary, church, monastery or, at last, a theatre company. Outcomes were even better if humanist enterprise could mediate between sites of learning and of wealth. Humanist theatre that was exclusively transmitted through the court, such as characterized Russia, never really flourished. Humanist theatre in the Polish court, which had stronger ties with the university, fared better by contrast. Such connections between court and university also jump-started English humanist theatre: Medwall had studied at Eton and then Cambridge; Skelton, another Cambridge graduate, repositioned the morality play early into secular, satirical terms, shadowing court politics, in *Magnificence* (1519).

Early Spanish humanist theatre similarly benefitted from points of contact between the court and university. Juan del Encina, a traveller to Italy like several English humanists, was educated at Spain's then-premier university at Salamanca. In Italy, Ludovico Ariosto, a recipient of humanist training with Augustinian monks and then at the University of Ferrara, was patronized by the court of Ercole d'Este, which began promoting humanist theatre in the 1480s. The illegitimate son of a sometime university physician, Angelo Beolco (Ruzante), associated with Padua's humanist intellectuals, such as Bembo and Speroni, and may have performed his first play at the University of Padua: *La pastoral* (1517). His reputation might have stayed there, however, had he not acquired the favour of Alvise Cornaro, a retired Paduan patrician, who patronized Ruzante for the rest of his career and staged his plays at his aristocratic villa.

The influx of new humanist professors, many of them from Germany, also generated theatrical productions that spread outside the confines of Charles University in Prague, inasmuch as they melded with urban processional traditions. There it was the alchemy of the humanist university and the newly founded Jesuit order that produced the most noteworthy theatrical productions. And in general the Jesuit educational mission, founded in a humanist tradition and taking drama as one of its main instruments, was productive of theatrical performance all across the vast extent of its geographical range, from Brazil to Sicily to Prague to India.[22]

VI

A map is a static visual instrument. Changes in the institutions sponsoring or occupying a given corner of our map across the period in question could occur at different times in different locations, and the tempo or fact of change in theatrical activity might result in marked differences from – and even contradict – the situation in another area of cultural activity, even in the same country. So for instance, to take the signal outliers in European theatre of the period, both Ireland under Lord Deputy Strafford (1632–39)[23] and Russia under Tsar Alexei Mikhailovich (1645–76)[24] saw the construction of permanent professional companies and venues for performance through the frank imposition by royal power of trends in theatrical culture imported wholesale from elsewhere (London and Paris, respectively), trends which had no basis in existing practice and hardly suited the local culture or economy. In the one case this was to buttress the prestige of the English colonial power, in the other to provide a rallying point and distinctiveness for a monarchy with absolutist aspirations. In both cases, these innovations required direct government support. In Ireland, rebellion soon caused this theatrical enterprise to collapse; in Russia, by contrast, the imported model persisted, but was heavily dependent on official patronage, and remained largely the preserve of a French-speaking elite into the eighteenth century.

Although the most important single development in institutional frameworks for drama over this period was the rise of resident professional drama, it is also important to recognize exceptions, holdovers and countercurrents in any general narrative of 'from festival to market'. What we repeatedly see is not so much a rhythm of 'emergence and replacement' as a more subtle one

INSTITUTIONAL FRAMEWORKS   33

of 'adaptation and occupation'. Religious festival drama continued, but it increasingly became an expression of political choices intertwined with, even dictated by, more centralizing regimes. In the seventeenth century, urban festivals still occasioned important theatrical activity, but were now likely to be devoted as much to secular as to religious themes. The urban marketplace was from the outset an important theatrical locus, but across these centuries the institutions feeding it and feeding *off* it gathered increasing stability, reach, and organizing force, and these changes drove new forms of organization. For example, after the return of the Medici rulers to Florence in 1512, the church-based spectacles staged by the *compagnie laudese* of the fifteenth century largely disappeared, but one in particular, that of the Annunciation, was retained and reconfigured to celebrate the glory of the ruling family.[25] In London in the late 1530s, the Midsummer Watch associated with a traditional saint's day metamorphosed almost without effort into the Lord Mayor's Pageant asserting the honour of the city, its mayor and his guild.[26] However, a similar reoccupation process failed in the case of the Coventry Corpus Christi plays, whose final performance in 1579 the young William Shakespeare might have seen. On their suppression, the Coventry burghers of 1591 unsuccessfully tried to build a secular historical drama on the old guild-pageant model.[27] But the final demise of Coventry playing coincided with recorded London performances of a history play now known as *The First Part of Henry VI* by William Shakespeare, where a similar narrative to the one that Coventry had proposed was staged by professional actors before paying audiences in a dedicated playhouse. We could take this coincidence as a handover emblematic of the complex intersection of religious, civic, secular and professional frameworks for theatrical performance in the late sixteenth century.

CHAPTER TWO

Social Functions

Audience Participation, Efficacious Entertainment

ERIKA T. LIN

In *As You Like It*, Jaques famously declares that 'All the world's a stage, / And all the men and women merely players; / They have their exits and their entrances, / And one man in his time plays many parts, / His acts being seven ages.'[1] This speech is often cited independently of Shakespeare's dramatic narrative as an exemplar of the *theatrum mundi* trope. What are less well known are the lines that immediately precede it, when Duke Senior says, 'Thou seest we are not all alone unhappy: / This wide and universal theatre / Presents more woeful pageants than the scene / Wherein we play in' (2.7.136–9). Seeing the sorry circumstances of other characters, the Duke positions himself and his men as spectators viewing 'woeful pageants'. Whereas 'All the world's a stage' is usually taken to mean we are all actors, the Duke stresses that we are also all *audiences*.

In early modern Europe, theatre was part of daily life, and people were regular beholders of many kinds of performances. The entire social hierarchy participated in these activities, from royalty and other elite who invested in elaborate entertainments to gallants who showed off at public playhouses to agricultural workers who engaged in holiday role-playing to the urban poor who witnessed civic processions. Yet it is much easier to articulate *who* witnessed theatrical activity than to figure out *how* they experienced performances. What did plays and playing mean to spectators? Why did they engage so enthusiastically with theatre? And how do we uncover the ephemeral feelings and sensations produced by those encounters?

This chapter starts by summarizing briefly what we know and what we don't – and what we can do about it. It begins with the basics: the social composition of early modern audiences and how they usually behaved at theatrical events. It then turns to the methodological difficulties of reconstructing spectator experiences – a decidedly non-trivial task. In the face of such challenges, one solution, I argue, is to adopt a cultural history approach. I focus in particular on historically-specific discourses and practices that circumscribed spectators' habitual ways of thinking and feeling. This strategy applies cultural history not so much to the stories within plays as to the medium of performance itself. It maps broader attitudes and practices that influenced not simply the content of dramatic representation but the act of theatrical presentation.

This chapter therefore concentrates on three main areas. First, in order to comprehend what it meant to experience a play, I examine early modern conceptions of sensory perception, especially seeing and hearing,[2] and I pay particular attention to how perception was gendered. Building on these cultural understandings, I then turn to religious practices and civic processions to reveal how spectatorship could also be ritually efficacious – and to think about when and how such understandings shaped encounters with theatre. Last but not least, I analyse unscripted entertainments – acrobatics, spectacle, dancing, festivity – to explore how audiences responded to these alternative modes of theatricality and how the affective impact of such performances shaped the social functions of drama.

These three areas cut across demographics, venues and occasions, but together they enable us to trace the culturally-specific constraints around spectatorship that structured early modern theatre as a medium. By examining what it meant to see and hear, what it meant to behold ceremonies, and what it meant to marvel at spectacle, we can better understand the cognitive tendencies and affective predilections that audiences brought with them to theatrical events. Exploring these varied social contexts also allows us to grasp more fully the far-reaching significance of performance as a cultural phenomenon that permeated all facets of society – and thus to appreciate more deeply the purposes of play(go)ing in early modern Europe.

AUDIENCE BEHAVIOUR

Who were the spectators at the now-canonical plays of Shakespeare, the famed performances of the *commedia dell'arte*, and the lowbrow antics of French farces and fools? At the top of the hierarchy were, of course, the nobility, who served as patrons for some playing companies as well as guests of honour at theatrical events. At the bottom were beggars, rogues and vagabonds – a category encompassing not only the poor but also, in certain contexts, actors themselves.[3] In between were 'the middling sort'. Whereas today we might designate this large group of people 'the middle class', early modern spectators would have understood themselves as radically different from others with similar financial resources. Traditional cultural divisions cut across economic lines and were most evident in differences of profession, education, affiliation and apparel. Although exact social formations, titles and ranks varied from region to region, the four classes found in William Harrison's 1577 'Description' of England exemplify the kinds of 'middling' identities that could be found across Europe: (1) aristocrats, including a broad range of nobility and minor gentry, (2) citizens and burgesses, (3) rural landholders, often farmers, who were commoners but respectable (in English, termed *yeomen*), and (4) artisans and labourers, including apprentices, household servants, and poorer agricultural workers.[4] In practice, these categories overlapped – civic offices were often held by wealthier artisans, for example – but they functioned as a powerful lens through which the social world was viewed.

It is therefore noteworthy that, across early modern Europe, despite a wide variety of dramatic genres and acting styles, the diverse social types that constituted the vast middle of society all converged at theatrical events. Moreover, at all social levels, women were avid participants in and consumers of theatrical activity.[5] This deeply heterogeneous audience was nevertheless unified in their lively, participatory behaviour. *Commedia dell'arte* spectators, for example, were extremely rowdy, not only in the open streets and the piazza but also in the indoor halls known as *stanze*. As Robert Henke notes, among the letters describing *stanze* performances in 1618 at the Teatro di Baldracca are references to 'continual chaos and noise in the theater' and 'continual din of the Florentine youth'.[6] The same was true in England, as is described in *The Fair Maid of the Inn* (1625), by John Fletcher and his collaborators. The Prologue to the play laments that unruly crowds often disliked well-crafted verse in favour of jigs, a mixed theatrical genre that involved bawdy skits combined with song and dance:

> A worthy story, howsoever writ
> For language, modest mirth, conceit or wit,
> Meets oftentimes with the sweet commendation
> Of hang't, 'tis scurvy, when for approbation
> A Jig shall be clapped at, and every rhyme
> Praised and applauded by a clamorous chime.[7]

In Spain's public theatres, the sound of whistles pierced the air whenever the *mosqueteros*, or spectators in the yard, disapproved of plays. Female playgoers, who sat in their own gallery section, the *cazuela*, also whistled and jangled their keys.[8]

This sort of raucous behaviour was not confined to the lower classes. In addition to the lively crowds who stood in the English amphitheatre yard, the Spanish patio, the French *parterre*, and the Italian piazza, minor aristocrats often behaved loudly and disruptively, too, and even made a nuisance of themselves by sitting onstage. As Gédéon Tallemant des Réaux put it in 1657:

> There is at the moment a terrible source of inconvenience at the theatre: namely that both sides of the stage are filled with young men sitting on cane chairs. They refuse to go to the *parterre*, even though there are often guards at the door, and pages and lackeys no longer wear swords. The boxes are very expensive and have to be booked in advance: you can be on the stage for an *écu* or half a *louis*, but it spoils everything, and takes only one arrogant rogue to disturb the whole house.[9]

The 'guards' to which Tallemant des Réaux refers were porters armed with swords. Quarrels over entrance fees were common enough, however, so that some were nevertheless injured or even killed in brawls at the door.[10] In the Spanish *corrales*, doorkeepers likewise sought to carry daggers in self-defence.[11] Conflicts over admission were instigated not only by rowdy soldiers and servants but also by those of ample means and an overblown sense of privilege. Juan de Zabaleta's *Día de fiesta por la tarde* (1666), for example, features a gallant who rudely pushes his way into the theatre without paying.[12] A similar incident at the Hôtel de Bourgogne took place in 1608, when a French gentleman breezed right by the Italian actor collecting admission – and then slapped him for good measure before ascending to his seat in the *loges*.[13] Even though the kinds of shows playgoers attended varied somewhat depending on social status, geographic location, and the occasion for entertainment, audiences across the board were boisterous and expressed themselves entirely without reserve.

RECONSTRUCTING SPECTATORSHIP

The energetic behaviour of early modern playgoers reminds us that theatrical spectators are never simply passive consumers but actively produce the performances in which they take part. Eric Bentley famously defined theatre as 'A impersonates B while C looks on'.[14] But audiences don't just 'look on' – they talk back, they make noise, they censure, they approve. That crucial role may be most visible in early modern dramatic prologues entreating spectators' patience and epilogues inviting their applause, yet less overt but equally important audience participation also takes place moment by moment during the entire performance. That invisible contribution continues to be essential to theatre today; what have changed, however, are the cultural norms that govern how expressive the audience is. At the Globe and other early modern theatres, spectators could see each other as well as they could see the actors, and they were not shy about making their opinions known. However, even when audience reactions are *not* manifested externally in lively or disruptive behaviour, performance still elicits playgoers' affective responses and relies on their perceptual and interpretive acts.

The question is how to recover these ephemeral thoughts and amorphous sensations. The crucial difficulty in assessing why early modern people went to the theatre and what they experienced there is the paucity of historical evidence: in the sixteenth and early seventeenth centuries, first-person accounts are few and far between, and those references that do survive are often idiosyncratic and governed by divergent generic conventions. Moreover, most people were illiterate. In England, for example, only about 20 per cent of men and 5 per cent of women could sign their own names as of 1558. Those figures had increased by 1642 to 30 per cent and 10 per cent, but these numbers are still incredibly small in absolute terms.[15] So even if people had been inclined to record their playgoing experiences, few would have been able to do so, and even fewer documents would have survived the vagaries of time. Even in our own era, the challenges of studying audience reception are significant. Despite widespread literacy today, there are theoretical difficulties with relying on textual accounts of playgoing, since spectators can usually only remember certain aspects of performances. Writing down those memories also reshapes audience experiences into narrative forms that may not resemble actual sensations and responses during the theatrical event itself.[16]

How, then, can we reconstruct early modern audience experiences? One possible solution is to take a cultural history approach by analysing *typical* ways of feeling and thinking. These historically-specific habits of mind were the ones taken for granted by actors and playgoers alike, the baseline assumptions that shaped not the particularities of any given individual's response but undergirded the entire cultural field on which those responses rested. This strategy accounts for the social heterogeneity of theatrical audiences and their inevitably idiosyncratic reactions by mapping the overall horizon of expectations beyond which performance becomes unintelligible.[17] Rather than focusing on dramatic *representation* – by, say, poring over legal records to understand onstage trials or reading through early modern marriage manuals to contextualize domestic scenes – I turn now to theatrical *presentation* by examining early modern experiences of spectatorship. This approach enables us to see how theatre functions not just as a backdrop to culture but as the very means through which culture is created and circulated, not simply as a social occasion but as itself a form of social production.

SENSORY PERCEPTION

How did early modern understandings of visuality and aurality influence experiences of theatrical spectatorship? Many texts from the period suggest that seeing and hearing were understood as forms of direct bodily contact. Scientific writings offered two complementary explanations for the workings of sight. Extramission theories held that vision occurred when rays of light shot out of the eyes and acted on the world like hands manipulating objects. Intromission theories asserted that all material substances emitted tiny particles, or *species*, that would fly into the eyes and impress themselves on the soft matter within.[18] Both notions of sight had important theatrical ramifications. Extramission theories were ascribed to performers, whose eyebeams were believed to strike spectators like missiles hitting a target; playgoers, in turn, were moved, physically and emotionally, by quite literally 'taking in' the show, in accordance with intromission theories. Sound also was thought to affect audiences in profound ways. Hearing, it was believed, occurred when external air impressed itself on the *animal spirits*, or aerated fluids, within the listener's body. These spirits circulated to the mind and the heart, producing physiological changes resulting in diverse emotions.[19] The materiality of this process suggests a palpable link between the producer and receiver of sound in the theatre. As described in the prologue to Thomas Dekker's *If This Be Not a Good Play, The Devil Is in It* (1611–12), a playgoer is spellbound when skilful actors 'tie his ear with golden chains'.[20] The organs of hearing were thus particularly vulnerable openings, as when Hamlet's uncle murders the old king with a 'leprous distillment' (1.5.64) in that orifice or when Iago pours metaphorical 'poison' (3.3.325) in Othello's ear.

Because seeing and hearing were thought to involve bodily penetration, theatrical spectatorship was powerfully imbricated in broader understandings of gender and sexuality. Such attitudes are most evident in responses to female performers in the *commedia dell'arte*. First introduced in the 1560s, these actresses were believed to seduce spectators in ways akin to Roman and Venetian courtesans. Giovan Domenico Ottonelli disparagingly comments that 'The face of the actress is an invitation to dishonesty. . . . Aristotle has written that women have two pupils in their eyes, in which they conserve a very powerful poison. And I note that even one glance is sometimes enough to steal the heart and affections of a spectator.'[21] Tommaso Garzoni likewise describes one tumbler who 'whetted a strange desire in the mob with her lascivious graces'.[22] When a group of acrobats performed in England in 1574, Thomas Norton wrote disapprovingly of the crowds who flocked to the 'unchaste, shameless, and unnatural tumblings of the Italian Women'.[23]

English antitheatricalists likewise asserted that theatre's visual and aural displays led to sexual debauchery. Philip Stubbes, for instance, insists that plays 'induce whoredom and uncleanness', not only through 'wanton gestures' but also through 'bawdy speeches' and 'such winking and glancing of wanton eyes'.[24] Stubbes's concern about the overthrow of 'maidenly virginity and chastity'[25] slides into fears of more transgressive forms of sexuality, when he worries that 'these goodly pageants being done, every mate sorts to his mate, every one brings another homeward of their way very friendly, and in their secret conclaves (covertly) they play the Sodomites, or worse'.[26] Playgoing, he argues, leads to (homo)sexual congress. Moreover, by describing these assignations as happening in their 'secret conclaves' and 'covertly', Stubbes focuses attention on interior space – as if watching and hearing plays were like being penetrated.

Or as another writer put it, plays are 'bawdy dishes delightful in taste', and their 'pleasing and ravishing' qualities are 'made more forcible by gesture and outward action', so that 'it cannot be, but that the internal powers must be moved at such visible and lively objects'.[27] Here, taste complements the other senses – an overlap that, as we shall see shortly, also informed devotional rituals around the Eucharist. Theatrical spectatorship is compared to eating, as if plays were food to be taken into the body and digested. That experience is simultaneously understood as both abhorrently violent and delightfully sexual: playgoers are moved emotionally, and their affective sensation is imagined as 'pleasing and ravishing'. A description of *commedia dell'arte* actress Vincenza Armani recounts her effect on viewers in similar terms. Her virtuoso performances famously moved audiences so much that spectators found themselves enthralled, 'accompanying her movements as if they had become the shadow of her body'. The verb used is 'rapisce' (enraptures) – a cognate of the English word 'rape' and in line with British accounts of spectacle as 'ravishing' playgoers.[28] The pleasures and perils of playhouse spectatorship are repeatedly gendered feminine, regardless of the sex of actors and audiences, both because they are morally dubious and because seeing and hearing were themselves understood as forms of physical contact.

RELIGIOUS AND CIVIC RITUAL

If early modern notions of sensory perception implied a form of bodily congress, theatrical spectatorship could never be quite neutral. The voyeuristic subject was never fully separate from the performance object. Theatre was, in this sense, efficacious: it acted on the body of the playgoer, implicating the beholder in what was beheld. How, then, did other forms of spectatorship at events intended specifically to be ritually efficacious, such as religious worship and civic processions, influence how audiences experienced theatre?

The most obvious difference between Protestant and Catholic believers in early modern Europe was the status of visual images. For Protestants, the Catholic devotion to saints was tantamount to idolatry. The main problem was not the honouring of holy men and women but rather the ritual modes used to venerate them. Among the most common was the practice of affective piety, in which worshippers would gaze upon an image for long periods of time. This act was thought to stimulate feelings within viewers that would move them spiritually in powerful ways. Contemplating *Pietà* images in which the Virgin Mary held her son's body, for instance, enabled greater empathy and identification with her suffering and loss and deepened beholders' sense for the fullness of divine love and sacrifice.[29] Even the Eucharist was primarily experienced visually, since most parishioners only took communion at Easter. In larger churches in pre-Reformation England, people even ran from chapel to chapel to view the Elevation, when the priest would hold the wafer above his head – a practice found also in late medieval Germany.[30]

Protestant Reformers rebelled against these forms of visual worship. In place of the sacramental gaze, true believers were to listen to the Word of God. As one religious pamphlet puts it, 'there is no passage more easy for the entry of vice than by the cranny of the eye'.[31] And as another polemicist describes, 'Of all the senses, none is more needful or useful than hearing. Of all the objects of hearing, none to be compared to the Word of God.'[32] This is not to say that changes in devotional ritual meant all religious imagery disappeared. The sacking of the monasteries and other iconoclastic acts were themselves represented visually (Figure 2.1), and Protestant martyrologies contained woodcut illustrations that were every bit as gory and graphic as their Catholic counterparts. However, greater emphasis was placed on hearing sermons, which were often understood as in competition with theatres. Antitheatricalist Philip Stubbes complained that plays enticed people to 'flock thither thick and threefold, when the church of God shall be bare and empty. And those that will never come at sermons will flow thither apace'.[33] Comparisons between

FIGURE 2.1: Iconoclasm during the reign of Edward VI of England. Detail from John Foxe, *Actes and monuments of matters most speciall and memorable, happening in the Church* ... (London, 1610). Folger STC 11227 copy 1, v.2 (page 1178).
Used by permission of the Folger Shakespeare Library under a Creative Commons Attribution-ShareAlike 4.0 International License.

preaching and performance were made by more neutral parties as well, such as a Dutch traveller who, upon visiting England in 1652, described sermons given in locations that were 'divided into boxes, just like a place where comedies are performed, except for a space in the middle where the common people stand'.[34]

Early modern civic processions drew on the same paradigms as devotional practices. Indeed, they often involved overlapping forms. Ecclesiastical pageants in Catholic early modern Italy, for example, often involved the public display of sacred icons or relics. Whether the artefact was paraded through the streets or set up in a fixed location while viewers processed around it, the ceremony was intended to ensure that many people would be able to receive the object's salutary effects by gazing upon it. As Edward Muir argues, the act of beholding was itself understood to be beneficial through the emanation of particles, or species, that would aid viewers spiritually – a belief that accorded with intromission theories of vision.[35] However, civic and church officials who participated in processions were not only reverential worshippers but also themselves on view (Figure 2.2). Their location relative to the spectator was thus likened to that of the holy image or icon – a power position. This form of self-display was typical of rulers across Europe, for whom being the object of the gaze was preferable to being its subject.[36]

Ritual processions were also aurally efficacious. At Rogationtide, English parishioners walked the perimeters of their land to renew boundary markers and reinforce communal memory, an annual ceremony accompanied by the ringing of church bells.[37] Bells were also a prominent feature of Queen Elizabeth's Accession Day celebrations, and when she went on progress through the countryside, she was inevitably greeted with music. The monarch and other dignitaries who exhibited themselves in processions also engaged crowds vocally, through what David Bergeron has called 'charismatic interdependence'.[38] Rulers would participate in gracious, improvised interactions with laypersons and formally involve the audience by, for instance, offering prayers and asking them to say 'Amen'. We might think of early modern playgoers' rowdy behaviour from yet another perspective, then: if being on display was a privileged position, perhaps theatrical spectators were such active participants not just because of looser standards around playhouse decorum but because attracting attention was socially beneficial. Seeing a play was all about *being* seen. Talking back was more socially prestigious than sitting quietly. The act of spectatorship – a mode of active participation – was essential for producing and ratifying sacred and secular authority.

Such cultural paradigms and practices have important consequences for the public theatres, in which processions were staged for audiences accustomed to efficacious spectatorship. The civic processions in Shakespeare and Fletcher's *Henry VIII* (1613), for instance, echoed real-life processions by actively positioning theatregoers as ritual observers. When the Duke of Buckingham, convicted of high treason, processes from his trial to his execution, one minor

FIGURE 2.2: Venetian procession around St Mark's Square. Giacomo Franco, *Habiti d'huomeni et donne Venetiane con la processione della Serma Signoria et altri particolari* . . . (Venice, 1610). Folger GT972. V5 F7 Cage (page 9). Used by permission of the Folger Shakespeare Library under a Creative Commons Attribution-ShareAlike 4.0 International License.

character says to another, 'see the noble ruin'd man you speak of' (2.1.54); the other responds, 'Let's stand close and behold him' (2.1.55). Both comments underscore their function as onstage spectators, the representational counterparts of actual playgoers. After the Duke's address to the crowd who 'thus far have come to pity me' (2.1.56), the first speaker exclaims, 'O, this is full of pity!' (2.1.137). As Marissa Greenberg has shown, such moments in plays drew on spectators' memories of actual processions they had beheld, and in doing so, they incorporated audiences more fully into the body politic by calling on them to bear witness to English history.[39] Moreover, if playgoers felt 'pity' (2.1.56, 137) for the Duke, their sensations would align them with spectators within the dramatic narrative. Such performance experiences called on – and called forth – audience members' affective responses, so that the presentational dynamics of performance, not just the story represented, functioned as potent acts of social production. Spectatorship at plays, in other words, was ritually efficacious, both within and beyond the theatre. Witnessing rendered such ceremonies legitimate; ceremonies, in turn, blessed beholders with salutary effects.

UNSCRIPTED ENTERTAINMENTS

The social efficacy of spectatorship also played an important role in the myriad *un*scripted early modern entertainments, such as acrobatics, dancing and sports. Audiences at such events often expressed admiration at extraordinary feats of bodily prowess. José de Acosta, for example, refers to the natives of 'new Spain' as 'so excellent dancers, as it is admirable' and reports that 'Some dance upon a cord, . . . others with the soles of their feet and their hams, do handle, cast up and receive again a very heavy block, which seems incredible but in seeing it.'[40] In describing Hispaniola's *casiques* (Figure 2.3), John Ogilby notes that their 'splendor consisted chiefly in dancing to his devotion'.[41] Ogilby's use of the word 'splendor' figures this performance as dazzling to beholders: the term also means 'show of riches' as well as 'brilliant light'.[42] Such reactions pertained not only to spectacles in the Americas, but also to those in Europe (Figure 2.4). One playbill, printed sometime around or shortly after 1627, advertised a performance 'wherein an Irish boy of eight years old doth vault on the high rope, the like was never seen' as well as 'other rare varieties of dancing, the like hath not been seen in the realm of England'.[43] Simon Goulart's account of 'Admirable . . . wonders of our time' similarly describes an Italian rope-dancer who would 'tie basins to his feet, and with them would run upon the rope, showing such nimble tricks, as they seemed impossible to them that had not seen them'.[44] In all of these accounts of spectacular acts, audiences expressed admiration at wondrous displays of physical skill.

FIGURE 2.3: Native dancers from the Caribbean island of Hispaniola. John Ogilby, *America: being the latest, and most accurate description of the New World . . .* (London, 1671). Folger O165, leaf 2H5 recto (page 217) [i.e., 317]. Used by permission of the Folger Shakespeare Library under a Creative Commons Attribution-ShareAlike 4.0 International License.

FIGURE 2.4: Tumblers and rope-dancers. Johann Amos Comenius, *Orbis sensualium pictus: hoc est, omnium fundamentalium in mundo rerum . . .* (London, 1685). Folger C5525, leaf S5 verso (page 266). Used by permission of the Folger Shakespeare Library under a Creative Commons Attribution-ShareAlike 4.0 International License.

SOCIAL FUNCTIONS

This sensation of admiration and wonder tends to be associated in modern critical theory primarily with spectator sports, the circus, or other extravagant entertainments. Jean Alter refers to this aspect of performance as its 'performant' function – that is, its presentational power distinct from its 'referential' function as symbol or story.[45] In early modern theatrical theory, however, admiration as spectacle had an important corollary in representational theatre. Learned discourses on Aristotle's dramatic theories often described *catharsis* as tragedy's ability to purge the spectator of harmful emotions through the experience of 'fear and pity'. However, there was also a long tradition that translated the first of these emotions not as 'fear' but as 'admiration', or *admiratio*. Whereas today we might think of these two feelings as quite different, for early modern writers they were much closer in meaning: both describe a kind of awe so overwhelming that, like an encounter with the divine, the viewer is left shaking with wonder, reverence and terror all at once. When Acosta and Goulart characterize bodily prowess as 'admirable', they invoke this sensation, which Renaissance humanists, following Aristotle, believed was produced by theatre.[46] A study of unscripted entertainments thus demonstrates how a cultural history approach can enrich and extend traditional histories of theatre: it was not simply that humanist discourses based on Aristotle influenced spectator responses to acrobats, but the latter also informed the former. Although watching acrobats and tragedy might seem to us to evoke very different sorts of feelings, both were understood in the same discursive framework by early modern writers. Theatre was not just in dialogue with *learned* dramatic philosophies prevalent at the time; a cultural history approach uncovers the broader *popular* beliefs and assumptions on which those philosophies rested.

While both representational theatre and spectacular displays of skill produced feelings of admiration in audiences, it is important to stress that admiration did not necessarily mean lack of participation. In the court masque, we find an example of theatrical activity intended explicitly as both spectacle and participatory performance. Indeed, it was also a major venue for female theatrical participation in England and France.[47] On 21 December 1635, for example, Queen Henrietta Maria's own ladies presented the anonymous French pastoral, *Florimène*, with Inigo Jones in charge of the mise-en-scène, which was a typically extravagant affair. The antimasque that followed featured a representation of 'A Man of Canada' who apparently had some terpsichorean skill. Upon entering, he declares, 'From Canada, both rough, and rude, / Come I with bare and nimble feet / Those Amazonian Maids to greet, / Which conquered them that us subdued.'[48] Like the rope-dancer described in Goulart who showed such 'nimble tricks' with his 'feet',[49] the indigenous man's 'bare and nimble feet' will facilitate his dance with the 'Amazonian Maids'.

Such royal entertainments participated in transatlantic dramatic networks that circulated problematic representations of native peoples. However, the juxtaposition of the 'Man of Canada' with Egyptians, Italians and Spaniards within the antimasque suggests a complex dynamic by which 'New World' otherness is compared to 'Old World' otherness.[50] Foreign personages, whether brown, white or red, all serve as exotic ornament, enhancing the Christmas season festivities and honouring the noble audience. Yet when played by courtiers, these outlandish 'visitors' also imply a collapsing of Other into Self. Within the frame of the show, the bodies of the aristocratic actors and the alien figures that they represent are mapped onto each other: they *appear* identical, complicating notions of racial difference founded on anatomical distinctions. In the broader context of the theatrical event, that overlap evokes a further way in which Other merges with Self: since both spectators and players were members of the court, the social ties that bind them together not only connect viewers to performers but also audiences to the foreigners being enacted. Marvelling at the wonders of the world involves active participation. Taking in spectacles from faraway lands involves literal incorporation.

In the Americas proper, the audiences for entertainments might be either native or European. William Bradford describes how local tribesmen gave the Europeans food 'entertaining us with joy', and afterwards 'desired one of our men to shoot at a crow'. When the colonists shot 'some fourscore off', the natives 'much admired it, as other shots on other occasions'.[51] At another indigenous feast a few days later, King Massasoit and his men 'went to their manner of games for skins and knives. There we challenged them to shoot with them for skins, but they durst not; only they desired to see one of us shoot at a mark, who shooting with hail-shot, they wondered to see the mark so full of holes.'[52] Native spectators are here described as responding in ways similar to the Europeans I discussed earlier: feats of prowess are 'much admired' and 'wondered' at across the board.[53] Another, more famous, incident took place when Thomas Morton and his fellows devised some 'revels and merriment after the old English custom' by erecting a maypole at Mount Wollaston, near what is now Quincy, Massachusetts.[54] After brewing 'a barrel of excellent beer . . . for all comers of that day', they 'brought the maypole to the place appointed, with drums, guns, pistols, and other fitting instruments, for that purpose; and there erected it with the help of savages, that came thither of purpose to see the manner of our revels'.[55] The colonists also made up a drinking song 'which they performed in a dance, hand in hand about the maypole, whiles one of the company sung and filled out the good liquor'.[56] Naturally, the maypole was deemed 'lamentable spectacle' by the Puritans at 'New Plymouth', who 'termed it an idol'.[57] Their fervent repudiation bespeaks the power of spectatorship: admiration and pleasure would cause Puritan onlookers to be integrated into a community they found debauched.

Although all of these incidents took place far from the royal palace, not to mention numerous rungs down the social ladder, they evince the same relationship between performer and spectator as we saw at Henrietta Maria's court: audience members are also participants, and watching the show is a form of social incorporation. The slippage between Other and Self in that antimasque can also be seen in Henry Spelman's narrative of his travels to Virginia in 1609–10. In describing Powhatan dancing, Spelman compares it to a Derbyshire custom: 'when they meet at feasts or otherwise they use sports much like to ours here in England as their dancing, which is like our Derbyshire Hornpipe, a man first and then a woman, and so through them all, hanging all in a round.'[58] The hornpipe dance may have taken several different forms, but this reference likely refers to a round country dance for couples that was popular especially at weddings.[59] When Spelman narrates what he sees, the distance between Indian and European shrinks, as his description of the action itself ('a man first and then a woman, and so through them all, hanging all in a round') applies equally to both. Moreover, comparing festive dancing in Virginia to marriage celebrations in England positions natives and colonists alike as taking part in socially significant ritual performance.

Since all these references are from a European perspective, it is difficult to know how indigenous peoples actually experienced such entertainments. What we can say, however, is that for colonists, witnessing nonverbal spectacles and participating in them were two sides of the same coin, whether they were watching native dancers or performing for them. European attitudes toward playing as a mode of communal life meant that, in a place with no playhouses, paratheatrical activities mattered all the more. Spectatorship was critical for weaving the social ties that bind – and thus vital for building a new community in a 'New World'.

CONCLUSION

In these many and varied instances, what becomes clear is that performance was absolutely central to early modern life. Theatrical activity was not just widespread, spanning disparate social strata; it was woven into the very fabric of society. Plays and playing had important consequences in the real world. Performance was *performative*, in Judith Butler's sense of the word[60]: it cited cultural commonplaces, but in doing so it simultaneously functioned as efficacious act, producing the discursive frames and material conditions that rendered it possible in the first place. Theatre, in other words, did not just reflect the world; it helped create it. For theatrical performances to take effect, to *make* effects, required the implicit social consent of large sectors of the population. In early modern Europe, that consent was integrated into the act of spectatorship itself. Seeing and hearing performance was a form of performative participation by which audiences ratified the very notion that performance mattered. In so doing, they actively affirmed their place in the social system, embodying their social roles not only by inhabiting their bodies through their eyes and ears but by incorporating the performance into themselves. Adopting a cultural history approach to early modern theatre highlights this crucial interplay between performance and social life. If all the world's a stage, then, to revise Shakespeare's words, theatrical spectatorship means that we are not all alone in this wide and universal theatre.

CHAPTER THREE

Sexuality and Gender

The Early Modern Theatrical Body

ERIC NICHOLSON

PREAMBLE

The early modern theatrical body performatively negotiated the imaginary and the real, the disciplined and the unruly, and the spiritual and the material in ways that both addressed and confounded these oppositions. Take, for example, the statue of *St. Teresa in Ecstasy* (Figure 3.1) in GianLorenzo Bernini's Cornaro Chapel (1647–52) in the Roman church of Santa Maria delle Vittoria. Bernini, himself a set designer and playwright, designed this chapel to resemble an integrated theatrical space: live visitors become similar to audience members, while in 'private boxes', half-figure marble portrait busts of the patron and his family members behold the central 'performance' of the enraptured saint. The nun's half-closed and trance-altered eyes, the angel's joyously radiant smile; her sensuously open and rapturously moaning mouth, his flawlessly smooth naked torso; her soft billowing robes, starting to slide off her body while he gently lifts her upwards: this illusionistic scene transmits the saint's account of her mystical 'transverberation', where she explains how her 'intense pain' made her feel extreme 'sweetness', and how, despite this being a spiritual rather than a physical pain, 'the body has some share in it, even a considerable share'.[1] Bernini's carefully controlled spectacle represents unruly forces that spark between the profane and the spiritual, the material and the imaginary. The body is both all too real and imaginatively transformed.

Because the practice of theatre itself depends on live human beings moving and interacting in shared times and spaces, the contested and ambiguous body

FIGURE 3.1: GianLorenzo Bernini, *The Ecstasy of St. Teresa*, 1647–52; Cornaro Chapel, Church of Santa Maria della Vittoria, Rome (Photo by Mauro Magliani for Alinari/Alinari Archives, Florence/Alinari via Getty Images).

lies always at the centre of its concerns. As attested in the vast amount of historical and critical studies dedicated to the subject since the 1980s, the early modern human body was not merely a physical entity – a functioning 'machine', as Hamlet calls it – but a site of scrutiny, redefinition, and complex, often innovative symbolic representation. In tandem with the multiple transformations of Europe and its relations with the planet's other continents, the body's cultural configurations were undergoing a process of dynamic change, debate and revaluation. For example, the development of clinical dissection, with its applications from medicine and surgery to the visual arts, practised amidst clerical opposition in both private and public spaces – eventually in purpose-built 'anatomy theatres' such as those of Padua and Leiden – led to growing rejection of the traditional Galenic 'one-sex, two-genders' model, along with an analytic treatment of the body 'in parts'.[2] This chapter, enlisting an interdisciplinary approach, focuses on how theatre became the best-suited vehicle for embodying the multiple complexities of this process. In a sense, theatrical dissections, experiments and transformations were being performed on gender roles, femininity, masculinity, marriage, adultery, and a variety of same-sex as well as heterosexual passions and desires.

FROM THE COURTLY TO THE UNRULY THEATRICAL BODY

In early modern theatre, to what extent did the sex of real bodies matter, and in what ways, according to their particular performance context?[3] One such context tended to promote formalized and gender-conscious performance, while giving prominence to women players: this was the milieu of the royal and aristocratic courts of Europe. From Lisbon to Vienna, from Naples to Edinburgh, the courtly theatrical body was on constant display, almost as much during daily rituals and ceremonies as during actual performances of plays, masques, *intermezzi*, ballets, operas, and the like. Personal attire was thus of utmost importance. In the late fifteenth to sixteenth centuries, masculinity was on prominent show, through the use of close-fitting and sometimes parti-coloured stockings, leading the attracted eye towards an often upward-thrusting codpiece. Femininity was likewise fashioned and refashioned in exhibitionistic terms, as hooped farthingales became wider, heeled shoes became taller, fabrics more expensive and elaborately woven as well as embroidered, and close-fitting bodices and corsets tighter, with protruding triangular 'plackets' or pointed 'stomachers' that directed gazes toward the (covered) female pudenda.[4] During the seventeenth century, the upper body would receive extraordinary attention at court, as both sexes wore earrings, bundles of ribbons, powders and rouge (women more than men), wigs (men more than women), and framed their faces with elaborate lace ruffs and immense fan-like collars. While men over thirty usually grew beards, a fashion emerged for sartorial opulence and carefully applied cosmetics that favoured the kind of 'effeminate' gender indeterminacy denounced by continental as well as English moralists and churchmen. When it came time to celebrate ceremonial occasions, in particular lavish and internationally attended weddings, the ostentatious theatricality of court life would be augmented by the production of sumptuous and carefully prepared events, whose professional casts and crews would accomplish spectacular sets, props, costumes, music, dancing and poetic recitation.

Since the curriculum of princely education encouraged the mastery of music, dance and spoken languages, members of royal and aristocratic families themselves were trained to perform with distinction for live and often large audiences. A premium was placed on the embodiment of 'grazia', or elegant grace, advocated by the speakers in Castiglione's *Book of the Courtier* (first published 1528). Male courtiers would deploy post-medieval courtship tropes, fighting jousts in resplendent armour, or entering in Roman-style costume on mythological floats, distributing flowers and reciting amorous verses for court ladies in attendance, as the gallant Don Virginio Orsini did during the famous Medici wedding festivities of 1589.[5] Don Virginio, who twelve years later would visit England and gain admiration there for his speaking Italian and dancing energetically with Queen Elizabeth, is a noteworthy exemplar of the male courtly performer who modulated games of homosocial competition through the use of theatrical virtuosity.

Variations of such games sometimes allowed courtly women to break free of their traditional position as passive onlookers and objects of competitive male desire. Special theatrical occasions could permit or even encourage women to become active players, assuming prominence as entertainers and potential role models. In sixteenth-century France, a group of court ladies known as 'l'escadron volant' (the flying squadron) gave cross-dressed performances on various occasions, and participated in major court productions such as Baltasar de Beaujoyeaulx's *Balet comique de la Royne* (performed in 1581, published in 1582). In this Italianate masque, la 'damoyselle de Victry' recited rhyming couplets 'with such distinction', the chronicler records, 'that those learned guests who until that moment had yet to meet her, immediately judged her vivacious mind to be capable of the most noble and most difficult things in all sciences and disciplines'.[6] The 'escadron volant' and other French female performers most likely took inspiration from visiting professional Italian actresses and singers, and in turn exported their kind of performance beyond Paris. Henrietta Maria, the French princess who became Queen of England in 1625, and her well-rehearsed women's troupe surprised local observers and impressed foreign ambassadors with their talents, in such productions as the pastoral *Shepherd's Paradise* of 1633. The testimony of an admiring Florentine spectator, who emphasizes the queen's 'grace' and 'regal' action, confirms that courtly women could enhance their status and reputations through theatrical performance.[7]

Henrietta Maria had a high-status female precursor in the palaces and banqueting halls of London: Anna of Denmark, the consort of King James I, who promoted the regular production of Ben Jonson's and Inigo Jones's masques. She and her ladies-in-waiting also took an active part in them as costumed dancers. In their doing so, biological differences as well as gender-related behaviour codes could become a complicating factor, for example, when Anna's six-month-pregnant body added to the unsettling effects of her wearing black greasepaint and pseudo-African attire as one of the daughters of the River Niger in *The Masque of Blackness* (1605). Records of dismayed audience reaction to this masque support Clare McManus's argument that while Queen Anna and her dancing colleagues were meant to represent the virtues of grace, fertility and earthly bounty, their physical embodiment of consummated female sexuality disrupted the political-aesthetic purpose.[8] In short, even the scrupulously fashioned courtly body could yield to instability and self-contradiction.

Like their counterparts on the continent, Queen Anna and her female co-performers faced the dilemma of publicly embodying their own spiritual, moral and intellectual virtues before live audiences, while at the same time risking association with the vicious impulses often staged in preceding 'anti-masque' dances and routines, such as that of twelve hag/witches in *The Masque of Queens* (1609), or of the 'she-monster' inspired by the Italian *commedia dell'arte*, who is 'delivered of six burratines that dance with six pantaloons' in *The Vision of Delight* (1617). Specific cultural and national practices could also condition responses to women's performances. In 1620s Paris, there emerged a vogue for burlesque ballet, favouring ludicrous and satirical *entrée* routines based on caricatured portrayals of lower and middle-class life. It was most likely a female version of this kind of grotesque dance that a group of elderly ladies performed in 1625 at the English court of Henrietta Maria, perhaps too boldly and comically for the tastes of their unimpressed English audience.[9] Rejecting the geometrically patterned and verbally programmed modes of preceding French courtly dance, the burlesque ballet productions of the 1620s foregrounded the dancing body itself, as well as parodic and potentially subversive energies more typical of popular and Carnivalesque milieux.[10]

In this latter regard, these Baroque productions show an affinity with the rich repertoire of French farces, which flourished in late medieval times but continued to influence European performance traditions into the seventeenth century and beyond. The unruly theatrical body, with its capacity to express social and political tensions through the prism of sexually related misconduct, was a defining element of the *farceurs*' productions. As stated in a 1541 decree of the Parlement de Paris, 'lascivious farces have led to infinite fornications and adulteries, to scandals, derisions, and mockeries'.[11] These magistrates thus tried to impose a traditional Christian belief that the staged portrayal of illicit sex would prompt audiences to perform equally illicit acts. The repressive officials, however, were in the minority, and most spectators probably applauded the farces for the same reasons that the censors tried to suppress them. Moreover, the farces' conditions of production tended to be festive, youth-oriented and boldly impudent. As cultural historians have shown, the worlds of 'misrule' and Carnival in early modern Europe were dialectically engaged with authoritarian institutions, and thus inclined towards public demonstrations and performances of inversion.[12] Favourite Carnivalesque themes like the 'woman on top', and youth overcoming old age, appear in the recorded paratheatrical activities of urban males' festive clubs and confraternities, such as the Compagnie della Calza (Companies of the Hose) of Venice, the Compagnie de la Mère Folle (Company of the Crazy Mamma) of Dijon, and the Abbaye des Conards (Abbey of Fucking Idiots) of Rouen.

The most theatrically active French youth societies, however, were the 'Basochiens', the junior law clerks and students of the Parlements of Paris, Toulouse, Rouen and Bordeaux. These all-male clubs cultivated their rhetorical and presentational skills through their part-time work as comic authors, trying facetious legal cases ('causes grasses') once a week. Just as importantly, the Basochiens became adept at the bawdy physical performance of both genders, playing favourite comical characters like the lecherous priest, the stupid and jealous husband (often a cobbler or tinker), and the self-assertive, sexually unsatisfied, and ingeniously scheming wife.[13] Such types, moreover, carried special transnational interest in early capitalist and Reformation-era Europe, as shown by the 'kluchten' farces frequently staged by the Netherlandish *rederijker kamers*, literary-theatrical societies whose members came from diverse social classes: an evident crowd-pleaser, depicted in numerous prints and paintings, was the 'Klucht van Plaeyerwater', with its curious husband who tries to spy on his wife and her lover by having himself carried into his own house inside a large basket (see the front cover illustration by Peeter Baltens: *Een opvoering van de klucht 'Een cluyte van Plaeyerwater' op een Vlaamse kermis* [A Flemish Kermis with a Performance of the Farce 'Een cluyte van Plaeyerwater']).[14]

Not surprisingly, several farces composed and performed by the Basochiens have a strongly juridical flavour, playing out a scenario of just compensation for a sexually related fault or misdeed, and directly appealing to the audience as virtual witnesses/jury members. Played by young cross-dressed law clerks, the 'wives' in these pieces often seek to escape from jealous, cruel and unusual restraint, and in doing so 'legislate' their own comic order of laughter and delight. The farce of *De deux jeunes femmes qui coiferent leurs maris* (Two Young Wives Who Doll Up Their Husbands, or literally 'who put headgear on/ mislead their husbands') opens with a couturier and a stockings-maker complaining of their being cuckolded and dominated, and vowing to reclaim their authority, by force if necessary (2.16–23).[15] When their wives appear, however, the two husbands soon capitulate, and in the end the two women succeed in placing female headgear on the two men, in full view of the audience.[16] The farceurs thus cajole their spectators to laugh at a scenario of gender-based role reversal, with a stress on public shame, and a sense of pillory-enforced justice: 'It will be a great big disgrace', cries the dressmaker at the prospect of his transvestite appearance. Fittingly, the outcome of the play refuses to condemn the wives for their fashionable dress and insubordinate actions.

The festive context of the Basochiens' productions allowed for alternative if not exactly 'feminist' visions of the unruly female body, as seen in stagings of the unequal social privileges of men and women. Theatrical travesty and cross-dressing could dramatize, in material form, the possibility for equitable compensation. In *La farce de celui qui se confesse* (literally, 'The Farce of the Man Who Confesses', but more pithily and wittily translated by Jody Enders as 'Confession Lessons'),[17] a woman named Colette, friend and neighbour to the wife of the philandering, physically abusive title character, disguises herself as a priest, and learns that the husband's lover is none other than her own daughter! As the two offended women plot to humiliate the wayward male, one of them declares that 'it seems that we two will make a charivari together', an explicit reference to the late medieval and early modern rite designed to shame members of the community who had allegedly transgressed the norms of marital propriety. As often as not, these supposed transgressors were remarrying widows or widowers, or an elderly husband with a much younger bride.[18] Thus the self-proclaimed charivari of Colette and the wife of 'Confession Lessons' is a suggestive variant, given that their target is not a woman who might be seen as ready to dominate or betray her spouse, but rather an adulterous, brutal and would-be domineering husband.

The fact that the players of these late-fifteenth- and early-sixteenth-century French farces were all male increased their proximity to the disordering facets of the charivaris. These shaming rituals inverted the apparatus and proceedings of a conventional wedding ceremony, substituting cuckold's horns for spouses' rings, discordant for harmonious music, and cross-dressing for heteronormative male and female attire. Nor were such histrionic activities limited to France: to name but two other countries, they were practised in Italy, where they were called 'mattinate', and in England, where obstreperous, satirical 'rough music' and the typically backwards 'Skimmington Rides' on a mule or donkey were enacted.[19] Men whose wives had purportedly beaten them would be impersonated by their neighbours, who would also sometimes cross-dress and play the part of the transgressing wife, admonishing female onlookers to remember their duty to obey their husbands. In the very act of asserting the patriarchal standard, however, these performances could call attention to the artificial and unstable qualities of that standard: their theatricality heightened the sense that men and women's sexual and marital relationships, as well as their gender, might be determined less by nature than by role-playing.

Records of several Italian 'mariazi', French farces, English jigs and other mocking skits, confirm the fact that staging real-life sexual episodes could bring distress and further loss of reputation to the parties in question. In 1602 in Skelton, Yorkshire, a certain Michael Steel took his case all the way to the Star Chamber high court, complaining that he had been brought 'into utter disgrace among his neighbours' after his adulterous liaison with his maidservant Frances Thornton had been represented by 'stage players who by practyce and procurement have at the ending of their playes sunge the same as a Jigg'.[20] Even prominent London theatre professionals sometimes collaborated on potentially libellous stagings of sexual and marital scandals. In 1624, Thomas Dekker, William Rowley, John Ford and John Webster co-wrote a lost play entitled *The Late Murder of the Son upon the Mother, or Keep the Widow Waking*, staged at the Red Bull Theatre in Clerkenwell. This docudrama was based on a criminal conspiracy that took place in July of the same year. The victim of this plot was the wealthy widow Anne Elsdon, aged sixty-two, and her primary abuser was the tobacconist Tobias Audley, aged twenty-five. With the help of two disreputable preachers, a prostitute and her procuress, Audley abducted Elsdon and dragged her from one London tavern to another, keeping her in a drunken stupor until he coerced her into a technically legal marriage with him. Eventually he removed various deeds, titles, and 140 pounds worth of gold, rings and plate from Elsdon's house, causing the widow's son-in-law Benjamin Garfield to take him to court. Before the case reached the Star Chamber, however, Audley had commissioned Dekker, Rowley, and several actors to write and perform 'one scandalous enterlude or play', with the intent 'to scandalize and discrace Anne Elsden and make her ridiculous to the world', and arranged for it 'to be severall tymes acted and played at the playhouse called the Bull'.[21] This was the same Red Bull Theatre that about five years earlier had served as the venue for the play *Swetnam the Woman-Hater Arraigned by Women* (anonymous, first published 1620). This lively comedy uses a male-to-female cross-dressing 'Amazon' character to ridicule, humiliate and convert its title character, based on the real-life misogynist Joseph Swetnam. In 1615, Swetnam had published the antifeminist tract 'The Arraignment of Lewd, Idle, Froward, and Unconstant Women', which received a series of convincing proto-feminist rebuttals credited to women authors. Thus the Red Bull, known for its rowdy, mainly working-class male clientele, could host a play that was notably sympathetic to women and their honourable reputations. Perhaps what matters most is the fact that dramatizing current controversies could increase attendance and profits, which would also explain why a playwright like Dekker – sometimes advanced as a candidate for the authorship of *Swetnam the Woman-Hater* – could champion an unorthodox, independent, cross-dressing, lute-playing and comically talented contemporary London woman like Mary Frith, alias Moll Cutpurse in *The Roaring Girle* (co-written with Thomas Middleton in 1610–11 (Figure 3.2)), and then help to victimize a cruelly exploited one with *The Late Murder of the Son upon the Mother, or Keep the Widow Waking*.

Moreover, Audley's theatrical humiliation of Anne Elsdon can be understood as a case study in both psychological projection and comic substitution. The unruly body, still governed in many people's view by the four humours – sanguine, choleric, phlegmatic and melancholic – codified by post-Galenic medicine, is again at stake here, since according to this system a sexually mature woman, as the 'weaker' and 'leakier vessel', was much more prone than a man to succumb to her bodily appetites.[22] Women's supposedly insatiable libido could be cited as justification for husbands to control and confine their wives, as a precaution against being turned into cuckolds. This prejudice could lead men to endow the object of their hazing routines and scornful laughter with vulnerable qualities that they feared in themselves. Thus Tobias Audley could have exploited the stereotype of the lecherous, dissipate widow in order to displace his own guilt in abusing his elderly 'bride'.[23] Instead of laughing at the young, cynical and greedy fortune hunter, the audience could have been

FIGURE 3.2: Frontispiece to *The Roaring Girle, or Moll Cut-purse*, 1611, by Thomas Middleton and Thomas Dekker. (Photo by Culture Club/Getty Images.)

invited to laugh at the sexually incontinent woman, whose volatile female fluids determined her outrageous actions.

The widespread but also contested assumption of female sexual incontinence, and the related fear of cuckoldry and being mocked through the sign of ironically impotent horns became a hallmark of many early modern European theatrical comedies as well as tragedies.[24] Their challenge as well as their popularity depended at least in part on two interrelated phenomena: first, that of female agency, since women who made horned 'beasts' or even 'monsters' of their husbands were perceived as becoming active, dominant individuals; second, that of collective theatricality, since husbands' anxieties about controlling their wives' sexual behaviour were embedded in a culture of public shame and shaming, where one's identity and status were formed, observed and policed as much by external communities as by internal conscience. The male and female bodies, whether actual or simulated, of the charivaris and analogous rituals tended to differ from the ones on display at court: if the latter strove to channel sexual energies toward harmony, symmetry and grace, with an agenda of marital concord and aristocratic procreation, the former accentuated the unruly, discontinuous and ambivalent aspects of human sexuality.

THE DESIRED, FABRICATED AND MARKETED THEATRICAL BODY

The physical configurations and material conditions of public performance spaces in early modern Europe favoured the pressing together of bodies, enabling playgoers to brush up closely against each other, and to see and be seen at very close range by actors themselves. Flamboyantly dressed, tobacco-smoking gallants would sometimes sit on the stages of Southwark theatres, while 'groundlings' of both sexes crowded together in the yard, not unlike the obstreperous, vegetable-throwing 'mosqueteros' of the Spanish 'corrales'. In the public theatres of Spain, women were segregated in the upper 'cazuela' or 'stew-pot' area, but they were still highly visible, and involved in the theatrical event, expressing favour or disfavour by loudly rattling bunches of keys.[25] The fact that licensed brothels were located near commercial theatres in cities like Florence, Seville, Paris and Southwark also encouraged the notion that the act of playgoing was akin to the act of frequenting prostitutes. Not only Counter-Reformation bishops and cardinals, or Protestant antitheatricalists, but also less polemical observers would sexualize the exchange between players and their customers. In his *Vices Anotimie* (1617), Robert Anton claims that performances of 'Cleopatra's crimes', 'Poppea's pride', and other lascivious lessons in lust and lechery are enough to 'turn a modest audience / To brazen-faced profession of a whore'.[26] Another London-based commentator, William Goddard, in his *Neaste of Waspes* (1615), fully conflates theatrical and sexual acting, in verses that explain how an actor is a whore, a whore is an actor: through the act of 'tiring', men simultaneously change their outfits and undergo sexual exhaustion.[27] In this context of (at)tiring, of getting into costume, it is pertinent to note that cross-dressing was widely practised by prostitutes, both on the continent and in England as a means of exciting clients' desire.[28] Pietro Bertelli's 1580s print of a Venetian courtesan plays on this syndrome, inviting the viewer to lift a paper flap and see the female figure wearing masculine breeches

FIGURE 3.3: Venetian courtesan with blind Cupid. Engraving by Pietro Bertelli, *c.* 1588. Reproduction made available by The Metropolitan Museum of Art Open Access for Scholarly Content program.

beneath her feminine dress (Figures 3.3 and 3.4). Likewise, the cross-dressing boy actors of the stage were often charged with homosexual prostitution, though opinions on this subject ranged from the puritanical to the tolerant and even indulgent. As Stephen Orgel makes clear, the majority attitude towards transvestite boy actors was that they posed less of a threat to social order and sexual identity than would professional public actresses, because of an especially English concern to police women's heterosexual behaviour.[29]

The correlation between theatrical role-playing and illicit sexual activity both attracted and repelled early modern Europeans. This ambivalent attitude befits the liminal status of the prostitute, sought after but reviled, dependent on patronage but also more autonomous than the majority of daughters, nuns, wives and widows of the era. The prostitute's transgressions of social and physical boundaries could extend so far as to confuse established categories of gender. John Taylor, in his pamphlet 'A Common Whore' (1622), argues that a 'meretrix'

> will soon decline
> *Mulier* into the gender masculine
> By her attire, of which sex she should be,
> She seems the doubtful gender unto me.[30]

FIGURE 3.4: Venetian courtesan with 'raised skirt' (flap of paper). Engraving by Pietro Bertelli, from *Diversarum nationum habitus* (Padua, 1591). Private Collection. (Photo by Fine Art Images/Heritage Images/Getty Images.)

Taylor's poem suggests that the prostitute's ambiguous persona was made all the more troubling by her promiscuity, her 'doubtful gender' reflecting her mobile circulation through the streets, theatres and social groups of the city. Further provocation as well as fascination derived from the prostitute's – and particularly the 'high-end' courtesan's – capabilities as a kind of theatrical performer. Nor did she need to speak a word: her body language, from a smile beneath a half-mask, to her gestures and hand signals, to her towering over men as well as women when she wore foot-high platform shoes could make a special appeal to onlookers' attentions.

While the actual prostitutes who could be seen in the public playhouses of Southwark, or in nearby 'bawdy-houses', were impersonated on stage by young male actors in English plays of the period, such impersonating would no longer necessarily apply to theatrical practice on the European continent after the 1560s. The talents and charisma of some female sex professionals were certainly more admired and emulated in Venice and other cities of Italy than in England. Whether or not particular courtesans came to join professional acting companies, the performative gifts of both kinds of professionals considerably overlapped: their proficiencies included singing, dancing, instrumental playing,

SEXUALITY AND GENDER

musical and theatrical improvisation—in short, the capacity to perform publicly in a variety of ways. Thus the professional actress's rise to acclaim can be linked to precedents established by 'honoured' courtesans of the early to mid-sixteenth century, such as Tullia d'Aragona (1508–56), renowned for her exceptional skills as a singer, poet and philosopher.[31] Despite the esteem accorded to such admired as well as 'honourably' desired women, stigmas attached to the prostitute's profession would afflict actresses through the following decades and even centuries. While Thomas Nashe shows a protectionist English bias in his declaration that 'our players are not as the players beyond the sea, a sort of squirting bawdy comedians, that have whores and common courtesans to play women's parts',[32] the early-seventeenth-century Spanish Jesuit Jaime Alberto even more prudishly decries theatres as 'the shrine of Venus', where 'vainglorious females' are 'enticements to sensuality', and 'actresses, interludes, gallantries, music, and dancing are the fifth essence of lasciviousness'.[33] His extreme antipathy can be seen as one of the comical targets in such contemporary Spanish gender-juggling plays as Guillen de Castro's *La fuerza de la costumbre*.[34] The actress-as-whore identification also could move beyond the pages of theological diatribes, and complicate the working lives of acting companies: for example, it appears in the Tuscan Granducal commissioner's 1576 ban on a travelling troupe from playing in Pisa, because of 'certain love affairs of the actresses'.[35]

The trope of enchantment by female performance had a long and complex history pre-dating the arrival of actresses and professional singers on continental European stages. Many late medieval and Renaissance moralizers defined the classical sirens as erotic temptresses, whose irresistible song could lead men to sinful doom; at the same time, the Neo-Platonic association of the sirens with heavenly harmonies and the music of the spheres nurtured a positive and at times reverential esteem for the professional female player. The now familiar term 'diva', literally 'heavenly one', comes into currency in this period. As Anne MacNeil, Rosalind Kerr and others have shown, the modern fetishization of the actress as a special being or 'star' begins in late sixteenth-century Italy – also emerging soon after in France, as Virginia Scott demonstrates – and gains dissemination through adulatory non-dramatic texts.[36] For example, Tommaso Garzoni writes in 1584 of the Gelosi troupe's renowned Vittoria Piissimi, calling her 'that Divine Vittoria who creates metamorphoses of herself on the stage, that beautiful sorceress of love who wins the hearts of a thousand lovers with her words, that sweet siren whose melodious enchantments catch the souls of her adoring spectators, and certainly deserves to be held the epitome of her profession'.[37]

In the previous decade, the Jewish playwright and impresario of Mantua Leone De' Sommi had dedicated over a hundred eulogistic lines to the multitalented Vincenza Armani, calling her an 'immortal goddess' adept at playing both the 'armed woman warrior' and 'the lovely young woman aflame with love', and capable of shining a 'divine light' when she wears a 'manly guise'. De' Sommi's verses were appended to an 'Orazione', published in 1570 by the Veronese actor Adriano Valerini in memoriam of 'la Divina Signora Vincenza Armani, Comica Eccellentissima'. In his oration, Valerini stresses the protean versatility of Vincenza, as he extols her acting, her writing the lyrics and the settings of her own sonnets and madrigals, and her almost superhuman singing and instrument-playing: like Orpheus, she could instantly convert her listeners' sorrow into happiness.[38] Among the crowd-pleasing turns practised by the *prime donne innamorate* of troupes like the Gelosi, dressing in 'viril manto' and playing the man was one of the most crucial. Thus De' Sommi's call for giving Vincenza 'eternal homage' occurs as the flourish to his praise of the actress's androgynous performative skills.

This cross-gendering motif recurs in encomia of the most famous of all early *dive*, Isabella Andreini (1562–1604), star and co-leader of the Gelosi with her husband Francesco. The masculine 'virtù' of Isabella works like a key signature in the orchestration of her 'virtuosa' persona, which will ensure her eternal fame. Her Flemish admirer and correspondent Erycius Puteanus declares that she is 'not only capable of male glory but in fact an equal partner in it', her French eulogizer Isaac du Ryer proposes that she 'is one of the gods, who has disguised himself as a woman, in order to ravish our souls through our ears and eyes', and her Italian supporter Torquato Tasso concludes his laudatory sonnet 'Bella d'Asia' with the lines 'Happy the souls, and fortunate the hearts / where with letters of gold Love imprints himself, / in your image, and wherein he is adored.'[39] In Tasso's elaborate conceit, Isabella is cast as the male love-god, but retains her own features, while pressing or imprinting – more like an 'active' Aristotelian male than a 'passive' female – into waxen hearts and souls her/his/Love's adored image. She was clearly a master of gender-inflected paradox, for her most famous routine, 'La Pazzia', required her to stay in lucid, 'manly' command of her specialized linguistic and kinetic techniques, even as she convincingly represented a female love-madness that could possibly communicate Neo-Platonic ideas.[40] Isabella also published non-theatrical as well as theatrical texts to shield herself from envious accusations as well as deadly obscurity. Her death in 1604, at the age of forty-two, followed all too soon upon the publication of her *Rime*, whose outstanding opening poem plays wittily on Isabella's 'finti detti', 'falsi miei dolori', and 'falsi miei diletti' performed 'nei Teatri' – in short, her seemingly true but actually false sayings, sorrows and delights – with woman/man gender alternations: 'hor Donna, hor / Huom fei'.[41]

Thus the 'Renaissance regime of *virtù*', as Guido Ruggiero puts it, meant that publicly performing courtesans, female singers and actresses had the power to delight and enchant their male clients and audiences, who in the process risked losing both prestige and their own masculine selves.[42] As bi-gendered *virtuose,* courtesans and actresses were capable of spoofing conventional distinctions and binary opposites related to both morality and gender. That Italian female theatre artists and their male colleagues were well aware of this spoof can be seen in the self-referential 'commedia dell'arte scenario' called 'The Portrait' ('il Ritratto'), published in Flaminio Scala's repertory *Il Teatro delle favole rappresentative* (1611). Here Vittoria Piissimi appears as the character Vittoria, a charismatic travelling diva who provokes adulterous yearnings in the married men of the city of Parma, and outraged reactions from their wives. Meanwhile, Isabella, the wife of Pantalone, is conducting an affair with the young gallant Orazio, who had given his lover's miniature portrait to Vittoria and thus caused much of the plot intrigues of the play. As if to ensure the wry, self-conscious send-up of prejudices against the professional actress, the Isabella character harangues Vittoria as a 'wandering whore', and at a certain point brings a 'page-boy' into her house, the suggestively named Lesbino, who is actually the young 'innamorata' Silvia in cross-dressed disguise. The overlay of homoerotic implications recalls one of the 'commedia dell'arte' players' preferred source-scripts, the comedy *Gl' ingannati* (The Deceived, 1532) by the Accademia degli Intronati of Siena, with its scene originally played by an all-male cast wherein the cross-dressed protagonist Lelia and Isabella, the young woman who has fallen in love with her/him, kiss each other repeatedly and passionately, in a way that is at once 'heterosexual', as well as both male and female 'homosexual'.[43] As elsewhere in early modern theatre, perhaps 'performatively polymorphous' would be the most appropriate term to use, even for Andreini, who constructed a public image of herself as a devoted wife and mother of seven children.

If women played their own roles on the continent, while talented teenage male actors emulated their versatile, charismatic, and poetically demanding performances on English public stages, the two distinct theatre cultures thus shared a fascination with female agency, especially as they often – in specular ways – staged how women could act themselves while acting as/like men. This demonstrative kind of staging sustains Peter Stallybrass's insight that the English theatre of this period organized gender through an ambivalent process of fetishizing, wherein contradictory fixations prevailed over general indeterminacy.[44] While Stallybrass's focus is on the English boy actor and prosthesis in Elizabethan and Jacobean plays, his argument can be applied to the 'playing with gender' enacted by professional female performers in Italy and other European countries. They might sometimes resemble courtesans, but their bodies were not for sale: instead, as they performed representations of sexual intrigues and relationships, for audiences that included large numbers of female spectators, they showed how women could be protagonists in every sense of the term, both on and off the stage.[45] This pattern again operates in specular relation to the phenomenon of transvestite boy actors, for as Stephen Orgel eloquently concludes – citing *The Roaring Girl* as a key case in point – early modern theatre

SACRED AND PROFANE THEATRICAL BODIES

While all-male public acting companies remained the norm in England until the mid-seventeenth century, there was a European tradition of organized all-female performance, which continued to thrive during the same period: Catholic convent theatre. Free from the stigmas and prejudices faced by women who performed before paying audiences, the nuns who wrote and staged plays within convent walls could do so with a confident sense of autonomy, in generally safe havens for female performance.[47] Whereas a monk or friar was enjoined to lead a life devoid of any erotic imaginings, a nun was mystically designated a 'bride of Christ', and could express her devotion to God in terms of spousal union and amorous passion. A century after Saint Teresa's time, a revealing case is that of Marcela de San Felix (1605–87), the illegitimate daughter of the renowned professional actress Micaela de Lujan and her lover Lope de Vega, the most prolific and successful Spanish playwright of the era. While this remarkable woman, who inherited her father's literary talents, took religious orders at the age of sixteen partially to escape living in proximity to Lope's promiscuous sexual habits, she also did so, as Electa Arenal observes, because 'the conventions of female monastic life gave her the opportunity to act in dramatic spectacles; ascetic language enabled her to describe the Brides of Christ as dynamic, active partners in the divine coupling.'[48]

Varieties of 'spiritual fun' ('spasso onesto' and 'ricreazioni') were also practised in early modern Italian convents. Elissa Weaver explains how a good part of this fun involved not only regular opportunities for talented women to prepare, rehearse, and express themselves in active, collaborative ways, but also the use of a semi-public forum – laypeople, including Medici dignitaries, sometimes were in attendance – to explore stories and themes related to women's sexual virtue.[49] Despite official opposition to nuns performing contemporary-style *commedie* rather than traditional *sacre rappresentazioni* (sacred dramas), and to their wearing of fine dresses, jewellery, wigs, beards, men's tights, and other profane costume pieces and accessories, many productions did use techniques similar to those that distinguished the nascent secular theatre of late-fifteenth- to early-sixteenth-century Italy. Some written and performed playscripts, like the *Commedia ovvero tragedia di Santa Teodora vergine e martire* (first published 1544) ironically recall the gender-switching of the performing nuns themselves. Thus, while it is true that basic assumptions of women as the weaker sex mark the majority of the saints' and other kinds of plays written and staged by early modern Italian nuns, the very fact of their production, their formative influence on intellectual women like Moderata Fonte (Modesta Pozzo), and their lasting success in printed and reprinted editions confirm that they offered a significant theatrical affirmation of the sanctified female body, mind and soul.[50]

Moving from the convent world to the much more public one of Spanish *autos sacramentales* (Sacramental Performances), one encounters evidence of how productions designed to promulgate Counter-Reformation doctrines could also bespeak the contentious approaches to sexual relations and identities that distinguish contemporary non-religious theatre. With generous church funding, the *autos* were vigorously promoted during the late sixteenth through seventeenth centuries, and performed during the late spring festival of Corpus Christi by professional as well as amateur players of both sexes. The scripts of these plays usually concluded with an affirmation of patriarchal hierarchies, but along the way indecorous sexual behaviour was often staged, and unconventional gender roles could be communicated. The material staging conditions of Spanish *autos*, as well as the entire occasion of their productions, also could permit even bolder and more provocative cuttings against the prevailing grain of gender fixity and sexual morality.[51] The actors and actresses of these religious pieces performed these plays on carts, moving from town to town: as a result, they suffered the standard accusation of vagabondage, and the prejudiced view that their travelling mode favoured promiscuity and dissolution.

In Spain as elsewhere, gaps between rigorous rules and flexible practices abounded. In Jesuit school theatre, for instance, restrictions were loosened to allow for bawdy talk and risqué jokes, while female saint characters, who often had to resist unwanted advances and attempts to seduce or violate them, were played by cross-dressed young male students.[52] This concession notwithstanding, the ban against boy transvestite actors on the public stages eventually became rigorous: this enforced a brutally homophobic (or anti-'sodomitic') bias in early modern Spanish culture, which shared the English anxiety that transvestism, whether practised by male or female players, would lead to effeminization and social decadence.[53]

While Jesuit authorities cited the danger of sexual immorality to justify prohibiting members of their order from attending Spanish public theatres (1582), at the same time they were organizing theatrical productions on a global basis, not only in Latin America but also in East Asian countries. Succeeding in converting thousands, the Jesuits flourished in Japan until Christianity was formally outlawed as a religion during the 1630s. As scholars like Thomas Leims have shown, Jesuit theatre in Japan was an artistically inventive activity, inclined to blend didactic Western Christian theatre with the native traditions of Noh and Kyogen.[54] This favouring of hybridization may have influenced the birth of a new Japanese theatrical art form, one which often expresses sensuality and amorous passion. In 1603, the charismatic female performer Izumo no

Okuni started to enact the dances and routines which would become known as 'Kabuki odori'. In later times, the compound 'ka-bu-ki' would be written in Chinese-derived characters meaning 'song-dance-skill'. This term, however, also can be translated as 'dances' ('odori') of a rebellious, non-conformist ('Kabuki') kind: by the early seventeenth century, the word 'kabuki,' originally meaning to 'bend exaggeratedly forward and over', had come to signify

FIGURE 3.5: Anonymous, detail of Izumo No Okuni performing in hybrid samurai and European costume, from the 'Okuni Kabuki Screen' painting, *c.* 1610, Kyoto (courtesy Kyoto National Museum Photographic Services).

outlandish personal display and transgressive behaviour, as practised by the so-called *kabuki mono*: these were young, often dispossessed samurai ('ronin') who wore outrageous costumes, grew their hair long and wild, carried elaborately decorated swords, and smoked four-foot-long pipes.[55] This male extravagance was imitated by Okuni herself, who sometimes performed in samurai outfits and swords.[56] Contemporary paintings also show how she incorporated European elements in her hybrid performances: a rosary with crucifix dangles from her neck, and/or she sports Portuguese male hats and trousers (Figure 3.5).

As she gained popularity, Okuni joined forces with other female performers as well as prostitutes. Travelling through Japan, these women created 'onna kabuki', or 'women's kabuki', which caused so many scandals that it was banned by the repressive Shogunate in 1629. Moreover, Okuni was a junior priestess/ shaman or 'Miko' turned public actress: while she helped to invent a secular theatrical mode, she retained associations with the divine world, for example in her mystically performing with the ghost of her ronin lover Nagoya Sansaburo. In this way, Okuni juggled the sacred and the profane for the sake of heterogeneous audiences who could enjoy seeing the masked, all-male, elite Noh theatre transformed into the unmasked, all-female, humble-class Kabuki.

Okuni's flamboyant, transcultural and transgendered body, both sanctified and parodic, would provide the model for later Kabuki practices, even as the practitioners of the art form became exclusively male, including the specialized transvestite virtuoso known as the 'onnagata'. Finally, as if to foreground her spectacularization of the individual female performer, Okuni devised early versions of the 'hanamichi', the raised 'flower path' runway that passes above the heads of the audience, who are thus forced to look up at gaudily robed, heavily cosmeticized, larger-and-more-dazzling-than-life figures. Like Bernini's rendition of Saint Teresa in Ecstasy, her performances invited viewers to transport their carnally erotic sensibilities towards a higher spiritual level, above and beyond the material means of theatrical representation.

CHAPTER FOUR

The Environment of Theatre

Urbanization and Theatre Building in Early Modern Europe

KAREN NEWMAN

Europe boasted no purpose-built theatres in 1400. Theatre was performed inside or just outside of churches, in piazzas, in streets, whether at random or in the great processions of the mystery plays, and in various indoor venues: great halls, municipal buildings and at court. In medieval Europe, 'theatre' did not carry a specific architectural meaning; it was an activity that took place in found spaces, but by 1650, purpose-built theatres had been constructed in England, Spain, Italy and France – in fact throughout Europe. Although theatre continued to be performed in the spaces where it had thrived in the medieval period, beginning with the rediscovery of Vitruvius' *De architettura*, with elaborations by Alberti, Serlio and others, the term 'theatre' was revived as a distinct type of architectural structure, legitimized by classical precedent, whence James Burbage's famous naming of the structure erected in Shoreditch, outside of London's city walls in 1576, 'The Theatre'. Cities and towns spurred the development of late medieval drama, and the acceleration of urbanization – demographic growth, commerce and trade – in the early modern period led to the construction of specially designated theatre buildings that located theatrical activity firmly in the urban landscape in what came to be called 'theatre districts'.

Early modern theatre in Europe, then, was performed in streets and plazas, inn-yards, courtyards and tennis courts, halls and banqueting rooms, schools and universities, and finally in purpose-built theatres and playhouses at court and in cities. Early theatre itself was as varied and heterogeneous as the venues in which it was performed, from the theatre of mountebanks, bear baiting, May-games, street theatre and the like, to celebrations of power in pageants, revels, masques, processions and entries, from religious drama performed on festival days to the classically inflected productions of humanist academies, from school theatricals in Latin to the highly organized performances of professional troupes such as the *commedia dell'arte* players and the English companies that depended on a royal or aristocratic patron. These multiple spaces were themselves situated in diverse environments that were changing profoundly: Renaissance theatre was a sociocultural event that needs to be understood not only by considering what happened on stage, but also by analysing the multiple arenas in which performance took place. In what follows I consider four major performance environments in Western Europe: streets and plazas, including fairs and markets; courts and aristocratic households; academies, schools and universities; and finally public commercial and purpose-built theatres. These arenas are not entirely separate, so I also point out the ways in which they sometimes overlap.

STREETS AND PLAZAS

Environmental and architectural historians have long noted the persistence of certain 'architectural objects' in urban environments. Theatres are a major example, which in the classical period were found all over the Mediterranean, and from the Renaissance onward, in a city of almost any size.[1] Yet in the Middle Ages, theatre took place in central open spaces of cities and towns such as the sixteen-hour cycle pageant performed in the Piazza Signoria that moved out through the streets of Florence on the feast of St. John in 1454, or the Misterio de Elche in Catalonia, which seems to date from the thirteenth century and is still performed today, or the Passion plays presented in towns in the north, including at Bolzano over seven days in 1514. As Lewis Mumford noted long ago, the medieval town was 'a stage for the ceremonies of the Church'.[2]

Theatrical production in the Renaissance shifted from such outdoor performances to indoor purpose-built theatres in urban environments, but street performance, and theatre in market places, fairs and plazas, continued to flourish throughout the early modern period. Passion plays, 'sacra rappresentazione', and mystery cycles continued to be performed in the streets into the seventeenth century, but secular activities of various kinds also shared the urban stage. From at least the thirteenth century, rituals and entertainments of various kinds were mounted by cities to celebrate accession, coronation, dynastic weddings and births, royal visits, and military victories. In the mercantile cities of the Low Countries, civic pageants and festivities celebrated

THE ENVIRONMENT OF THEATRE
73

guilds and their trades as well as religious holidays and are said to have been the
prototypes for London's civic pageantry.[3] Renaissance princes admired the
Roman triumph witnessed by the survival of triumphal arches in various
locations throughout Europe and North Africa. The triumph metamorphosed
into the related phenomenon of the royal entry that marked a monarch's or his
consort's theatricalized entrance into a capital or other city, or his or her
accession to the throne.

Entries consisted of an ordered procession by the lavishly costumed royal
household through richly decorated city streets lined with civic dignitaries and
the public. Beginning with relatively minor officials and liveried servingmen
and ending with the nobility and royal family, such processions mirrored the
social hierarchy.[4] Yet it would be a mistake to assume an entry simply celebrated
royal power and status before a passive audience, for crowds of spectators
asserted their presence by cheering noisily, pushing and shoving, by causing
what Malcolm Smuts has termed 'deliberate pandemonium'.[5] Particularly
important entries came to be accompanied by street pageants that punctuated
the processional route and that were mounted by the city, its guilds or other
corporate groups, such as London's annual Lord Mayor's procession which
took place regularly from about 1535 and which came to include pageants
written by well-known playwrights.

Renaissance princes increasingly found narrow medieval streets marked by
tokens of a city's wealth and authority unsuited to the celebration of their power
and began to configure urban space in new ways, with new, broader urban axes,
and monuments and allegorical tableaux that reflected the prince's significance
placed along processional routes. As many commentators have observed,
perspective was closely allied to this new configuration of space since it 'emphasized
the order imposed upon space by the political master of that space'.[6] In court
performances, the monarch was seated where the illusion produced by perspective
was most fully realized, and spectators were seated according to their status in
relation to the monarch. Thus perspective enabled, and imposed, hierarchy.

Streets were not the only spaces deployed by princes and city governments to
celebrate their power and prosperity. Public spaces – the piazzas of Venice and
other Italian cities, the Pont Neuf in Paris, English town commons, the Frankfurt
Book Fair in what is now Germany – all boasted theatrical performance of
varied kinds: buffone or clowns, acrobats, mummings, jigs and dances, masques,
and plays. The Pont Neuf in Paris, for example, built at the end of the sixteenth
century, was distinguished from previous bridges by its open plan, part of a
reconfiguration of the street as a public space for the flow of traffic that began
to characterize urban development in the early modern city. The Pont Neuf was
not lined with several storeys of shops and houses, as was London Bridge, or
Paris's earlier Pont au Change, but instead was open, a space suited both to royal
processionals and urban promenade. It offered a perspective looking toward the

Louvre as well as pedestrian space where ballads and street poetry were sold, and performances of charlatans took place. The most famous and popular were Tabarin and his partner/master Mondor, purveyor of pomades and unguents, who in his performances on a collapsible platform or trestle stage (Figure 4.1) joked about sex, religion, work, politics, health and more.[7]

Marketplaces and seasonal fairs were also environments in which theatre flourished, and there is considerable evidence of fierce competition for licenses to perform at the most popular marts. Ben Jonson records in his eponymous play, *Bartholomew Faire*, the puppet theatricals that were a part of one of London's most important fairs held at Smithfield from the twelfth century until the Victorian age. The mart at Frankfurt in what is now Germany had by the sixteenth century become a major European market where goods of all sorts were sold and exchanged and a major centre of the continental book trade. From all over Europe, and also from England, came not only printers, booksellers and merchants, but humanists, writers, travellers, players and more. Considerable evidence documents the presence and popularity of travelling players from England, the so-called 'Englischer Comoedianten', in the Low Countries and Germany reaching Vienna, Prague, and even Gdansk from the 1580s through the first half of the seventeenth century.[8] Famously the English actor Will Kemp travelled to the Low Countries with Leicester's Men in 1586 where an outdoor performance at Elsinore provoked such excitement that the audience broke down a wall between the Town Hall and the house of the Town Clerk. The English comedians who travelled the Continent demonstrate the overlap between so-called 'street theatre' and other more situated theatrical forms. From occasional court performances, to more sustained sojourns at the courts of German princes, to a major presence in the theatre of several German

FIGURE 4.1: Théâtre de Tabarin, 1620s. Abraham Bosse, engraver. Bibliothèque Nationale de France.

THE ENVIRONMENT OF THEATRE

cities, the number of troupes travelling and performing on the continent increased in the first decades of the seventeenth century and seems only to have been slowed by the advent of the Thirty Years' War.

From first-hand accounts of visitors to the Frankfurt Book Fair and from other archival sources, we know that English troupes regularly performed there. Fynes Moryson famously disparages the players out of England for merely 'pronouncing pieces and patches of English playes', but their expert deployment of gesture and action seems to have attracted enthusiastic audiences.[9] The London actor Robert Browne travelled with various troupes on the continent over some thirty years. When playing at the Fair, Browne's troupe seems to have stayed regularly at a particular inn in Frankfurt, the Sanduhr, whose proprietor undertook extensive, and expensive, building renovations in order to transform its inn-yard into a suitable venue for performance.[10] In 1620 his widow outlines these investments in her ultimately successful appeal to the city authorities who had initially denied the players' petition for permission to perform. The travelling troupes employed not only English actors, but foreign comedians as well, and thus fostered a theatre that was multilingual and what we might today term transnational, and they performed in varied theatrical environments, from the halls of princes to the inn-yards of market towns like Frankfurt. Travelling players scoured Europe in the late-sixteenth and early-seventeenth centuries – Italian *commedia dell'arte* troupes toured as far away as England, the Low Countries, and Spain, often performing in the halls and banqueting rooms of aristocratic households; in France they eventually won their own theatre in Paris under the auspices of the French king.[11] Fairs like the Foire St Germain, located just outside the precincts of the city of Paris to the south between Saint-Germain-des-Prés and Saint-Sulpice, featured trained animals, puppetry, tightrope walking, tumbling, actors performing farces with quack healing and the like on wooden stages. The fair performers apparently represented competition to the established theatre since the licensed troupe at the Hôtel de Bourgogne brought lawsuits against them to prevent their playing. Molière himself, excluded early in his theatrical career from the licensed theatres of the French capital, toured the provinces performing plays indoors and out that drew on both *commedia dell'arte* scenarios and indigenous French farce, in cities and towns throughout France (Figure 4.2).

COURTS AND ARISTOCRATIC HOUSEHOLDS

Plays and entertainments were performed at court and in aristocratic households throughout early modern Europe. In Italy, comedies based on classical models but written in the vernacular began to be performed for aristocratic patrons: already in the 1470s and 1480s at Ferrara, revivals and recreations of the comedies of Plautus and Terence were being produced at the instigation of Ercole I. Ariosto's *La Cassaria* and his *I Suppositi,* based on classical models,

FIGURE 4.2: French and Italian characters from the *commedia dell'arte* with Molière, artist unknown, 1670. Dea Picture Library, Getty Images.

were produced there in the first decade of the sixteenth century at Carnival. Italian comedy and dramatic performance influenced the development of theatre all over Europe: in 1512 in England, for example, on Twelfth Night, Henry VIII, disguised along with other courtiers performed 'after the manner of Italie, [in what was] called a maske, a thyng not seen afore in England'.[12] These English masques, sometimes involving a pageant wagon of sorts, took place in various courtly venues, wherever the itinerant court travelled, both in banqueting halls and even at times in the Queen's chamber.

Already with the Plautine *Cassaria* we find the use of a city prospect as the backdrop for the action. But it is Bibbiena's *Calandria* that is often said to herald the birth of modern comedy in Italy. Like many early Renaissance comedies, it mixes a plot from Plautus with borrowings from Boccaccio and Italian *novelle*. Its action involving gender confusion and conflict among the mercantile middling sort, the very persons whose enterprise and rise prompted the success of the Italian city-states, is set in an urban space. *Calandria* was initially produced at the court of Urbino under the direction of Baldassare Castiglione, author of *The Book of the Courtier*. Productions of the sort Castiglione mounted in Urbino for Elisabetta Gonzaga, Duchess of Urbino, were designed to demonstrate and celebrate princely power and to show aristocratic patronage of the fashionable new humanist learning.[13]

But the most important early performance of *Calandria* took place in Rome in 1514 when the play was presented before an audience of noblemen and women, and men of the church surrounding Leo X. At his election to the papacy and for his entry into Rome, the first Medici pope had constructed a wooden theatre on the Campidoglio in which a production of Plautus was performed in addition to various other theatrical events including plays and processions that celebrated princely power. In the hall in which *La Calandria* was performed, an elaborate perspective set of the city of Rome was designed by Baldassare Peruzzi. Thus the performance set mimed the very environment in which the play was produced; it celebrated Leo X's power and his patronage not only of the theatre, but of the city itself since he commissioned a number of building projects, notably the reconstruction of Saint Peter's, and was patron to painters such as Raphael whom he commissioned to decorate rooms in the Vatican. Leo X served as pope between 1513 and 1521, and notoriously offered indulgences – remission by the pope of the temporal punishment in purgatory sinners faced even after absolution – for contributors to his project for rebuilding Saint Peter's.

Humanist study of ancient authors on architecture, especially Vitruvius, the Roman compiler of classical architectural forms, and Italian painters and architects' interest in perspective, prompted treatises, visual renditions of the 'ideal city' (Figure 4.3) and set designs such as Peruzzi's perspective of Rome that was the backdrop for the 1514 production of *Calandria*. Theatrical sets often mirrored the urban space in which plays were performed, as was the case for the scene designed by Baldassare Lanci in 1569 that took place in the Salone dei Cinquecento of the Ducal Palace (Figure 4.4) and which uses Brunelleschi's Baptistry as its focal point. But as Marvin Carlson has pointed out, later sets displaced the Baptistry from its central position in Lanci's design and instead moved the Ducal Palace with its tower, symbol of the power of the Medici, to centre stage.[14] All over Italy, and in Spain with which Italy had close ties in this period, the vernacular comedy based on classical models was performed,

FIGURE 4.3: *View of an Ideal City*, attributed to Luciano Laurana, fifteenth century. From the Galleria Nazionale delle Marche, Urbino, Italy. Art Media/Print Collector/Getty Images.

FIGURE 4.4: Perspective view of Florence with the Palazzo Vecchio and Brunelleschi's dome of Santa Maria del Fiore. Baldassare Lanci, circa 1570. Gallerie degli Uffizi, Gabinetto Fotografico delle Gallerie degli Uffizi.

initially as part of Carnival in private halls and banqueting rooms. Soon, however, theatre was performed on other holidays and occasions, in more public spaces, as in Florence between 1576 and 1653, when travelling troupes played in a large third-floor room, known as the 'Stanzone delle Commedie' or room of the comedies, or *zanni,* behind the Uffizi in the quarter known as the Baldracca.[15] This room was also sometimes called the teatrino della Baldracca, or 'whore's theatre' since it was located near a brothel.[16] It had a fixed stage and designated spaces for the actors, and attracted not only paying bourgeois audiences but also the ducal entourage that had access via a palace corridor and could watch performances protected from view by a grate.[17]

Plays were staged both by resident companies under the patronage of a prince or noblemen, and by itinerant players who moved from cities and great households, to seasonal fairs and markets, staging a mixed repertory of plays and entertainments. We see evidence of such performance in the plays themselves: the main action of Shakespeare's *The Taming of the Shrew,* for

THE ENVIRONMENT OF THEATRE   79

example, is performed by players come to 'offer service to your lordship' just as Hamlet's *The Mousetrap* is performed by itinerant players who stop at Elsinore and perform in a hall before the court. But it is worth remembering, as Phil Withington has observed about England, that 'city commonwealths, cities and boroughs' made up between 80 and 90 per cent of the touring destinations of the Queen's Men, 'vastly outnumbering alternative sites such as the country house, royal palaces, universities or cathedral liberties'.[18]

Whereas Machiavelli's great comedy *La Mandragola* was first performed in Florence at the house of Bernandrino de Giordana in 1520, by the mid-sixteenth century, Italian princes and aristocrats had begun building theatres within their palaces, in Florence, Parma, Rome and elsewhere. Most were rectangular, with level auditoriums and proscenium arches. But at Sabbioneta, a town in the province of Mantua built according to Renaissance theories of urban planning, one of the earliest freestanding theatres was built between 1588 and 1590, the Teatro all'antiqua designed by Vincenzo Scamozzi. The theatre at Sabbioneta was based on Palladio's designs for the Teatro Olimpico in Vicenza discussed below and can still be visited today.

In 1589, for the celebration of the Medici marriage of the Grand Duke Ferdinand to Christine of Lorraine, months of preparation preceded the fortnight of festivities that included a sports match, animal baiting, tilts, a naumachy or mock sea battle, as well as the performance of a learned comedy with a perspective set of Pisa performed by the Sienese academy, the Intronati. Between acts, *intermezzi* or musical interludes that included dance and extraordinary special effects caused a sensation and were repeated for performances by the Gelosi, the leading *commedia dell'arte* troupe of the period. Both the *commedia* performances and the five-act learned comedy, *La Pellegrina,* revised for the nuptial performance, took place in the Uffizi theatre in the Granducal palace. It is worth remembering that Sebastiano Serlio's well-known generic sets for tragedy, comedy and pastoral or satyr plays (Figures 4.5 and 4.6) are included in his book on architecture because he assumes any palace should have a theatre.

The history of Whitehall Palace in Westminster demonstrates the development of royal building for theatrical entertainments in England. When Henry VIII confiscated York Place from Wolsey and renamed it Whitehall, he also acquired land between his new palace and the Thames where he built a number of buildings designed for theatrical entertainments and other sorts of aristocratic leisure activities such as tennis, tilts and tournaments. Great halls in the palace were used for the performance of plays and masques. Subsequently in 1581 Elizabeth I built a temporary banqueting house on the site of the present hall, for entertainments connected to her marriage negotiations with the Duke d'Alençon. It remained in use for twenty-five years until James I replaced it with a permanent building completed in 1609. That building burned in 1619 and was replaced by the Banqueting House that still stands today; it was designed

FIGURE 4.5: Tragic scene: theatrical scene design by Sebastiano Serlio (1475–1554), illustration from *Treatise on Architecture*, Book II, 1545. Milan, Museo Teatrale (Scala). (Photo by DeAgostini/Getty Images.)

FIGURE 4.6: Comic scene: theatrical scene design by Sebastiano Serlio (1475–1554), illustration from *Treatise on Architecture*, Book II, 1545.

THE ENVIRONMENT OF THEATRE

for the performance of masques by the architect and theatre designer Inigo Jones who was much influenced by Italian theatre architecture and scene design. In 1629–30 Jones redesigned a cockpit dating from Henry VIII's building of Whitehall to become the first English court theatre, the Cockpit-in-Court, but the Banqueting House and the Great Hall remained the venue for important court productions.

ACADEMIES, SCHOOLS AND UNIVERSITIES

Humanists used drama for both teaching and learning. 'Playacting occasioned learning in language, diction, gesture, attitude and sententiae', not only in schools and universities, but also in the Renaissance academies established in Italy and elsewhere in Europe by humanists and their patrons interested in sharing ancient texts, reviving the ancient theatre and studying classical antiquity.[19] The academies were, in fact, a major force in theatrical activity. The Accademia Olimpica, a group of noblemen, artists and academics interested in the new learning in Vicenza, initially presented theatrical performances and entertainments in a moveable wooden theatre designed by Palladio, also a member, and set up in a municipal building, the Palazzo della Ragione. Subsequently in 1579 the academy petitioned the city for space and licence to build a permanent theatre, the Teatro Olimpico, housed in a medieval building remodelled according to Palladio's interpretation of ancient Roman theatres, and finished by Scamozzi after Palladio's death. The Teatro Olimpico had a stage designed as a triumphal arch and a distinctive feature that drew on the Renaissance discovery of perspective: a set design of five *trompe l'oeil* hallways constructed of wood and plaster used for actors' entrances offering urban street perspectives to audience members sitting throughout the semi-elliptical raked hall (Figure 4.7). Its inaugural offering was Sophocles' *Oedipus Rex*, and the Scamozzi-designed perspective sets represented the gates of Thebes.

In Siena there were competing 'academies', the Intronati, who had performed Bargagli's *La Pellegrina* for the wedding festivities of 1589, and the Congrega dei Rozzi who bonded together for the performance of *commedia villanesca* based on indigenous dramatic forms. The humanist Intronati collaborated in playwriting and performance and their most famous play, *Gl'Ingannati,* was first performed in Siena in 1532. One of the earliest vernacular comedies of cross-dressing and mistaken identity, it was a precursor to Shakespeare's *Twelfth Night*; there is evidence of a version played in England at Cambridge already in 1546–47.

In 1510–11, a play by Terence was performed at King's Hall, Cambridge, the first known classical play to be performed at Oxford or Cambridge.[20] Many of the earliest English Renaissance plays, *Ralph Roister Doister* modelled on

FIGURE 4.7: Interior of Teatro Olimpico, Vicenza, Veneto, Italy. Stefano Politi Markovina, Getty Images.

Plautus's *Braggart Soldier* and written by Nicholas Udall, headmaster of Eton, and *Gammer Gurton's Needle,* written at Cambridge by one Mr S, were written for performance in schools. *Gammer Gurton's Needle*, as we learn from the 1575 title page of an early printed edition, was 'played on Stage, not longe ago in Christes Colledge in Cambridge', but its subject matter – five acts on the loss of a needle – was popular. As Alan Nelson has shown, more performances of plays and other dramatic activities are recorded at Cambridge in mid-century than in any other town in England, including London, a level of activity that suggests a desire amongst the colleges to compete with the continental academies and demonstrates the importance of Cambridge for the formation of some of the most important dramatists of the English Renaissance. Between 1540 and 1560, colleges at Cambridge introduced statutes requiring a certain number of dramatic performances annually that generally took place in college halls on temporary trestle stages. At Cambridge buildings remain today largely as they were in the sixteenth century when such school plays were performed and the halls themselves may have been designed with dramatic performance in mind.[21]

The performance of plays by boys and young scholars was intended to teach moral lessons and to improve oratorical skills. The Scot George Buchanan, a pre-eminent neo-Latinist of the period, taught at the renowned College of Guyenne in Bordeaux, a college with a strong dramatic tradition that included

THE ENVIRONMENT OF THEATRE

among its dramatists and actors not only Buchanan, but Joseph Scaliger and Montaigne. Famously Racine wrote both *Esther* and *Athalie* for performance before Louis XIV by the Demoiselles of the boarding school begun by his second wife, Madame de Maintenon, at St Cyr.

Yet drama not only represented the high ideals of humanism and humanist education; it also provoked outbreaks of violence and misrule. When Elizabeth visited Oxford in 1566, so many people attempted to see the play presented in Christ Church hall that a staircase collapsed killing three men. In February 1610–11, competition between St John's scholars and Trinity students for entry into Trinity hall to see a comedy led to violence and provocative action on the part of the stage-keeper, 'part bouncer, part torchbearer, and part usher'.[22] A wall was pulled down by St John's men for ammunition, and college windows were broken. What these and records of other incidents show, however, is that violence was a regular part of the play season, and that on the evening of the Trinity riots, there were two staged 'performances' in tandem, one on stage within Trinity hall, the other outside at the college gates.

In England, choirboys at the royal chapels of Westminster, Windsor and St Paul's were trained not only in music, but also as young actors who performed at court before the Queen. During several of her royal progresses through the English countryside, Elizabeth I visited both Oxford and Cambridge where she was presented a series of plays, mostly in Latin. When she was in residence at any of the royal palaces in the vicinity of London, however, the plays performed at court were in English. Spectators watched not only the play, but the monarch who was sometimes seated on the stage itself: as Stephen Orgel observes, 'the central experience of drama at court . . . involved not simply the action of the play, but the interacting between the play and the monarch, and the structured organization of the other spectators around him.'[23] For a production in 1605 in Christ Church Hall at Oxford, the first in England to use perspective sets and movable scenery, James I's seat was determined by optics with the King perfectly placed in terms of the perspectival vanishing point. His entourage, however, objected that the royal seat was not high enough, and the audience could not fully see the King. In the end, the King's seat was moved so that he was perfectly visible to the spectators, but could see the play only from afar, and hear it not at all.[24] As Elizabeth is reputed to have remarked in 1586, 'we princes . . . are set on stages, in the sight and view of all the world dulie observed; the eies of manie behold our actions.'[25]

From the 1480s, an important venue of dramatic performance in the Low Countries were the Chambers of Rhetoric, or *rederijkerskamers,* literary or dramatic societies in some respects not unlike the Italian academies. The word 'chamber' is linked to the expression *kamer houden* (to hold a meeting), thus Chambers of Rhetoric also indicates a room or location in which meetings of the society were held.[26] By the sixteenth century, every town – and even villages – in the Dutch- and French-speaking 'Burgundian Netherlands' sponsored these groups and their performances, which were staged on scaffolds erected in market squares and other public spaces, or in their designated meeting rooms in public buildings. The Dutch *Elckerlijc,* often said to be the source for the best-known English morality play, *Everyman,* won first prize in the *rederijker* contest in Antwerp in 1485. Evidence suggests competition among cities and towns, among rival groups within various cities, and later even between members of the chambers of rhetoric and the travelling English troupes.[27]

Not unlike the Chambers of Rhetoric were the English Inns at Court, located between the City of London and Westminster, in the area that develops in the course of the seventeenth century into London's West End. Though ostensibly for the training of lawyers, they early on became centres of intellectual and literary activity, where young men congregated to pursue distinction, pleasure and advancement, or as a contemporary described them, they were 'a kind of academy of all the manners nobles learn'. In his *Characterisimi* (1631), Francis Lenton claims young men of the Inns showed a marked preference for 'Shakespeare's plaies instead of my Lord Coke', the well-known English jurist (sig. F4). In fact, the Inns were a centre of theatrical performance, particularly during Christmas festivities and at Carnival. Famously the Middle Temple law student John Manningham recounts in his diary that on 2 February 1602 'at our feast we had a play called *Twelfth Night, or What you Will*', performed in the Middle Temple Great Hall which was some 100 feet in length, with a 60-foot high oak double beam ceiling and carved wooden screen. Not only comedy, but also tragedy was performed in schools and at the Inns during holiday festivities: the first English tragedy, *Gorboduc* or *The Tragedy of Ferrex and Porrex* was performed at Christmas revels by the gentlemen of the Inner Temple in their hall in 1561–2; a few days later the play moved to Whitehall where it was performed before the Queen.[28]

Drama was an important part of the curriculum of the many Jesuit colleges founded in the sixteenth century, including those in what is now the north of France that were established to educate the boys and young men of recusant English families. But the first recorded dramatic performance at a Jesuit college was at the Collegio Marnertino in Messina in 1551, only three years after the first Jesuit school was established. It is estimated that between 1650 and 1700, some 500 continental Jesuit colleges performed at least two plays annually. Additional theatricals were produced for special occasions before mixed audiences made up of college members, royal and aristocratic invitees, and general audiences made up from the colleges' surrounding population. These school productions were performed not only in college buildings, but also at court and in the public squares of towns and cities.[29]

PLAYHOUSES AND PURPOSE-BUILT THEATRES

Until the mid-sixteenth century, the early modern 'concept of theatre had included no sense of *place*'.[30] Though the Teatro Olimpico is the oldest surviving Renaissance theatre in Europe – other somewhat earlier and contemporaneous theatres in Italy have not survived – it did not bring about a shift to purpose-built playhouses, for it was built on the model of Roman theatres for a humanist academy, interested in classical theatre and classical learning, and engaged in many civic and literary activities. *Oedipus Rex*, the play for which the theatre was built, seems to have been performed there only once. Scamozzi's extraordinary perspective sets were permanent, unsuited to the moveable sets and machinery popular in Renaissance Italian theatre. The Teatro Olimpico was from the outset used for meetings, entertainments and diplomatic business, including, for example, the reception of a delegation of early Japanese converts to Christianity touring Italy with their Jesuit escorts in 1585. During the early modern period, it was never a public theatre.

Yet already as early as 1517 archives show that tickets to performances in private houses were sold in Venice, long before the establishment of commercial theatres. Records show that, increasingly, entrance fees were charged for theatrical performances, and commercial theatrical ventures of various sorts were attempted in Italy and elsewhere. In Spain and in France, religious confraternities and charitable institutions controlled the spaces in which, initially, religious drama had been performed, but they began to rent out their venues to secular troupes. Attendance grew and the confraternities came to depend on the drama as a source of funding, while municipal authorities and moralists demanded incessantly that theatre be banned from cities and towns all over Europe. Despite the objections of civic authorities, public demand and lucrative receipts ensured continued performance and eventually prompted the construction of permanent theatres. In Spain such theatres were called *corrales*, and in Madrid at least, they were outdoor theatres with rectangular yards, often sharing walls with other town or city buildings, centrally located near the Calle del Príncipe, in a respectable neighbourhood near the social and commercial city centre, as Margaret Greer has shown.[31] The *corrales* had a platform stage, some six feet above the ground, with a tiring house as in England, trap doors and a discovery space. Spectators sat in galleries and boxes on each side, or for those who couldn't afford such seating, stood in the yard or pit, as in London. In France, courts in which the precursor to tennis or *jeu de paume* was played were often used as temporary theatres in the sixteenth century (Figure 4.8). The Swiss traveller Thomas Platter tells of an Italian troupe that initially rented a tennis court in Avignon in which to perform, but when audiences dwindled, they moved to the open air, performing on a trestle set up on the Pont au Change.[32] The plan of the *jeux de paume* is sometimes said to have dictated the rectangular theatre design typical of later Parisian theatres. A platform was

FIGURE 4.8: Charles Hulpeau, *Le Jeu royal de la paume*, 1632. Bibliothèque Nationale de France.

erected at one end of the court, and galleries and benches for spectators were placed on the sides and at the back.

The major theatre in Paris throughout the second half of the sixteenth and much of the seventeenth century was the Hôtel de Bourgogne, built in 1548 in the precincts of the Dukes of Burgundy on the edge of the Marais, east of the Louvre, where many of the great aristocratic families built *hôtels particuliers* in the late sixteenth and early seventeenth centuries. The Hôtel de Bourgogne was controlled by the Confrérie de la Passion that had a monopoly dating from the

THE ENVIRONMENT OF THEATRE

fifteenth century for the production of mystery plays. But in 1548, the Parlement de Paris banned the production of Passion plays that had provoked increasing objections on religious grounds. That decree along with the humanist interest in classical theatre we have already traced in Italy and elsewhere, prompted interest in secular drama, and the Confrérie increasingly leased the Hôtel de Bourgogne to travelling troupes, especially the *commedia dell'arte* companies, and even upon occasion to English players. The Hôtel de Bourgogne was a rectangular theatre, with a pit and a tier of seating at the back as well as galleries or boxes on each side.

Other theatres followed the Hôtel de Bourgogne in Paris including the Théatre du Marais and the Théatre Guénégaud, the only theatre of the period located on the left bank. Cardinal Richelieu built a private theatre in the Palais-Cardinal in 1641, the first theatre in France to boast a proscenium arch; it eventually became the theatre of Molière's company and came to be called the Palais-Royal near where the Comédie Française stands today. Whereas the Spanish *corrales* accommodated some 2,000 spectators, in France the Hôtel de Bourgogne was much smaller, accommodating some 500, with sight lines compromised by seating onstage and steep loges at the rear of the auditorium, and no raked seating. The Marais and the Palais-Royal both had a sloping floor, with gallery seating on the sides.

By the middle of the sixteenth century in England, records indicate that plays were being performed not only at court by the boys' companies and by the adult actors, but in inn-yards with galleries such as the Bull and the Bel Savage on Ludgate Hill, and plays continued to be performed in such venues up to 1595. But the inn-yards in which plays were performed were within the City boundaries and thus under the jurisdiction of City authorities who were hostile to theatre. In 1567, a theatre called the Red Lion was built east of Aldgate and immediately prompted complaints from civic authorities. So when James Burbage came to build his 'Theatre' in 1576, perhaps prompted by an act of the Common Council concerning commercial performance in 1574, he chose the liberty of Holywell, in Shoreditch, to locate his playhouse. The liberties were areas that remained independent of the City's control after the dissolution of English religious houses in the aftermath of the Reformation. They have often been portrayed as areas of iniquity where taverns, brothels, gaming and alehouses, bear-baiting rings, marketplaces, even leprosaria were located. Burbage's project was sanctioned by his membership in Leicester's men, and royal patents licensed them to perform in the city of London as well as the liberties. Soon after the Theatre was built, another theatre, the Curtain, was built near Moorsfields, also outside the City's jurisdiction, but the city authorities nevertheless continued to object. In 1583, for example, the Lord Mayor complained of 'the assembly of people to plays, bear-baiting, fencers, and profane spectacles at the Theatre and Curtain', but the actors did not suffer harassment silently; they complained in turn to the Privy Council that the City of London was depriving them of their livelihood.[33] Most of the later public theatres were also built in the liberties south of the Thames: the Rose (1587), the Swan (1595), and the Globe (1599). Commentators have claimed that the liberties were ambivalent, liminal spaces that offered a destabilizing, subversive cultural geography in which the Elizabethan and Jacobean theatre could flourish.[34] More recently, however, historians have tempered these claims and recognized that the playhouses and the acting companies were embedded in urban corporate institutions, the Court and market culture, and the guild system, and were not in any simple opposition to the City of London.[35] The liberties and suburbs housed actors, criminals, lepers and prostitutes, but they also accommodated the great houses of the elite, the shopping streets of the burgeoning West End, and the living quarters of parvenus, in short, buildings and activities indistinguishable from London proper.

The new playhouses thus ringed the city to the south, with additional theatres in the northern suburbs, and theatrical venues to the west in the Inns of Court (Figure 4.9). Burbage's 'Theatre' may have been polygonal, as were

FIGURE 4.9: Detail, Claes Jansz Visscher, view of London. From *Londinum florentissima Britanniae urbs*, part 2 (London, 1625). Used by permission of the Folger Shakespeare Library under a Creative Commons Attribution-ShareAlike 4.0 International License.

THE ENVIRONMENT OF THEATRE

many subsequent English public playhouses that may have housed as many as 3,000 spectators, with a raised platform stage and a pit around which were vertical galleries with covered seating for higher paying customers. The rectangular apron stage thrust out into the yard and included a trap door, a balcony or upper level, and a tiring house. A reconstructed approximation of Shakespeare's Globe stands today some 750 feet from the site of the early Globe. Plays were also performed in an indoor playhouse within the City walls in Blackfriars, a former priory, by boy players between 1576 and 1584, in an upper room converted from a refectory into, as the disgruntled landlord complained, 'a continual house for plays, to the offense of the precinct'.[36] But in 1596, James Burbage bought the freehold of an adjacent set of rooms that he turned into a larger indoor playhouse also known as Blackfriars. Complaints from the neighbourhood initially prevented the adult players from performing there, but from 1609 until the closing of the theatres in 1642, the King's Men began performing regularly at Blackfriars, particularly in the winter months. With powerful patrons, guild organization, and permanent theatres in which to perform, the companies became increasingly settled and professional. By 1600, theatre had come to include a sense of place throughout Europe.

'TRAGEDIANS OF THE CITY'

At Act 2 Scene 2 of Shakespeare's *Hamlet,* in response to Hamlet's melancholy observation that 'man delights not me', Rosencrantz is led to wonder 'what lenten entertainment the players shall receive from you' who come 'to offer you service'. In these lines we find allusion to many issues and features of Renaissance theatre we have considered thus far – travelling players, theatrical entertainments at time of Carnival, players 'serving' a royal patron or lord and performing in his hall. Hamlet then asks, 'What players are they?' and Rosencrantz answers, 'the tragedians of the city'. There follows allusion to contemporary rivalries between the boy actors and the adult companies – *Hamlet* was performed in the 'Citie of London' in 1600/1, during the period in which the civic authorities attempted to ban performance in the City, and before, as we have seen, the adult companies were allowed to perform at Blackfriars. But more important for our purposes than the debates about company rivalries, or whether or not *Hamlet* was in fact performed in the City, as claimed on the title page of the 1603 quarto of *Hamlet* (Q1), 'tragedians of the city' returns us to the special role played by urban environments in the success of early modern theatre.[37] The period saw remarkable urbanization in Western Europe; while Venice and Antwerp dominated the urban landscape of Europe in the sixteenth century, by the 1590s Paris and London had outstripped them both. London and Paris saw a remarkable demographic explosion: London's population quadrupled between 1580 and 1650; Paris was larger earlier, but both cities boasted populations of some 400,000 by the mid-seventeenth century. It is estimated that some 3,750 immigrants were needed annually to fuel the extraordinary demographic growth of London, and Paris similarly depended on an influx of immigrants to regain and sustain its growth following the precipitous decline in its population during the wars of religion.

Immigrants were attracted to cities by opportunity and by what in the English context is sometimes termed 'betterment' migration, as children from middling provincial backgrounds sought their fortunes in the expanding commercial and manufacturing arenas of the metropolis. Plays often recount the experiences of such immigrants, their struggles to succeed, their country manners and susceptibility. And the plays and other urban texts performed an important role in promoting and idealizing commercial success and urban life. Whereas, initially, city perspectives were used in Italy and elsewhere as the set for plays, increasingly urban life became the subject of the drama itself. English city comedy in the early decades of the seventeenth century is famously concerned with urban subcultures, with con-artists, tradesmen, artisans and apprentices, thieves, prostitutes and petty criminals, rubes agog at the city with its street life, exchanges and fairs, its lively commerce. Its characters flock to London in search of fortune, preferment and cash and its characteristic mode is satire. French city comedy is different: its characters are members of a young urban elite in search of romance, intent on urban pleasures, on fashion, entertainment, and amatory adventure. Its plots depend on confusion, mistaken identity and intrigue – also features of English comedy – but rarely on gulling, theft and roguery. Yet both employ a language of exchange and value in the realm of human relations that suggests the impact of what has been termed the 'consumer revolution' taking place across Europe in the late sixteenth and seventeenth centuries. As London expanded westward, city comedy began to be set in the emerging, fashionable West End. English plays by James Shirley and others staged both in the public theatre, and at court for the French Queen Henrietta Maria, began to express 'standards of civil conduct and bodily deportment often associated with Continental norms and practices'.[38]

Demographic urbanization is an important material definition of cities, but scholars of urbanization also study what is termed the urbanization of society. Rapid growth, population concentration, and the development of large-scale, coordinated activities – the exchange of goods, the delivery of resources such as water and trash collection, coordinated movement through space – fostered an unprecedented concentration of both financial and cultural capital and promoted distinctive urban behaviours, social geographies, and new forms of sociability in the early modern city. Audiences grew, contact with various forms of literacy spread literacies, and cultural producers and consumers were drawn to urban centres that proffered social knowledge that was one of the principal axes of stratification in early modern Europe; at the same time, cities offered more sites for social exchange across such boundaries. In short, early modern cities were environments that fostered theatre – both as an institution and as the subject of drama itself.

CHAPTER FIVE

Circulation

Aristocratic, Commercial, Religious and Artistic Networks

PAVEL DRÁBEK

It was brothers, not others, whom they [the early European observers] wished to find.[1]

Under the stairs of a cardinal's Roman palazzo of the early sixteenth century, a polyglot company is getting the meals ready for the grand company upstairs. The hectic preparations are led by a Spanish butler Barrabás, attended by Miguel the Valencian, Fabio the Italian, Petiján the Frenchman, a generically named German called Tudesco, who speaks in Latin but swears in German, a Biscay (Viscaíno), another Italian (Canavario), yet another Frenchman (Metreianes; Maître Jean) and others – in a medley not dissimilar to Shakespeare's *Cymbeline* (1608).[2] The company boast of the greatness of their respective nations and countries, metaphorically bringing different tastes and ingredients to this international cuisine. This is the layout of Bartolomé de Torres Naharro's *Comedia Tinellaria* (1516), a witty farce written in Italy and performed before Pope Leo X, several cardinals and courtiers, but published in Spanish Toledo. What Torres Naharro (*c.* 1485–*c.* 1530) presented here and in his other plays, such as *Comedia Soldadesca*, was a multicultural Rome – a supreme Renaissance metropoly. Such a perspective – looking at the everyday, mundane world of real life characters, seeing the world as a *theatrum mundi* – was both a pastime and an instrument of contemplation of secular life, and theatre was a mode of understanding the fast-changing reality. The palace in Rome of Torres Naharro's comedy is the heart of pre-Reformation Europe and a metaphorical kitchen where different nationalities meet, squabble, and boast of some unique feature of their countries – the great Spanish army, the great city of Lisbon, the renowned brothel of Valencia, the University of Paris. It is also a place where different social strata intersect – the clerics with their aristocratic ambitions, aristocrats and courtiers proper, servants, tradespeople, comedians, and humanist intellectuals – such as the playwright himself: a Spaniard based in Italy, imbibing the comedies of Terence and Plautus as well as Machiavelli and Aretino.[3] Torres Naharro exploits the comedic potential of the international glossolalia and the *mingling of kings and clowns* – an absurd, and yet realistic depiction of the Renaissance world.

This chapter presents the different networks of circulation in early modern theatre – along (1) the aristocratic paths; (2) the trade routes; (3) the international missionary travels of the church; and (4) the peregrinations of the early literary authors: the Renaissance intellectuals and artists. These networks were never discrete – aristocrats and clerics shared blood and political ambitions; they were often patrons of artists and intellectuals, who were in turn often practising a non-theatrical trade. Many of them had education from Church-run schools and their first experience with the theatre can be traced back to school drama and lessons of rhetoric.

ARISTOCRATIC NETWORKS

In November 1627, the Prague Castle (Hradčany) saw a double coronation – Eleonore of Gonzaga of Mantua, second wife of the Austrian Emperor Ferdinand II Habsburg (1578–1637), was crowned Queen of Bohemia on 21 November, and the Emperor had his son (by his first marriage), Archduke and Hungarian King Ferdinand III (1608–57) crowned King of Bohemia on 24 November. The entertainments marking the prolonged ceremonies lasting till the Lent of 1629 may serve for as good an example as any of transnational circulation in the early modern period. The famous Mantuan *commedia dell'arte* troupe *Comici Fedeli* performed *La Trasformazione di Callisto e Arcade* by Cesare Gonzaga di Guastalla, inspired by Ovid's *Metamorphoses*, with stage machinery constructed by architect (scenographer) Giovanni Pieroni. The production was denoted as a 'sung comedy' in a number of terms – 'commedia cantata', 'commedia in musica', 'comedia recitata in musica con intermedi' and 'pastorale in musica'. An eyewitness reported that the *Comici Fedeli* led by their *capocomico* Giovan Battista Andreini 'pleased the Emperor in Prague so much that he almost never went hunting'.[4] Apart from this company, the English comedians' troupe led by John Green and Robert Reynolds performed at court with their clown Pickelhering. Third, the Prague Jesuits mounted a tragedy called *Constantino Magno Victore* (27 January 1628),[5] probably performed by the students of their college, perhaps supported by professional actors. And last

CIRCULATION   95

but not least, the festivities were accompanied by other spectacles: so fireworks, chivalric jousts and tournaments would be interspersed (on 5 and 6 February 1628) with 'a comedy by the English; and on the following night, a comedy by the Italians, other shows of jesters who danced and of puppeteers'.[6]

Events such as these were characteristic of the early modern court culture: the heightened aristocratic ambitions in international politics were realized through a combination of marriages, political subjugation and occasional warfare, and theatre played a crucial mediating role. Court players – musicians, actors, dancers and other performing professionals, often summatively referred to as 'players' (English), 'comici' (Italian), 'Instrumentist' (German) – were not only employed to entertain the international congress on these occasions but also as crucial instruments of these ambitions. In the earlier decades of the Renaissance, aristocratic events preserved late medieval chivalric cultures – with tournaments, jousts, chivalric sports (such as *running at the ring*), equestrian carousels and processions; they also incorporated the characteristically Renaissance pastimes, such as the Italianate court masques, royal entries, fireworks, stagings of nautical battles or the ever-changing fashionable dances – and theatre plays. As early as 1347, the English *ludi* included 'masked dancers wearing animal heads'; the vernacular lore of mumming was gradually enriched by the Italian fashion of the *masque*. The historian Edward Hall was the first to use the term 'maske' 'to describe the revel on Twelfth Night 1512, when Henry VIII and eleven gentlemen arrived at court in disguise "after the manner of Italie"'.[7]

Documents of later festivities suggest the growing trend of theatre circulation along aristocratic networks: Italian *commedia dell'arte* actors performed at the marriage of Crown Prince Wilhelm of Bavaria and Princess Renata (Renée) of Lorraine in Munich in 1568; of Charles IX of France (Valois) and Archduchess Elizabeth of Austria (Habsburg) in 1571; or at the marriage ceremonies of Renata's niece Christine of Lorraine and Grand Duke Ferdinand de' Medici in 1589.[8] English comedians were invited to the court of Frederick II of Denmark and Norway at Elsinore (Helsingør) in 1585 and again in 1586; the latter troupe has been identified as that of the Earl of Leicester (and three of the actors later became Shakespeare's colleagues) and continued in their successful tour of Germany and Scandinavia.[9] It is of importance that the Danish patron was father not only to Anne, the later wife of James VI and I of Scotland and England, but also to Elisabeth, who married Heinrich Julius of Braunschweig-Lüneburg, who employed English actors and musicians at his court in Wolfenbüttel and was himself an aspiring playwright.[10] This German-Danish dynasty of Oldenburg continued to employ the descendant English troupe, led by Robert Browne: in 1592, these actors and musicians performed at Nyköping in Sweden at the marriage of Duke Charles of Sweden (Vasa; later King Charles IX) and Princess Christine of Holstein-Gottorp. In 1596, the troupe performed at Copenhagen at the coronation of King Christian IV (Oldenburg); among the guests were his sisters Anne and Elisabeth and their husbands, King James VI of Scotland, and Duke Heinrich Julius of Braunschweig-Lüneburg.[11] Perhaps by extension throughout North German aristocracy, the English actors gave three performances at the Silesian Jägerndorf (now Krnov in the Czech Republic) in 1610, at the second marriage of the influential military leader Johann Georg of Brandenburg, Duke of Jägerndorf, and Duchess Eva Christina of Württemberg.[12]

It is perhaps unsurprising that these itinerant actors' forays in and out of court were – as far as can be learned – sponsored by aristocrats; they were aristocratic envoys, although the extent and remit of their diplomatic missions will probably always remain unknown ambitions. The theatre with its ability to cross political boundaries and overcome cultural barriers was well served in the aristocratic international forays. In 1583 Elizabeth I of England established her own troupe, the Queen's Men, as a touring company, comprising select players from several troupes of aristocratic patrons, who had been making themselves (unduly?) visible at internationally attended court events and in publicizing their family names across England and beyond.[13] It was perhaps for a similar reason that James I, shortly after his accession to the English throne in 1603, decreed that theatre companies were to be associated exclusively with patrons from the royal family.

Aristocrats saw the theatre as an important part of their self-fashioned image. Travel accounts, diaries, and friendship albums[14] document aristocrats' and other travellers' ardent interest in performances of all kinds. So, for instance, the Czech aristocrat Jindřich (Heinrich) Hýzrle of the Chods, on his grand tour – which was part of the aristocratic families' upbringing combined with diplomatic missions – visited most European metropoles, describing them as cosmopolitan centres populated by foreigners and as bustling crossroads of theatre activities.[15] In 1593, aged nineteen, he accompanied his patron, the Archduke Ernest of Austria (brother to Rudolph II Habsburg, the Holy Roman Emperor). During the Christmas festivities in Würzburg he records that 'the Jesuits held a most beautiful comedy one day' (p. 41); on arrival in Namur,

> the streets were all decorated with many lamps and fiery instruments, with beautiful theatres constructed, on which Roman histories were figured. On the streets we passed, music was heard playing but no musicians could be seen, since streets were planted with trees. And there was certainly much to look upon. On the following day, His Majesty kindly held a grand a banquet and dance.
>
> On the third day, we went to the château and watched sixty comedians who gave an exquisite pastime in the yard. That is, 30 in green clothes and 30 in yellow, who drew against each other from two lines (on the side positions) in a military manner, with drummers and trumpeteers (p. 45).

On his later travels he describes Paris and London as places of theatrical and performative pastimes, attended by an international community. Hýzrle was not primarily interested in the popular theatre, unlike other sole travellers such as Thomas Platter, but rather in the political theatre and ceremony. He was clearly fascinated by the grand ceremony organized by the Mayor of London for James I and his court. Hýzrle was invited as 'the King observed the courtly custom, as if at a theatre production, that he summoned all foreigners who were aristocrats, asked them along, placing them to see better in the forefront of his trains' (p. 145). As Hýzrle observes, international aristocratic politics, self-fashioning and theatre existed in a customary symbiosis. The sovereign's magnitude was manifested to the transnational world of the early modern metropolis by means of explicitly theatrical performances – such as the grand ballet and masque that Hýzrle describes in amazement, adding that the 'most rare theatre was to be seen on the sumptuous dishes laid out on many tables' (p. 145).

The close connection between an internationally fashioned sovereignty and a transnational theatre dramaturgy was evident in many aspects of the public life. The symbiosis is masterfully portrayed in *The Roman Actor* (1626), a play Philip Massinger wrote as his entrance ticket to the prestigious King's Men, then under the patronage of Charles I. It is not incidental that Massinger harped on the Stuarts' diplomatic forays and politics of the early phase of the Thirty Years' War – their entanglement with Habsburg Spain, their ambivalent support of the Protestant League and their crypto-Catholic leanings (Charles' mother, Queen Anne of Denmark, was a Catholic). *The Roman Actor* has two protagonists – the tyrant Domitianus and his actor Paris, who is martyred to his draconic jealousy. Massinger wrote not only a metatheatrical *tour de force* but also a first-rate *politicum*: it has not been acknowledged yet that Massinger based his play partly on Lope de Vega's 1606 tragedy *Lo fingido verdadero* (translated as *The Great Pretenders* or *Acting is Believing*), which in turn reworks the popular Jesuit dramatic plot of the actor-martyr St Genesius. In so doing, Massinger not only developed the great tradition of Shakespearean tragedy of the London stage but also concocted it with the High Baroque of Continental Europe. It holds for his play at least as much as for the German Baroque tragedies what Walter Benjamin observed: 'In the Baroque, the tyrant and the martyr are the Janus heads of the crowned'.[16] Massinger's actor-martyr Paris, and the entire company of the King's Men at the Globe just outside London's city walls (on the south bank of the Thames) and in the private Blackfriars playhouse, were indelible parts of the crowned sovereignty.

Along the same lines, when the Puritans took complete control of London after the outbreak of the Civil War in 1642, they banned all theatre activities of the royal companies. The fact that performances continued, showing sketches, clowneries or 'drolls' – as Francis Kirkman documents them in his popular *Wits, or Sport upon Sport* (1662) – suggests that the Puritans' closure of the theatres was not so much directed against performances as such but rather against plays, actors and their playhouses, indivisibly connected to their royal patrons, for whom they represented a powerful political tool – a shop window of their public influence. The modelling of the modern transnational world on the aristocratic stage was part of early modern politics. While in many early modern countries, such as Italy, France, Germany, Austria, Denmark, the Netherlands or the Scandinavian states, theatre was an instrument of aristocratic pastimes and ambitions, in England and in Spain, theatre developed into a new form: it became an institutionalized and architectonic embodiment of the nation led by aristocratic sovereignty.[17]

COMMERCIAL NETWORKS

English theatre soon established itself as a striving business in the many playhouses around the capital. Until recently, most existing research has focused on the London scene and neglected the more characteristic professional theatre practices outside the metropoly. The London theatre culture of the Elizabethan, Jacobean and Caroline eras (1567–1642) has often been presented as a precocious type of 'national theatre' that played a key role in the formulation of the modern English identity; its transnational dimensions have been, quite logically, sidelined. It is only relatively recently that English drama of Shakespeare's age has been approached as a crossroads of cultures rather than just the sedentary seat of a growing empire. Travelling in English theatre was more than a mere necessity in the times of the theatres' frequent closures due to outbreaks of plague; extant playhouse wills suggest that early modern English actors did not share our modern division of labour: they were *players* in more than one sense (actors, musicians, entertainers) and often had family trades that they continued to pursue in some fashion. Leaving aside the anecdotal evidence that William Shakespeare secretly traded in wool and lent money,[18] his partners and shareholders had trades. Among them was Robert Browne (1563–*c*. 1621), a one-time shareholder in the King's Men, who had a successful career in mainland Europe as a troupe leader, performing in France, the Netherlands, Poland and mainly the German-speaking countries.[19] He was also involved in other trades, such as importing dogs, bears and apes for the King's pastimes.[20] The Browne family had an additional performative activity; extant documents suggest that both in England and in mainland Europe they performed with puppets or 'motions' as they were called – a term ranging from puppetry proper to automata, mechanical Nativity shows and visions of the world.[21] These performative activities combined their fashionable style of 'English comedy' with the ancient mystical art of puppetry and also complemented their portfolio in emulating with the 'Italian comedy' of the actors *dell'arte*. The early modern fascination with the mechanics of God's creation served as an effective medium of transnational circulation in the theatre; puppeteers and performers of automata, often recruiting from artisans (joiners, carvers, sculptors), travelled Europe throughout the early modern period until deep into the nineteenth century.[22]

The connection between theatre and trade had had a long standing, from medieval travelling professional performers and other 'masterless men'[23] – jongleurs, acrobats, bearwards, fencers, troubadours, minnesingers, minstrels, puppeteers, and trickster figures such as Shakespeare's Autolycus of *The Winter's Tale* (*c*.1610), who sells gloves, masks, bugle-bracelets, necklace amber, perfumes, golden coifs and stomachers, pins and poking-sticks, not to mention ballads for any occasion. In the professional theatre, actors retained the associated trades and their close connection with commerce, although in a sublimated and waning form. While the phenomenon of late medieval mystery plays organized within guilds seems to have transformed into the institution of holy processions and public functions of civic fraternities and sororities that often included theatrical elements,[24] itinerant actors partnered with tradesmen, performing at the same marketplaces and travelling along the same trade routes. So the rise of the *commedia dell'arte* was closely connected with the activities of the Italian merchant class.[25] On a grand scale, theatre was perceived as a marketplace[26] and it followed the model laid down by commerce. Apart from that, performing was perennially connected with healing: quacksalvers, charlatans, mountebanks, magical healers as well as more respectable itinerant physicians and surgeons travelled with an entourage that extolled their art and their goods by performative means. One strand of late medieval theatre devolved from Easter ceremonies – not only in the solemn staged enactments of the *Quem quaeritis* (Whom do you seek?) and the *Hortulanus* (Gardener) sequences but especially in the *Unguentarius* (Ointment Merchant) episode derived from Mark 16.1–2 and Luke 23.56 and 24.1, in which the three Marys come to buy balms and ointments for the body of Christ. The *Unguentarius* coincided with the marketplace tradition and offered an opportunity for secular farce – the earliest scripts date to the late 1300s.[27] Borrowing some of the sublime, divine mystery of the Easter miracle, travelling quacks performed acts of magical healing, accompanied by histrionics. This tradition continued and intensified in the early modern period, with some quack doctors' troupes counting over 100 members – as was the case of the German charlatan Johann Andreas Eisenbarth (1663–1727), who employed actors, singers, acrobats, rope dancers, contortionists and others to attract attention to his medical prowess.[28] It was well into the eighteenth century that actors often associated themselves with medical practice as their art's *genus proximum* – most notably the famous Viennese Hanswurst Joseph Anton Stranitzky (1676–1726), who prided himself in his 1707 university certificate of a 'Zahn- und Mundarzt' (tooth and mouth doctor), who elaborated his healing through cure by laughter.[29] The continuing tradition of performative medicine was far from exclusively a male affair; female attendants and assistants of the quack were in evidence throughout history.[30]

Italian comedians *dell'arte* often combined their theatre activities with commercial skills, laterally connected with the theatre. So the famous Flaminio Scala (1552–1624), an *innamorato* (young lover) in Francesco and Isabella Andreini's *I Gelosi* troupe and author of the invaluable scenario collection *Il teatro delle favole rappresentative* (1611), had a secure business at the Venetian Rialto as owner of a perfume shop.[31] His actor-colleague Pier Maria Cecchini (1563–1645) 'submitted patents to the Medicean and Gonzagan courts for inventions regarding silk production, soap manufacturing, and milling[; and] the Mantuan court granted him the exclusive license to sell perfume products.'[32] Similarly, Drusiano Martinelli and Vincenzo Belando had commercial connections while in Antwerp, extending throughout the Germanic world, France and England.[33]

It is of interest that, during the sixteenth century, the European centre of commerce transferred from Venice to Antwerp.[34] The arts, and the theatre in particular, followed the same trend, with a delay of a few decades: with the gradual move of commercial activities from Italy to the Hanseatic space of the Netherlands, England and the Baltic, the theatre fashion shifted from the earlier Italian to the novel English comedy.[35] In around 1610, a public playhouse known as the Fencing School was built in the Hanseatic Danzig (Gdańsk) perhaps on the model of the Fortune playhouse of London.[36] The performances given there catered for the sizeable community of English merchants; while the merchants circulated English goods and material culture, the English players mediated the theatrical culture as well as other cultural merchandise, namely fencing.[37]

The fashion of English comedy, predominant throughout western, central and northern Europe from around 1590 to 1650, had dovetailed with the high tide of the Italian comedy and Italian puppet theatre, peaking between the years 1560 and 1620. In a similar vein, Dutch and German companies formed the fashion of the following generation until they were supplanted by French and Spanish dramaturgy that swamped most of Europe in the wake of the Peace of Westphalia of 1648 and uncannily shadowed the international politics of the last Spanish Habsburgs and the French Valois.[38]

A number of early modern English theatre professionals came from different trades related to theatre making, with a significant presence of women in these professions.[39] James Burbage was a trained joiner who became actor, builder and founder of the first semi-permanent purpose-built stage, the 1567 playhouse at the Red Lion Inn, and later the Theatre playhouse in Shoreditch, outside London's northern city gates. Associations of actors with inns and public houses were also longstanding: not only as resorts for travellers but also as venues for social gatherings and the burgeoning public sphere. With this historical backdrop, it is unsurprising how many early modern English plays feature an

CIRCULATION   101

inn – from the opening comical routine of *The Taming of the Shrew* (as well as
the anonymous *The Taming of a Shrew*), through the unmotivated comic relief
in the popular *Mucedorus* to Shakespeare's Falstaff scenes located at Boar's
Head or Ben Jonson's late comedy *The New Inn*. The great tragedian and
benefactor Edward Alleyn was the son of an innkeeper in Bishopsgate in
London; Shakespeare's collaborator George Wilkins was an innkeeper himself;
and Shakespeare's godson and self-crowned heir William Davenant was son to
the keeper of the Crown Inn at Oxford.[40] The trade of innkeeping was conducive
to performance, and the inns as social spaces of encounter as well as common
venues of theatre performances played a crucial role in theatre history.

The image of having a declared trade outside the theatre was not merely an economic
necessity but also a legal self-protection. The Vagrancy Act published in England
in 1572 posited that

> All and everye persone [. . .] havinge not Land or Maister, nor using any
> lawfull Marchaundize Crafte or Mysterye [. . .] shalbee taken adjudged and
> deemed Roges Vacaboundes and Sturdy Beggers.[41]

Given that the Act explicitly names 'Common Players in Enterludes &
Minstrels', it was necessary for theatre itinerants to have a declared 'merchandise,
craft or mystery' to avoid persecution. The fact that actors continued to be
associated with the ancient itinerant trades is evidenced by the link between
theatre and animal-keeping – well into the eighteenth century, bears were staple
characters in Baroque opera. In London in 1610/11, actor Edward Alleyn and
manager Philip Henslowe were licensed to keep two white bears and a lion,
among others;[42] these beasts were presumably used in court masques, in
processions and other public spectacles, although it is rather unlikely that they
were employed in playhouses; given Henslowe's ambitions for the post of the
Master of the Revels, a fully equipped depository was a key asset.[43]

The image of the theatre as a marketplace was strengthened with the growing
overseas exploits and the need for communicating news and information.
The stage, as a natural space of novelty, served to communicate these and
theatre became a metaphorical marketplace of information, a knowledge
laboratory that modelled humans interacting with new realities. It became a
proto-journalistic information mass medium, a point highlighted brilliantly
by Ben Jonson in his plays, namely in *The Staple of News*.[44] Grafted onto
well-established genres – such as the medieval fictitious travel narrative, the
romance or even the pastoral transformed in the fashionable genre of Italian
tragicomedy – novelties from afar were presented on the stage and became an
indelible part of modern identity. Such is the case of English popular drama:
Christopher Marlowe's *Doctor Faustus* (*c.* 1589), a modern morality play based
on a German popular story, which in turn transformed a late medieval genre of

magician tales; Marlowe's play carries the spectator through the modern world – into the Pope's Rome and into several continents. *The Travels of the Three English Brothers* (1607) by John Day, William Rowley and George Wilkins is a travel play combining a Mandevillian narrative with transnational politics of its time.[45] Similarly, Thomas Dekker's *Old Fortunatus* (1599) is a popular morality adapting a German folk tale (also dramatized by Hans Sachs), combining it with novel realities: starting in the city of Famagusta (Cyprus), it takes its heroes into other countries, including England. In this way, old genres and stories were used as vehicles to convey news of the greater world.

Spanish plays, often structurally Italianate tragicomedies (called *comedia nueva*), combined generic features of medieval hagiographies and miracle plays with popular romance narratives, and were used to address up-to-date themes – be they the corruption and degeneration of the declining Spanish Habsburg empire, the anxieties of modern spirituality in a rapidly changing world, or the Mediterranean military tensions between the Christian world and the Ottomans. By extension, these stories travelled further into Europe – naturally entering the professional theatre in Paris and London, as is the case of Pierre Corneille's *Le Cid* (1636), based on Guillén de Castro's *Las Mocedades del Cid* (acted in Valencia in 1618), or of Lope de Vega's *Lo fingido verdadero* (1606), which found another life not only in the above-mentioned 1626 play by Philip Massinger on the London stage, but also in two competing French plays of 1644/5: Nicolas-Marc Desfontaines' *L'illustre comédien ou Le martyre de Saint-Genest* and Jean de Rotrou's *Le véritable Saint Genest*. Cervantes's Mediterranean-conflict tragicomedy *Los baños de Argel* (1615) was adapted for the King's Men by Philip Massinger into his *The Renegado* (1624), which updated the post-Lepanto Spanish politics for the English–Spanish maritime relations in the early years of the Thirty Years' War.[46]

Transatlantic exploits and missions in Indonesia, the Far East and the West Indies inspired a host of new plays – such as Shakespeare's *The Tempest* (1611), which elegantly combines the enchanted world of an Italianate *commedia dell'arte* scenario with topical news from the West Indies, or John Fletcher's *The Island Princess* (*c*. 1620), which is based on two Spanish books of exploration of the Portuguese politics on the Indonesian Moluccas (Maluku) Islands.[47] In this way, the commercial theatre stage also played a role later taken over by journalism – mediating and commenting on news from all around the world.

CHURCH NETWORKS

The early modern church recognized the pastoral and didactic power of theatre and explored its potential in spreading the faith and knowledge. In the sixteenth and most of the seventeenth centuries, clerics were often patrons of the arts and of the theatre in particular, more so than in the later times. Early Baroque theatre of religious orders and schools, in what may be a seeming paradox, made ample use of the secular joys of the world, often deploying songs, dance and spectacular effects for the entertainment of its audiences. Apart from the Catholic Church, the Lutherans – unlike the austere Calvinists – were among the first Protestants to make innovative use of performative and theatrical tools, realizing their benefits for education – such as language instruction manuals with dramatic situations to act out in class.[48] For instance, the Spanish-based Catholic monk William Bathe of Ireland published his *Janua linguarum* (The Gate to Languages) in Salamanca in 1611. The Protestant scholar Jan Amos Komenský (Comenius) adapted it for his *Ianua linguarum reserata* (The Gate of the Latin Tongue Unlocked; Leszno 1631), which was in turn translated into a dozen European languages within a decade, followed by translations into Turkish, Persian, Mongolian, and Armenian.[49]

Jesuit schools, established after the approval of the 'Formula of the Institute' in 1540, competed with the powerful didactic successes of Lutheran schools and developed the theatre culture even further, making it obligatory for pupils to participate in plays that helped memorize as well as enact the knowledge. Jesuit colleges were established throughout Europe as well as in overseas outposts of the missions. The model turned out to be highly successful, surviving for several centuries, as the Jesuits' school system with its heightened social awareness soon came to dominate the communities of cities and towns they occupied. Theatre activities, realized by college students, were often open to families and the wider public, satisfying the cultural needs for a theatre venue or even successfully competing with professional theatres.[50] Jesuit school drama had its national specifics, with the French and the Italian being more classicist, while the German tended more towards a mixture of genres and styles, and until the decree *Ratio studiorum* (1599) tended towards secular practices.[51]

Of a such transnationally mixed nature was the work of Joseph Simons (*c*. 1595–1671), an English-born Jesuit, whose five Latin tragedies (*Tragoedia quinque*) published in Rome in 1656 bring together an array of international inspirations: Shakespeare, Dutch, Spanish, and Italian drama. While they fulfilled the necessary didactic agenda, they drew on a transnational dramaturgy for their effect and further circulated it. This was an effort to compete for audiences with professional theatre companies, as the Polish scholar Jan Okoń has observed discussing the style of mid-seventeenth-century Jesuit plays: 'It is a Shakespearean model of tragedy, though taken rather from the dramaturgy of the English Jesuit Simeons – and not so much from *Hamlet* but from *Richard III* and *Macbeth*. And also from *Othello*.'[52] Simons's plays were further performed throughout the Jesuit Europe as well as adapted by several dramatists of various denominations (for instance, his *Leo Armenus* was first performed in the English College in Rome in 1645 and shortly after rewritten in German by Andreas Gryphius and published in Breslau [Wrocław]).

Apart from Jesuit schools, the Catholic Church also operated the less known but more religiously tolerant Piarist schools, which also made ample use of theatre as a didactic tool and were operating on a system similar to the Jesuit schools. A telling example of the possible influence of school drama on professional theatre at an intersection of international cultures can be found in a little known early seventeenth-century Piarist play entitled *Representation Von S. Bonifacii wunderbarlichen Kampff und Lobwürdigen Sieg* (A Representation of St Bonifatius [of Tharsus] his Miraculous Struggle and Praiseworthy Victory). The play was performed in Mikulov (Nikolsburg) in 1639, for the two junior sons of Count Ferdinand Joseph von Dietrichstein. The surviving German synopsis shows parallels between this religious hagiography, the style of the Italian *commedia dell'arte* and the English travelling actors' comedy, anticipating the structure of the High Baroque dramatic genre of *Haupt- und Staatsaktion*.[53] At the same time, the comical character of the *Representation* was the Solomonic fool Marcolf, who shares features not only with the Arlecchino but also with the English clown Pickelhering. The allegorical figures of the bad and good angel dressed in human clothes and well known from English drama – such as in the 1616 B-text version of Marlowe's *Doctor Faustus* or in Thomas Dekker and Philip Massinger's *The Virgin Martyr* (1620), a play that enjoyed great popularity in Germany throughout the seventeenth century.[54] It is highly likely that the Nikolsburg-born Johann Georg Gettner, a leading German comedian performing in the style of English comedy, studied at the Piarist college. The spectacular genre of a hagiographic school play would have given him almost everything necessary for the genre that he practised in his professional years, touring Austria, Bohemia and Switzerland.

Jesuits operated also far outside the boundaries of Europe and used the theatre to fulfil their missionary agenda. The theatre served as an effective means of spreading Christianity in many outposts – from India, Japan, Brazil, Mexico, Peru to Paraguay. One period report from India claims that 'Nothing has attracted the poetry-loving Indians more effectively than our plays.'[55] Recent research has analysed historical documents on the theatrical activities of the Jesuits in America and in India. The missions to Mexico and Peru among the Aztecs and the Incas drew on performances of symbolic dances and dramatized legends.[56] In Bungo (Japan) Jesuits performed cycles of sacred plays that combined elements of Japanese genres and the Spanish *autos sacramentales* – permanent school theatres were established in the colleges at Nagasaki, Arima, Osaka and Miyako.[57]

The influence of school drama (mainly of the Jesuit provenience) on early modern professional theatre was profound. Although hard evidence is lacking, the fact that most of the leading professional playwrights in Spain and France (as well as some in England) had Jesuit education and perhaps first encountered the theatre through them – Lope de Vega, Miguel de Cervantes, Molière or Corneille, to name a few – must have played a significant role in their artistic formation.

INTELLECTUAL NETWORKS

It was not only in religious education and in the overseas missions that school drama was used. A significant part of instruction at lower levels as well as at university were lessons of rhetoric, derived from Latin – the pan-European *lingua franca* – as well as from Greek. Humanist education, drawing on classical authors, created a transnational community of intellectuals; although it was never formalized, let alone institutionalized, there is a host of evidence of the exchange of ideas along these humanist routes. Theatrical evidence can be found in the late Elizabethan play of *Sir Thomas More*, which portrays the encounter and scholarly discussion between Thomas More and Erasmus of Rotterdam (Scene 8).[58]

Outside grammar schools, it was mainly in law schools that dramatic techniques were deployed. Apart from the classical rhetorical practices, a special category was the casuistical training based on Seneca's *Controversiae* – a set of rhetorical texts centred on a controversial situation. Students would distribute roles within such a situation and enact a law case; in so doing, they practised not only their rhetorical skills but also their abilities to react promptly to their opponents' propositions. While this didactic technique belonged to the classical tradition, it also inspired a number of novel writing – within the casuistical tradition and the highly performative culture of *mental reservation*.[59] The importance of this classical tradition of rhetoric and casuistry for early modern theatre was decisive.[60] An example of casuistry engendering professional theatre are a group of plays in the John Fletcher canon – most of which are based on Spanish sources – deriving from particular Senecan controversies: such is the case of *The Queen of Corinth* (1617, by Fletcher, Massinger, and Field), *The Double Marriage* (*c.* 1621, by Fletcher and Massinger), or the apocryphal *The Laws of Candy* (*c.* 1624, probably mostly by Ford).[61] The theatrical productions at the London Inns of Court may have been harnessed by a common denominator of law education and the professional theatre – the refined skills of rhetoric and role-playing within a controversial situation. John Fletcher and other early modern dramatists departed from these conventional routines and ostentatiously displayed their plotting and rhetorical skills in a public forum, establishing themselves as modern authors and original thinkers.

While many early modern theatre practices retained the traditional elements of residual orality and the pre-individual authorship, the period also witnessed the birth of the modern intellectual – an individual of sufficient social and geographical mobility, capable of purely rational judgement conditioned exclusively by his or her knowledge and experience. The playwright Andreas Gryphius (1616–64) was one such figure – a Protestant intellectual from Silesia who became the founder of German classical tragedy. He spent most of his life travelling, moving relatively freely throughout a Europe that presented a plethora of ideas, views, and novelties. Shortly after the first performance of

Simons's tragedy *Leo Armenus* (1645), Gryphius probably encountered the play on his travels to Venice and Strasbourg (which had an important Jesuit college) and reworked it polemically at Liège (which also had a Jesuit college) into his first tragedy, *Leo Armenius* (1647).[62] Not long after, he adapted Shakespeare's *A Midsummer Night's Dream*, probably from a Dutch version, and created the hilarious domesticated *Absurda Comica, oder Herr Peter Squentz: Schimpf-Spiel* (*c.* 1649). His play was, in turn, adapted and performed at the Premonstratensian Monastery in Prague in 1662;[63] the text is deposited in a manuscript collection and entitled '*Ein Nagelneues Spiel, traurig und lustig*' with the probably pseudonymous author Bartholomeo Schepelius. Gryphius's tragedy *Ermordete Majestät, oder Carolus Stuardus* (The Murdered Majesty, or Charles Stuart, 1657) was written in the Shakespearean style and dramatized the recent execution of Charles I of England.[64] Although claims that Gryphius's plays were performed by late seventeenth-century English troupes are probably unreliable, there is little doubt that his dramatic output operating within a broad European dramaturgy had a lasting effect on the theatre.

Intellectual and creative freedom was a new reality and the relatively little populated world still warranted unlimited curiosity in exploration and in finding novelty. In the wake of the aristocrats' grand tours, intellectuals undertook travels in search of knowledge and learning. The great theatre scenographer Inigo Jones (1573–1652) brought overwhelming innovations from his travels to Italy – and so did the court dramatist and poet Samuel Daniel (1562–1619), who visited Italy in 1591, probably met with the modern creator of tragicomedy Giovanni Battista Guarini (1538–1612), and brought a copy of his *Il pastor fido*, which he translated into English in 1602.[65]

These late humanists and early intellectual individualists were relatively rare in the early modern period; nevertheless, the phenomenon of the itinerant international scholar and theatremaker, unattached to an aristocrat, a professional company, a trade or a church mission was a novelty in this period and anticipated the theatre cultures of the following centuries. A transnational culture was its indelible part, at least until the nationalist movements of the late-eighteenth and nineteenth centuries obscured this grand vision. Theatre played a crucial role in disseminating these notions – it was truly a *theatrum mundi* that modelled the modern self and a world of individual freedoms, while rethinking the Classical heritage and the tradition of the powers that be.[66] The early modern period was also a time when the dramatic reader came into existence: many intellectuals had no access to live performances but could vicariously enjoy them through reading. Playtexts were copied in hand and also printed, advertised and sold. This devolved into a thick network of a reading public of a truly transnational dimension with an intellectual awareness far surpassing any national limits – such as when the 1623 Folio edition of Shakespeare's complete works was advertised at the Frankfurt Fair in the preceding year.

CIRCULATION   107

A less conspicuous, yet perhaps even more characteristic symptom of this growing transnational culture of circulation is the case of two plays that were found in the library of Maria Josepha Harrach, daughter of a late seventeenth-century Austrian ambassador in Madrid; on return, she married Count Künburg of Mladá Vožice (Jungwoschitz) in central Bohemia. Her library survives there, among it a 1647 edition of *Don Quijote* and especially two manuscript plays by Calderón: *El Gran duque de Gandía* and *No hay que creer ni en la verdad*, considered lost until discovered there in the early 1960s.[67]

Thomas Weelkes in the second part of his madrigal *Thule, the Period of Cosmographie* (from his collection of *Madrigals of 5 and 6 parts*, 1600) places the reflective individual with a heightened theatrical vision amidst the staggering business of the modern world:

> The Andelusian Merchant that returnes,
> Laden with Cutchinele and China dishes,
> Reports in Spaine how strangely Fogo burnes,
> Amidst an Ocean full of flying fishes.
>> These things seeme wondrous,
>> yet more wondrous I,
>> Whose hart with feare doth freeze,
>> With love doth frye.

Not only is the meditation in the refrain offsetting the amazed mind of the singer; the very conceit of Weelkes' madrigal is indicative of the ever-changing artistic fashion: Weelkes clearly found inspiration in one of the first books of madrigals by Claudio Monteverdi and imported his novel aesthetics into England – as in the onomatopoeic leading of the voices, the striking use of dissonances and augmented fourths (the 'forbidden interval' of church music) and the suggestive chromatic sequences. Weelkes' madrigal does indeed 'seeme wondrous' and the composer himself was a self-fashioned 'Merchant that returnes' from afar, loaded with exotic goods. In effect, this madrigal may be seen as an emblem of the early modern artist, exploring the world in its transnational dimensions and mediating it through performance.

CHAPTER SIX

Interpretations

Antitheatrical Thinking and the Rise of 'Theatre'

STEFAN HULFELD

Only a transnational approach that departs from nationalist historiographies can fully show what was ideologically at stake in early modern theatre, because ideological attacks on and defences of the theatre drew upon cultural anxieties and aspirations that crossed geo-linguistic boundaries. From the mid-sixteenth century on, professional theatre prospered across Europe and the figure of the professional actor and (in most places besides England) actress distinctly rose in prominence. In reaction to such success, many religious figures both Catholic and Protestant fiercely opposed the theatre on the moral grounds that it promoted immoral behaviour both in its onstage fictions and in the perceived loose morals of its mixed-gender, cohabitating acting troupes. In turn, the besieged actors defended their art in treatises and dialogues on the same moral grounds by which they had been attacked and by printing scripted versions of what had often been improvisational material, enlisting print culture as a self-legitimating if not ideological defence. To be sure, some religious institutions, such as the newly formed Society of Jesus, appropriated theatrical performance (crucially amateur and not professional) for moral and indeed theological purposes. For their part, humanist elites promoted the idea of reviving ancient theatre as a vital cultural institution at the heart of civic society. But neither the utopian project of the humanists nor the actors' own self-defence really valued the actors themselves as autonomous artists. The actor tended to be justified on grounds more moral than aesthetic. Moreover, there was still distrust, even among many actors themselves and certainly among humanists, of real corporeal bodies moving in space and time.

HUMANISTS ON ACTING

It is not known if Petrarch ever actually climbed the summit of Mont Ventoux. Perhaps he was merely indulging in self-staging through literature. Be that as it may, Petrarch's account did lead eminent scholars like Jacob Burckhardt to mark 26 April 1336 as an epochal threshold and to declare Petrarch as one of the first modern humans for his subjective observation of the landscape. But it is precisely Petrarch's bifurcation of the body and the mind in the letter – fundamental in his Augustinian allegorization of the mountain's ascent – that poses theatre and theatrical performance as a problem in early humanism. For the perhaps fictional mountaineer, body and mind remain remarkably separate. After his first attempts on the chosen 'broad path' have failed miserably, Petrarch transfers his thoughts 'from bodily things to spiritual things'. He draws an analogy between his climbing and an *iter spiritualis*, a spiritual journey, and complains about his 'body destined to fall under the heavy burden of its limbs', since 'the swift immortal soul . . . can do it in the twinkling of an eye without any need to pass through space'.[1] Later, as Petrarch lauds the life of a hermit in *De vita solitaria* (1346–56), he refers negatively to theatrical matters, both concretely and metaphorically. The 'scena' among the public places and the 'charlatans' and 'jesters' among the groups were among the things he did not at all miss in his solitude. He describes urban life as dominated by constant flattery, a craving for admiration, and trickery. To sum up, he labels ostentation and applause as poison to the soul. But the most surprising outcome of Petrarch's seclusion is his invented ability to ignore urban life even while forced to remain in the city. He pretends to have mastered his senses to such a degree that they do not perceive what they perceive.[2] Thus in his denial of being either the producer or the recipient of any sort of deception, Petrarch has asserted a twofold claim to being antitheatrical.

More than a century later, Giovanni Pico della Mirandola argued quite similarly. In his *De hominis dignitate* (On Human Dignity) from 1486, which is renowned as a humanist keynote speech about free will and man's perfectible nature, the body is still regarded as the major obstacle in the struggle to climb the narrow path of virtue. According to Pico, individuals who are acutely aware of their bodily needs exist on the same low level as plants or animals, as evidenced by their incapacity to perceive much more than vain illusions and figments of their imagination. By contrast, he describes his ideal, the philosopher, as a *purus contemplator corporis nescium*, representing a deity accidentally encased in human flesh.[3] The loathing felt for the body and the lust and mortal

INTERPRETATIONS

sin associated with it on the one hand, and the ideal view of human beings as pure minds whose fleshly clothing is alien to the spiritual self on the other, constitute a deep strain in humanist anthropology.

Later on, humanists were forced by degrees to acknowledge the theatrical dimension of social life. Rodrigo Borgia was elected Pope in 1492, assuming the name Alexander VI, and with him, the Papal Court became a perfect object of study for analysing the theatrical aspects of political power. In this regard the Pope's example provided Niccolò Machiavelli with credible support for his contention that the theatrical personation of morality trumps genuine morality for political leaders wishing to be effective. According to Machiavelli, men are so simple and so subject to present necessities, that the prince 'who seeks to deceive will always find a willing audience'.[4] And Machiavelli did not fail to mention that to 'entertain the people with festivals and spectacles at convenient seasons of the year' was one means of gaining renown.[5] Machiavelli coolly analysed the political performances of his day, illustrating with well-chosen examples his contention that for a Renaissance prince any sort of staging was justified to achieve his political ends.

In this intellectual atmosphere, and on the eve of the schism within Western Christianity, an authority like Desiderius Erasmus found it imperative to campaign for moral values, but he also duly noted the performative ironies of politics. In his *Institutio Principis Christiani* (1516), he dared to ask: 'If a necklace, a scepter, royal purple robes, a train of attendants are all that make a king, what is to prevent an actor who comes on stage decked out with all the pomp of state from being called king? What is it that distinguishes a real king from the actor?' Erasmus's answer was that insignias of power only symbolize good qualities if the spirit of a ruler is rooted in sovereign virtues. Otherwise they will be interpreted as 'accusations of vice'.[6] Erasmus certainly knew that this was an idealistic answer and a suitable view for an educational treatise. But beyond this, he obviously remained concerned that social relations were produced by theatrical means, often in contradiction to ethical principles. His *Colloquies* (1518) are full of scenarios in which Machiavellian logic is reversed, demonstrating that deceit is tolerable whenever it serves ethical purposes.[7] Still, he had reason to doubt whether societies and social relations would ever be founded on rationality and transparency and adopted the jester's persona to depict a very cheerful *theatrum mundi*: his ambiguous and ironic praise of folly is rife with theatre metaphors (Figure 6.1). Folly herself explains the world in Erasmus's *Stultitiae Laus* (1509–11) and claims to be the tutelary goddess of all social relationships, which, she claims, are generally based on deceit and illusion. According to her description, social life is a happy game played by people who are constantly cheating each other or themselves – in short, a human comedy.

These representative thoughts by humanists addressing the impact of acting on social life clearly manifest the most fundamental element of contradiction in

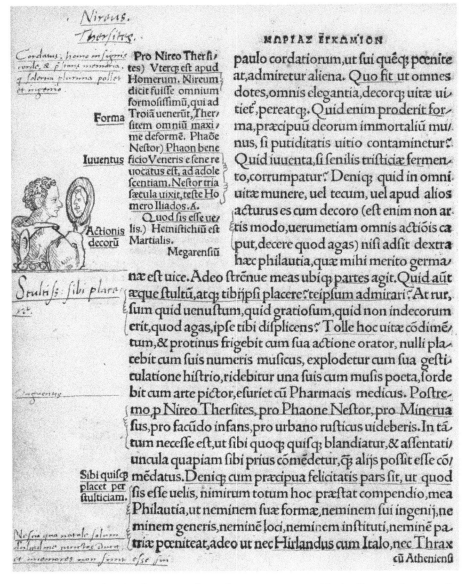

FIGURE 6.1: A sketch of Hans Holbein the Younger in Desiderius Erasmus' personal copy of the 1515 edition of his *The Praise of Folly*, held by the Kupferstichkabinett (Department of Prints and Drawings) of the Kunstmuseum Basel.

the evolution of modern theatre. Not surprisingly for Western thinking, the realm of truth tended to be spiritual – namely, bodiless and imperceptible. The human body was seen to be constantly in danger of causing ostentation, temptation, and fraud, whereas human perception was considered unable to discern the crux of a matter among the shimmering illusions. Most of the theatre metaphors in humanist writings refer to this alleged 'shortcoming' among human beings, while at the same time, any kind of acting carried the connotation of deception. Yet had this been treated as an everyday problem, the related 'dangers' would only have been considered even more valid in terms of professional theatre. There was hardly any legitimation of professional acting in mainstream early modern intellectual currents, and in their own artistic apologias, professional actors were forced into educational and moralistic frameworks. On the whole the contradictory process of ideological attack and professional success has yet to be adequately described in the theatre histories of Europe, and any future work will face some methodological problems. For the most part, theoretical accounts of early modern theatre are divorced from most forms of early modern performance. This is because theoretical interest oscillates between an idealized theatre of ancient times and a yet-to-be-implemented theatre in the future. In the printed pamphlets of the period that professional actors wrote to defend their vocation, even they mostly argued for adopting the dominant perspective. Depicting themselves as respectable citizens, good Christians, and merchants of honest pastimes, they denied having any supernatural powers at their disposal (dealing with such powers was basic to the business of the churches). Thus individual actors argued that their profession was (or could become) anything except what it was known for. All in all, the handed-down theoretical reflections did not necessarily deal with the practice of the time, and the most vital practice of the time resulted in moral statements rather than a language of explicit theory.

'RENAISSANCE THEATRE': ASPIRATIONS, FAILURES AND THE TAMING OF THE ACTORS

The Renaissance discourse about theatre and drama evolved in three major fields, which are defined by the names of ancient authorities: Vitruvius, Terence and Plautus, and Aristotle. The reception of the edition of Vitruvius's treatise *De architectura* inspired aspirations for regaining a noble ancient institution – both in the architectural and social sense – in the middle of tomorrow's society. Although Vitruvius's work had been handed down in medieval manuscripts, he had to be 'rediscovered' by the humanists. The comedies of Terence were renowned during the Middle Ages, and certain passages from his works were used for rhetorical education in schools, mainly mediated through Aelius Donatus's commentary. Six of the latter's plays were collected in the magnificently illuminated manuscript *Térence des ducs* at the beginning of the fifteenth century; at the end of that century, an edition of several illustrated prints of his plays appeared. Furthermore, the interest for ancient comedy was boosted by the rediscovery by Nicholas of Cusa of twelve Plautus plays in 1425.[8] The previously unknown Plautus comedies – namely, *Epidicus*,

Menaechmi, and *Miles gloriosus* – turned out to provide an important impetus for humanist theatre practice. Plautus's plays were staged from Pomponius Laetus's Accademia Romana and the court in Ferrara to the halls of the *Compagnia della Calze* in Venice, and from Italy and Spain to Germany.

A closer look at the Renaissance humanists' utopian project permits a deeper understanding of a type of theatre whose high cultural aspirations were not dampened by its limited success and practical impact. With the words 'Venio ad spectacula', Leon Battista Alberti introduced his chapter on theatre buildings, which is the seventh chapter of the eighth book of his *De re aedificatoria* (1452). This work was inspired by Vitruvius, but went far beyond his Roman role model by describing an architect as the guarantor of a happy and safe life for all urban dwellers. Further, Alberti was aware that architecture depends on sociological structures. His fourth book contains reflections on social differences and their underlying causes, revealing the republican spirit of its author. In his ideal city, he declared, 'some buildings are appropriate for society as a whole, others for the foremost citizens, and yet others for the common people.'[9] After the succinct launching of a new topic, Alberti refers to an antitheatrical episode in ancient times, purely to confirm that he in no way intends to cast aspersions upon contemporary clerics and guardians of public morals for hindering spectacles. After having satisfied the expected sceptical reader with this remark, he cunningly turns to Moses to highlight the positive impact of social gatherings. According to Alberti, Moses had introduced celebratory feasts and he, the Renaissance man, presumed to know why: 'His motive, I might suggest, was but the desire to cultivate the minds of the citizens through concourse and communion, and to make them more receptive to the benefits of friendship.'[10] It can be hypothesized that with this Old Testament twist, Alberti was expressing a first basic definition of spectacles in his ideal city. His wording in Latin reads 'conciliis et communione civium mitescere animos', with which he explicitly addresses the citizens and points out the necessity of festivals for social cohesion. In a next step he develops his theatre theory, presuming that the Grecian and Roman forebears had introduced and continued to organize spectacles in their cities for two reasons: pleasure and utility. Alberti's explanations make clear that with this dual legitimation he was addressing two types of spectacles: namely, the dignified scenic ones in theatres on the one hand, and the competitions in the amphitheatres and circuses on the other. He associated the former with peaceful leisure and the power to 'encourage intellectual energy and mental ability'; the latter, with belligerence and their effectiveness 'in developing toughness and strength of body and soul'.[11] Alberti's humanist idea of *spectacula* was based on community spirit and was addressed to the citizens, although it is sometimes unclear whether he is proposing an actual theatre of the future or merely contemplating an ideal one of the past.

INTERPRETATIONS

To a certain extent the dignity he ascribed to the *theatrum* reflected the dignity of architecture as a pioneering art. But during the second half of the fifteenth century, the humanist idea of theatre obviously developed into a symbol of a lost cultural institution at the heart of a civic society. In Pellegrino Prisciani's codex bearing the title *Spectacula*, he translated and expanded Alberti's theatre chapter (*c.* 1501). Prisciani's working environment was the court of Ercole I d'Este, Duke of Ferrara, where beginning in 1486 the court's performers and poets played comedies by Plautus and Terence in Italian during the carnival period. Prisciani is also regarded as one of the organizers of these classical theatre festivals, which is probably why he made the effort in his translation of Alberti's theatre chapter to be more precise on some points than was the original. In this spirit he added an important explanation of the humanist notion of *theatrum*, borrowed from Cassiodorus:

> The Athenians were the first to transfer this rural principle [i.e., community festivals and sacrifice rituals] to urban spectacles; they called it 'theatro,' which means *visorio*, where a vast crowd was able to see and be seen from a distance without any visual obstruction.[12]

This type of architectural structure that permits everyone to see and be seen equally well – with its implication of equality and social transparency during the festive gathering of citizens – represents the culmination of Alberti's theoretical reflections concerning the functionality of spectacles. For the Renaissance humanists up to the philosophers of the Enlightenment, the notion of *theatrum* was connected with an envisioned utopia. This utopia involved a reflective society that would meet at theatrical festivals where sight and gaze were mutual and equal, thus allowing a certain transparency of the social construct to be realized during a festival. Although the subject cannot be dealt with in detail here, it should at least be mentioned that this thought, inspired by a particular interpretation of the theatre festivals in Athens, was a long-term driving force in the relationship between theatre and citizenship.[13] One result of this comprehension of theatre was the rejection of professional actors: significant models of society, from Thomas More to Jean-Jacques Rousseau, postulated a need for festivals, dances or sports, while they rated professional theatre dispensable.

In 1486, Giovanni Sulpizio took on the responsibility for the *editio princeps* of Vitruvius's *De architectura*. This dedication had but one aim: namely, to convince Cardinal Raffaele Riario, renowned for his love of the fine arts and architecture, to let a *theatrum* be built. Both Sulpizio and Riario had supported the activities of the Accademia Romana, led by the Roman orator Pomponius Laetus, who had pioneered the reintroduction of ancient Roman feasts and used his pupils to stage comedies by Plautus beginning in 1483.[14] The editor

Sulpizio tried to encourage his patron's ambitions by remembering that these representations in antique style educate the people and entertain it with honest spectacles, adding that no other entertainment is capable of such noble seduction.[15]

Thus in the time span from Alberti's treatise (*c.* 1452) to the first edition of Vitruvius (1486) to Prisciani's 1501 elaboration of Alberti, Renaissance humanists in Italy brought forth a utopian idea of theatre inspired by their knowledge of classical theatre buildings and spectacles and their consciousness that a new era might be dawning.[16] The splendour of the transparent *visorio*, where citizens used their leisure time to enjoy and educate themselves or strengthen their bodies and understanding was praised, while the crucial question of *how* to reintroduce this cultural forum with republican spirit into the Italian duchies remained undiscussed.

The whole project was destined to fail, and it failed splendidly. Shortly after the first theatre experiments at several academies had taken place, erudite comedies, like Machiavelli's outstanding republican-spirited plays, either had to be performed in very private settings,[17] or they were absorbed and exploited by the courts. Under the influence of the latter, vernacular comedies became some sort of pretext to show sensational and extravagant interludes, dominated by stage machines, music, and decorations. With this, the development of a theatrical space *all'italiana* within the sphere of the Medici festivals led to the opposite of the projected *visorio*. Only the prince and his kinfolk were granted a perfect view of the scenery, from their place on the platform in the middle of the auditorium, while most of the other spectators could see the prince but not necessarily what was happening on stage – at least, not without restriction.[18] The Teatro Olimpico in Vicenza represents another attempt to recreate a classical theatre: the Accademia Olimpica appointed Vincenzo Palladio to create a pocket-sized antique *theatrum* inside a barn with an open sky painted on the ceiling of the auditorium.[19] This very special theatre building thus became the material manifestation of the impossibility of creating a public discourse in a transparent forum by artistic means. There is a basic paradox inherent in the evolving 'idea' of theatre as inspired by the reception of Vitruvius at the Medici festivals or the Teatro Olimpico. These performances and their venues are regarded as 'Renaissance theatre' by theatre historians, who point out the artistic value of the architecture, the staging techniques, and the performances. But if a social or political function were the major criterion, did a Renaissance theatre in the sense of the *visorio* ever exist? It probably did but must be sought elsewhere. Glenn Ehrstine convincingly describes the staging of Reformation plays under the skies of Berne from 1523 to 1555 as being community theatre employed to overcome a crisis.[20] The playwrights were council members, and the actors were their sons. The aim was to legitimize and rationalize the new faith, and also to enforce the sense of a common bond,

INTERPRETATIONS

but yet the aesthetics were borrowed from the mystery plays. Despite the traditional and simple form of the stage and the staging techniques, the humanist idea of theatre was functionally represented in these performances, while in the so-called 'Renaissance theatre', this idea tended to be turned into the opposite.

As stated above, the reception and staging of the comedies by Terence and Plautus were a decisive driving force in the evolution of the early modern theatre. All over Europe from the last quarter of the fifteenth century into the sixteenth century, academies, guilds, grammar and convent schools, universities, courts, and others staged or declaimed these dramatists in Latin or in translation. Professional actors and affiliated writers adopted scenes and plots, and for the authors of the vernacular erudite comedies, Plautus and Terence provided the models. The double impact of *prodesse et delectare* according to the *Ars Poetica* of Horace and the wreath of honour won by recapturing the antique spirit were legitimation enough. In addition, Terence's plays served as the theoretical basis for a kind of comedy aimed at moral improvement, while for public performances, Plautus's comedies were generally preferred. To name these very different authors in the same breath was advantageous, as one of the false twins was fit for theory and the other, fun to stage.

One major misunderstanding of Terence at the time reveals that scholars had a specific problem in comprehending the nature of theatre. The concept that human beings have an intellectual capacity for improvement and virtue but are encased in sinful flesh, together with the tradition of ancient rhetoric separating *vox* and *actio*, led the men of letters interested in Terence to gain a rather idiosyncratic idea of acting. An illustration displayed in the aforementioned *Térence des ducs* (*c.* 1410) shows the noble author Terence in the lower half handing over a precious book to two armed messengers. In the upper half is a round *theatrum*, where the well-dressed *populus romanus* attends a performance. Within this *theatrum* is a stage house called the 'scena' where 'Calliopius' sits with the book provided by Terence and declaims the text of the play while four masked *joculatores* dance and gesticulate[21] (Figure 6.2).

This illustration gives us a clear idea of the theatre that was typical for the late Middle Ages as well as for the early modern period, where *declamation* as the positive, intellectual ingredient of performances and *gesticulation* as the negative and lascivious part, remained strictly separate. This division of acting into two parts, one virtuous and intellectual and the other sinful and physical, was motivated by medieval authorities who proclaimed that jugglers able to compose and declaim *res gestae* would find mercy in the Christian state, while those performing lascivious 'gesticulations' must be condemned.[22] That is why one Calliopius became the first role model for honest actors. We see him depicted in many of the illustrated Terence prints of the late fifteenth century. A Carolingian editor encouraged this misunderstanding, referring to

FIGURE 6.2: Title page of a codex held by the Bibliothèque de l'Arsenal in Paris as Ms. 664. The illustrated codex contains six comedies by Terence and was ordered around 1410 by the third son of King Charles VI, Louis duc de Guyenne. After his death a further duke was in possession of the codex, from where the usual designation *Térence des ducs* stems. Paris, Bibliothiéque Des Arts Decoratifs (Library) (Photo by DeAgostini/Getty Images).

the late-antique grammarian Calliopius, who was mentioned in some few codices, by generally writing at the end of his Terence manuscripts such phrases as 'Ego caliopius recensui' ('I, Calliopius, have reviewed [this text]').[23] Scholars from the thirteenth to the sixteenth centuries tended to mistranslate the verb *recensere* here as 'to declaim' instead of 'to review'. Their misinterpretation is not insignificant, since the stage Calliopius was motivated by the need for a positive notion of acting, and the *actio* of an antique orator was an acceptable model for defining early modern acting. The director of the 1585 *Oedipus Rex* performance in the Teatro Olimpico, Angelo Ingegneri, solved this problem by dividing the actors into separate visual and auditory parts. In his theoretical writings, Ingegneri explained that theatrical performances consisted of three elements: the *apparato* (the theatrical space, scenery, stage machines, costumes, etc.), the *actio* (the voice and the actors' [decent] gestures), and the *musica*. On the one hand, the bodies of the actors in his concept became part of the scenery and were therefore a pictorial element. On the other hand, the actors' gestures became subdued, with only decorous movements allowed that would underscore

INTERPRETATIONS   119

the meaning of the spoken words.[24] Acting became limited to the auxiliary function that it had traditionally held in the rhetorical context. With this, early modern theatre theory eliminated the compelling gesticulations of jugglers and their bodily 'obscenities', which for many centuries had served as the main arguments as to why theatre undermined moral values and should therefore be shunned by Christians.

Above all, the response to Aristotle's *Poetics* led to an aesthetic discourse on drama. The rediscovery of his *Poetics* was first and foremost a very difficult endeavour because of the philological questions it raised. Compared with Vitruvius and the Latin comedy, the critical occupation with the *Poetics* started quite late – namely, in 1548 – with comments by Francesco Robortello, followed by the most significant contributions, made by Julius Caesar Scaliger in 1561 and Lodovico Castelvetro in 1570. Through them, the debate on the impact of drama and theatre proved to be non-controversial. It seemed obvious to them that 'the imitation and praise of virtuous men incites men to virtue; the representation and condemnation of vice serve as deterrents'.[25] But in the shadow of this agreement, controversial standpoints concerning the interpretation of key concepts like *mimesis* or *catharsis* were widely discussed with increasing vehemence in most of the other European languages.[26] This broad discourse transformed the description of Greek tragedy by Aristotle into a normative guideline for modern authors, and from the point of view of Aristotle's *Poetics*, scholars repeatedly felt the need to complain about the 'dramatic monstrosities' in Italy, England, or Spain, where mixed-type dramas became public successes. Around 1604–8 a notable exponent of this development, Lope de Vega, was forced by his fellow members of the Academy of Madrid to provide his own doctrine after having written 483 dramas for the stage. His speech made clear that it was not for lack of knowledge that his dramas were not written in line with Aristotle's *Poetics*, defending him with cited comments by Donatus Aelius and Francesco Robortello. Nevertheless, Lope de Vega was forced to admit that all of his dramas 'except six gravely sin against art', although he was sure that 'though they might have been better in another manner, they would not have had the vogue which they have had; for sometimes that which is contrary to what is just, for that very reason pleases the taste'.[27] Thus, neither ignorance of the classical rules nor his reluctance to accept them, he says, made him an anti-Aristotelian, but rather, the need to 'write in accordance with that art which they devised who aspired to the applause of the crowd; for, since the crowd pays for the comedies, it is fitting to talk foolishly to it to satisfy its taste'.[28] Even one of the stars of early modern theatre justified his practical knowledge by referring to dominant theories, the expectations of the crowds, and related economic aspects, yet was not willing or able to develop his own idea of theatre as an art form.

THE BODY OF PROFESSIONAL ACTORS

The defenders of comedies and actors, especially those actors defending themselves, such as Thomas Heywood with his *Apology for Actors* (1612) or Niccolò Barbieri with his *La supplica* (1634), confronted the antitheatrical propaganda with two major lines of argumentation at their disposal. First, they alluded to such authorities as Cicero and Thomas Aquinas in order to prove the necessity of leisure time and recreation after hard work. In his *Summa theologica*, Aquinas had explicitly addressed the question of whether the *officium histrionum* could be regarded as an honest vocation, and Saint Thomas was convinced that it was possible to fulfil it decently, provided that actors 'use no unlawful words or deeds in order to amuse, and that they do not introduce play into undue matters and seasons'.[29] A 'true use' (as Heywood put it) of comedies in the early modern times was easily outlined by applying a quotation attributed to Cicero by Aelius Donatus, according to which comedies are 'an imitation of life, a mirror of custom, an image of truth'.[30] Second, the 'antiquity' and 'ancient dignity' of actors, to which the next two chapters of Heywood's *Apology* are dedicated, culminated in Cicero's apology for Quintus Roscius Gallus (*c*. 162–62 BCE), who became the most prominent role model for actors in the early modern period. This wealthy Roman actor, born a slave and later elevated by Sulla to the Equestrian Order, praised by Cicero for his talent and his grace, had everything necessary to prove the fruitful opportunities of virtuous actors in a refined society.[31]

But the difficult struggle of early modern actors to find a basis for their existence or even social recognition limits the historiographical significance of such writings and argumentations. Actors and scholarly defenders of comedy were forced to pretend that theatre, as the best possible pastime, functioned as an effective exchange of moral values, as a school for good manners, and as an instrument for improving society. They also discussed their acting techniques as if the metaphor of the mirror or rhetorical gestures could fully define their skills. Yet it is hard to believe that professional actors interpreted their art in such a limited way.

To obtain a less idealistic idea of the practice of professional actors, one can, for example, consult the diary of Thomas Platter, covering the time span from 1595 to 1600. As a medical student he travelled from Basel to the University of Montpellier and completed his stay abroad with a tour through France, Spain, the Netherlands, and England. He took note of numerous theatrical events belonging to popular culture, including stage performances by amateurs or students. He also attended performances by professional actors of every kind in major cities, yet his viewpoints and the brevity of his reports do not correspond with evaluations made by theatre historians today. In February 1596 he witnessed a little troupe in Avignon, consisting of a French actor, a woman, and a boy, playing a 'French comedy' with 'strange dances and jumps'.[32] His most

INTERPRETATIONS

comprehensive description was inspired by an Italian troupe in Avignon three years later, where a certain Ian Bragetta performed with his troupe of four men and two women over a period of several weeks. First they played pastorals and comedies in the Jeu de Paume hall, about which Platter comments that the farces with Pantalone and Zanni were skilfully performed with words, dances, gesticulations, and jumps. But the troupe gave concerts as well, and the actors imitated all sorts of animals and birds and performed the magic trick of the allegedly 'beheaded maiden'. Since the audience in the hall decreased after a while, they began to perform outside on a trestle stage, where they showed dances and played comedies again, but now in conjunction with the sale of ointments and pills. Platter describes in detail some of the mountebank interactions between Zanni and the doctor and how they communicated with the purchasing public.[33] In January 1599 Platter arrived in Barcelona, where he reports visiting the Corral de Comedia several times. He was most impressed by this type of theatre building, pointing out that everyone was able to see what conspired on stage. He was also impressed that the income from the stage performances served to sustain the local poor. He mentioned that the stories of the plays were quite bizarre and highly entertaining. Yet while offering detailed accounts in the next pages about the skills, dances, jumps, and tricks performed by the French ropedancer Buratin, he failed to write a single word about the Spanish actors.[34] Some jugglers later, he arrived in Paris in July 1599, where he went to the Hôtel de Bourgogne to see the French actor Valleran le Conte and his Comédiens du Roi. Platter briefly acknowledged the 'funny French comedies in verse' but emphasized the farces played at the end of them. The latest gossip and all sorts of (love) affairs in Paris, Platter reported, were confided to Valleran le Conte, who worked these stories into his farces with his comrades and then performed them without delay, intermingled with all sorts of buffoonery, so that Platter's jaw dropped, especially when he knew about the persons and deeds portrayed in this way.[35] In September 1599, on the 21st to be precise, he was in London and saw a performance of *Julius Caesar* at the Globe Theatre. He, the tourist, was obviously impressed that there were 'about fifteen actors' involved in this tragedy and admitted that the players' acting was 'gar artlich' (most artful or skilful). But instead of describing what he meant by this attribute, Platter preferred to focus on the marvellous dances at the end of the performances that were executed by four men, two of them dressed as women.[36] Some days later he went to the Curtain Theatre, where he saw a comedy worth retelling, at least in his estimation. An Englishman courting a young maid eliminates rivals from 'all kind of nations' and defeats them all, except for the one from Germany. But the winner and his valet get drunk and quarrel, whereupon the servant bashes his master over the head with a shoe, so that the Englishman ends up with the young maid after all. Following this account, Platter explained that every day after two o'clock, two or three comedies were performed in different playhouses in London and proceeded to describe how these houses were built. He also happened to mention the presence of prostitutes in the London playhouses. Concerning the actors, he emphasized that they were splendidly dressed.[37]

Of course, Platter is an individual with his own way of looking at things and remembering them afterwards and perhaps his language skills, or lack thereof, are one explanation for why his theatre reports show more interest in the visual than the verbal. But at least two obvious things are remarkable. First, Platter himself never discussed his theatre experiences in terms of morality, but in terms of fun, entertainment, and amazement. Second, around 1600, small juggler troupes or a troupe of Italian commedia players and charlatans still dominated the definition of comedy and professional acting and the professional actors still showed artistic links to this breeding ground of their profession. In general, according to Platter, jumps, dances, brawls, buffoonery, parody, humorous gesticulations, and strange stories were still the essence of theatrical entertainment. But the writing actors, fighting for a reputation and an income, had many reasons to deny this state of their art; they behaved very much as Miguel de Cervantes depicted them in his play *Pedro de Urdemalas* (1615 or earlier). Pedro is some kind of a trickster, becomes a thief and a tramp, then an actor, and finally an actor at court. As soon as he arrives at court, he gives a speech praising the noble art of acting and lambasting the popular stage performances for their lack of verisimilitude.[38] Actors defending their stage business by means of academic arguments tended to define theatre as a rational communication about seemly and ethical behaviour, while their adversaries were afraid of its uncomfortable sensuality. But, as far as we know, the hostile view of professional theatre as a public arena where well-built bodies were exposed and strange fantasies created was the more precise one. The antitheatrical writers' fascination for a theatre they regarded as a 'Temple of Venus' and 'negotium diaboli' (according to the church father Tertullian) and their description of it were probably more in line with what early modern audiences were interested in seeing than were the discourses about morality. That is why antitheatrical writings can be interpreted as a form of negative poetics about professional theatre[39] (Figure 6.3).

But what kinds of materials are available to ascertain how the main figures of early modern theatre history, the professional actors, interpreted their artistic opportunities or their specific contribution to a society in transition? Considering that the actors' explicit utterances have been bowdlerized, a deduction has to be made from what is known about their performances. There is certainly enough material to examine this crucial question available in the prologues of improvising actors like Stefanelo Botarga or Domenico Bruni,[40] the 'fantaisies' and 'plaisantes imaginations' of the French actor Bruscambille,[41] the interludes of Miguel de Cervantes or the Spanish 'Gracioso' Juan Rana[42] and the plays by

FIGURE 6.3: Frontispiece of the 'scherzo carnevalesco' entitled *Scola di Pulcinelli*, printed in Roncilione in 1676. A copy of this *commedia ridicolosa* is held by the Biblioteca Casanatense in Rome.

Lope de Vega, the plays of actor-playwrights like William Shakespeare, and the scarce number of extant accounts by contemporary spectators (for example in travel reports). In addition, the metafictional scenes in plays must be considered as a source for the actors' poetics. So far, there has been a lack of answers on a European level to these questions of how the professional actors viewed their opportunities or social contributions. One could assume that an acting theory deduced from the above-mentioned materials would be as international as that of the Renaissance humanists, despite some obvious differences in the ensuing national theatre traditions.

Actors everywhere in early modern Europe were fascinated with inventing scenes showing that social relationships were based on simulation and dissimulation. Many early modern theatre scenes reveal the impact of pretence on politics, love, and daily business affairs. Professional actors and actresses, widely considered to be impostors per se, time and again showed in staged acts how social relationships and dominant truths were constructed – which means that they demonstrated a similar sensibility to the humanist philosophers while choosing a different angle (except for Erasmus, who temporarily adopted a buffoonish point of view). The actors neither idealized a society consisting of bodiless philosophers nor promoted the ascetic ideal. Instead they emphasized the capacities of the body, whose basic function in European comedy consisted of connecting the individual's existence with the universe. This meant that allusions to taboo bodily functions involving eating, excretion and procreation served as source material for the European professional comedy, which also juxtaposed bodily needs and desires in a confrontation between secular and religious ideals. Furthermore, the awareness that the body is involved in the construction of reality inspired professional actors to play exactly with this condition of social life, showing off corresponding mechanisms. Such plays reached their pinnacle with the construction of other worlds or even the otherworld through strange gesticulations. From the clash of fantasies of this grotesque kind with fictional works denoting real life, the early modern theatre focused on conditions of human existence in a broad sense.[43] As a *pars pro toto* of this theatrical philosophy of life, one can quote Prospero: 'We are such stuff / As dreams are made on; and our little life / Is rounded with a sleep.' And with the descent of Prospero, one returns to the ascent of Petrarch, with Prospero adding: 'And what strength I have's mine own, / Which is most faint.'[44]

But such perspectives on human existence, shared by many actors and some humanists, were marginalized in the further evolution of early modern theatre. The intensive and long-lasting debates about the status of theatre in the culture of the time led to a solid compromise, defining a restricted art of acting meant to emulate the everyday life of the average, ethically minded citizen.

During the whole controversy, theatre lovers and haters alike agreed that theatre, because of its visual communication, was the most viable medium for influencing even the uneducated masses. The critics in particular showed an enormous respect for theatre as a 'living book'.[45] Accordingly, the pro- and antitheatrical polemics and the legislation of the early modern era should now be seen as a competition to define the rules for this powerful medium. The Catholic and Protestant churches, the educational institutions, the courts, and the authorities of the growing cities all had distinct expectations regarding the times and places, the repertoires and casts, the aesthetics, and the aims of the expanding theatre industry. In 1904, Emilio Cotarelo y Mori edited the still-stunning publication *Controversias sobre la licitud del teatro in España* (Controversies About the Admissibility and Usefulness of Theatre in Spain), offering 739 pages of treatises, commissioned expert reports, and legislative texts from the Spanish theatre controversy between 1486 and 1868. This collection permits a study of the complex power struggle among the relevant cultural players in their efforts to possess and define the visual mass media called 'comedy' or 'theatre'. They exchanged ethical, aesthetic and economic arguments that resulted in manifold turnarounds in the course of the centuries. (Since the debate was raging throughout Europe with shifting confessional preconditions, it is a pity that such a collection does not exist on a European level.) A significant example from this debate, representing a typical case of conflict of interest, is the document containing a formal request made in 1598 by the city of Madrid to King Philip II of Spain that he revoke his edict prohibiting any theatrical representations due to such unfortunate circumstances as the repeated national bankruptcy and the death of his beloved daughter

Catalina Micaela. In addition to employing the usual argument that theatre was an educational medium in general and one associated with the Feast of Corpus Christi in particular, the town authorities pointed out that professional theatre was the source of a substantial portion of the funding for hospitals and poorhouses. For their part, the city officials promised to proceed with the 'moderation' or 'reform' of the shows by eliminating all the scandalous and lascivious elements.[46]

In this official document, like most of the contributions to the controversy of whether to promote or prohibit theatre, the difficult working conditions of the professional actors and actresses were not addressed in the slightest. Instead, the actors were treated like an available commodity to be used for defined purposes whenever needed, while both friends and foes of modern theatre totally rejected 'shameful gesticulations', 'lascivious dances', and 'frivolous songs'.[47]

Generally speaking, this meant that the theatrical elements most admired by Thomas Platter on his tour of European theatre cultures around 1600 had to be sacrificed for the integration of theatre into urban culture. Although edicts and censorship turned out to be powerless in controlling the actors and actresses, yet as the antitheatrical paradigm gradually became the heart of modern theatre and acting theory, 'progress' became unstoppable. Perhaps the most decisive outcome of all of the theatre polemics in the early modern period was that 'nature', verisimilitude, and authenticity became the most desired qualities in acting and theatrical production while these same qualities were paradoxically praised as being the opposite of 'theatrical'.

CHAPTER SEVEN

Communities of Production

Lives In and Out of the Theatre

WILLIAM N. WEST

... one man in his time plays many parts ...
– Shakespeare, *As You Like It*

But how can you perform this human comedy without rehearsing it?[1]
– Calderón, *El gran teatro del mundo*

One touchstone of modernity is the shift that Charles Taylor has called 'The Great Disembedding', a tidy phrase for a less easily grasped set of changes in how people experienced their participation in groups of different scales and kinds: familial, professional, civic, confessional, among others. According to Taylor, under modernity, associations are understood to be chosen by those in them based on shared interests and secured by their actions, rather than assigned outside of human control.[2]

In Europe between 1500 and 1700, institutions of theatre and performance were part of these changes in social organization, indeed often at their forefront. Performances and the communities that produced them became less firmly fixed in traditional social contexts, both actually and in how they represented themselves. Travelling players crossed what seemed settled linguistic, cultural, and religious boundaries, everywhere revising senses of community. Visiting London in 1599, Swiss physician Thomas Platter noted that the English preferred not to travel but 'experience in their plays what is happening abroad'.[3] This was not an unworkable strategy. Italian *commedia* troupes were touring France, Spain, and the German states by the early 1570s.[4] Around 1600, travelling English companies called often enough in Gdansk that a playhouse was constructed for them.[5] Plays travelled, too. In the 1670s the repertoire of a company in Bavaria included works by Kyd, Marlowe, Shakespeare, Lope de Vega, Calderón, Andreas Gryphius, and the Dutch playwright Joost van den Vondel, as well as Italian operas.[6] The oldest extant script of Calderón's *El gran teatro del mundo* is in Nahuatl, translated in colonial Mexico.[7] Opponents of theatre railed against its capacity to muddle distinctions between ranks, races and genders; in 1582 an English opponent of playing described its audience as an 'assembly of Tailors, Tinkers, Cordwainers, Sailors, old Men, young Men, Women, Boys, Girls, and such like'; 'The cat and the dog will be joining in soon!' protested a 1688 French comedy.[8] The novel organization of playing troupes as joint-stock companies in France and England or as contractual associations in Spain, the repurposing of guild structures by *Meistersinger* in southern Germany, the sponsorship of plays in Italy and the Netherlands by learned academies, and the distribution of audiences throughout Europe by the fees they paid created new social orders that overlaid existing ones, sometimes transgressing them and sometimes reinforcing them but invariably reconfiguring them.

Many of these theatrical, performative reorganizations of lines of division and inclusion assumed forms Robert Weimann has described as 'self-authorizing'.[9] Self-authorizing institutions maintain a degree of autonomy, however precarious, precisely by asserting their limits and contingencies. Early modern communities of production explored with great self-awareness how the manifold practices of performance forged new communities. Often these were fleeting ones: circles around a street mountebank, the crush of spectators in a playhouse. But there were also more lasting institutions, like playing companies organized along lines familiar from households, guilds or merchant ventures; charitable confraternities that sponsored performances; disciplinary institutions that monitored them; suppliers of costumes and food; and even theatre's opponents, who found in playing a focus for their social critique. To note the importance of self-authorizing, elective associations in early modern communities of production is not to demarcate 'traditional' from 'modern' forms of performance, much less of community. It is, however, to recognize how the development of 'disembedded' social formations reinterpreted even 'traditional' ones. For instance, around Chester before 1530, attendance at a civic pageant signified little beyond one's lively presence in one's parish. By 1575 such participation could be interpreted, and possibly decried, as inclination to Catholicism; by 1625 it might signal loyalty to the monarchy, and therefore be lauded. This chapter examines some of the communities of production in early modern playing across Europe as the theatre they produced became increasingly 'disembedded' and elective.

Whether participating in a playing community was a lifelong project or an occasional interlude, the varied institutions of performance demanded different investments from participants at different stages and conditions of their lives. Thus even among very different group formations – international touring companies of *englische Komödianten* or *commedia dell'arte*, individual actors under contract in a Madrid *corral*, or a troupe subsidized by the Sun King's 'gratifications' – there were distinct social as well as theatrical roles for boys, youths, women, men, and aged people. In a lifetime one person might play many of these parts, and at different times experience differing kinds of association (Figure 7.1). Tracing communities of production along the axis of an imagined lifespan reveals a general trend towards elective association that is nevertheless not a linear account of increasing liberal individuality. For if increasing 'disembeddedness' and freedom of association is the large-scale story of early modernity, it seems likely that individuals experienced smaller-scale differentials of freedom and compulsion cyclically, as their possibilities of association and action changed with their age and status.

FIGURE 7.1: The Seven Ages of Life. From Jean Corbichon, *Des propriétés des choses*, French translation of Bartholomeus Anglicus, *De proprietatibus rerum* (Lyons, 1486).

CHILDHOOD

Despite the age-old association of children with play, a child is probably less free than he or she will ever be. In 1604, a four-year-old future Louis XIII was so taken with the performance of English players touring Fontainebleau that for the next few days he played at being an actor, declaiming 'tiph, toph, milord' in a deep voice and marching around with big steps. 'Let's go see mama', he told his tutor, 'we're actors.'[10] But in general, for children playing was not proverbial child's play. In early modern theatre history children are generally visible only when they are at work, either as more or less compulsory performers or as audiences addressed with a view to correcting their physical, intellectual or spiritual development. Children's most prominent connection with playing in early modern Europe came through widespread practices of theatrical performance in schools. But children must often have been accidental audiences of performances, too; Flaminio Scala recounts with crisp distaste seeing audience members kneeling in front of their children or children hanging from their mothers' necks.[11] Children sometimes travelled with parents or other relatives in playing groups. A list of members of a Spanish company from 1625 includes three children, described as 'beautiful representers'.[12] Molière encouraged his company to bring their children to rehearsals to observe their 'uninhibited responses'.[13] But children's actual responses to the work of playing are hard to locate.

Because theatre was imagined as almost miraculously edifying, many progressive schools during the period required students to present plays, usually in Latin.[14] The performance of classical drama was revived in early modern Europe literally as an academic exercise, in which children were both performers and the trainable audience: watching plays vividly instilled edifying lessons, while acting in them taught public speaking, Latin, and 'shedding useless modesty'.[15] As early as the mid-1480s the students of Pomponius Laetus performed Seneca's *Hippolytus* in Rome; one of them, William Lily, returned to England to become master of St Paul's School, where theatrical performance continued to figure deeply.[16] From the mid-1520s Luther's friend Philip Melanchthon had his students in Wittenberg perform classical plays; the 1599 Jesuit *Ratio studiorum*, which standardized teaching practices at Jesuit colleges from Quito to Goa, mandated regular performances of all pupils.[17] Richard Mulcaster, head of London's Merchant Taylors' School from 1561 to 1586, and of St Paul's from 1596, was an early proponent of educating students through performance, among them Thomas Kyd and Thomas Lodge. Lope de Vega was educated as a boy in the 1570s at a Jesuit college in Madrid; in the 1610s Corneille studied at the Jesuit College of Bourbon. It seems no coincidence that adult professional playing in England, the *nueva comedia* in Spain, and the *querelle de Cid*, which affirmed neoclassical dramatic unities in France, each follow the institutional spread of educational performance by about a generation.

Despite Counter-Reformation conflicts, the essential practices of children's performances did not vary greatly among Catholic, Protestant, and less overtly confessional schools. Jesuits emphasized the educational performance of plays, as well as declamations, spectacles and processions, from the 1540s, but so did Calvin's lieutenant Theodore Beza, who wrote the school play *Abraham sacrifiant* (1550) in French for a popular audience.[18] Montaigne reported playing 'the leading parts in the Latin tragedies of Buchanan, . . . and of Muret' as a boy at the College of Guyenne in the 1540s. George Buchanan was an impassioned Protestant, Marc Antoine Muret a Catholic, but they agreed with Montaigne that 'Acting is an exercise that I do not disapprove of for young children of good family . . . after the example of the ancients', appropriate even for princes.[19] The craft of playmaking and the brief community it created sometimes could offer temporary shelter from more pressing demands of confessional identity.

That school plays were claimed as educational did not mean they could not be profitable as well, although rarely for the children who performed. School groups regularly offered plays at courts in England and Germany, the schoolmaster customarily receiving a 'gift' in return. Enterprising masters might admit spectators to additional performances, exacting admission for the good of their charges or pocketing it for their trouble. Mulcaster's students performed what were disingenuously described as 'rehearsals' for money in the Merchant Taylors Hall until 1574, and in 1581 the landlord of Blackfriars, which eventually became an indoor playhouse for Shakespeare's company, complained that one schoolmaster 'pretended unto me to use the house only for the teaching of the Children of the Chapel, but made it a Continual house for plays'.[20]

In England, choir schools like St Paul's or the Children of the Chapel extended familial and apprenticeship models of community to children involved in performance. Groups composed of younger, less enfranchised members who depend for sustenance and favour to a powerful central figure, who in turn receives the benefits of their labour, reappear throughout early modern theatre, not only in the context of children playing. English players arriving in Münster in 1599, for instance, are described in the city chronicle as 'all of them young and lively fellows except for one rather elderly fellow who was in charge of everything'.[21] It is in many ways the patriarchal image of a family (Figure 7.2). Masters of the chapels royal could impress even unwilling boys into a performance community as choristers. In 1600 one boy's father protested that a master 'for his own corrupt gain & lucre' and 'to [his son's] great terror and hurt' did 'haul, pull, drag, and carry [him] away to the said playhouse in the Blackfriars . . . there to detain and compel to exercise the base trade of mercenary interlude player'.[22] In this protest we may hear a rare echo of a child's voice. Or perhaps it is only another adult voice, laying a different claim to a child.

FIGURE 7.2: Harlequin with a family of Harlequins. From Tristano Martinelli, *Compositions de rhétorique de Mr. Don Arlequin* (Lyons, 1601), page 48. Bibliothèque nationale de France.

COMMUNITIES OF PRODUCTION

Professional companies in England and France radically repurposed existing guild and apprentice practices to secure boys – and in France, girls – as players.[23] Many adult players in England were freemen of one of the London livery companies. This entitled them to practise the trade of their company, which as players they did not, and to apprentice and train boys, which they frequently did – in the profession of playing.[24] Relations between boys and masters could be quite warm, filial as well as paternalistic. While touring, John Pyk, one of Edward Alleyn's apprentices, addresses an affectionately teasing letter to 'my loving m[rs] mistress Alleyn', and signs it 'yo[r] petty pretty prattling parling pig'.[25] Here may be a real child's voice, although even this letter is written in Alleyn's hand. Apprentices could play women's or other roles until their maturity, at which point they were released from service and made free members of the nominal company of their master. Some boy players worked in the theatre in adulthood; others did not or could not, both in England and elsewhere.[26] In any case children's roles, onstage and off, were so different from what they could be called upon to do as adults that the passage from one status to the next was far from certain.

YOUTH

Fifteen years after Louis XIII had played at being an actor, the king pardoned Mathieu Lefebvre for an 'error of his youth': 'Finding himself too old to continue with his studies he was allured and attracted by frequentation with others to compose some tragedies, comedies, pastorals ... which he even performed in public over a period of a few years'.[27] Lefebvre had taken a while to recognize his 'error': from 1608 to 1619, then called Laporte, he had led one of two prominent Paris playing companies. 'Too old' for schooling but not ready to join 'the gravest and most serious people', the figure of Lefebvre emblematically links youth, irresponsibility and theatre. Regardless of actual facts, people at the cusp of adulthood were cast by early modern culture at large as simultaneously consumers and producers of theatre. Adulthood was imagined to be when one put away childish things like playing, but stage-playing could be taken up like an interval between manageable childhood and responsible maturity.

As a category of incipience, youth differs from childhood not in years but in degree of autonomy. Boy players in England, bound as apprentices, could be in their early twenties, but still imagined as a kind of child, useful and obedient; unsupervised, the same figure becomes a *Lusty Juventus*.[28] Corneille's *L'Illusion comique* (1639) represents the theatre itself as a virtual adolescence. In it, a worried father is shown increasingly dire and improbable visions of his wayward son, first as a desperate lover, then a servant in a love quadrangle, finally an ageing, unhappily married nobleman murdered by a younger rival. It turns out that the son has become an actor, and the father is seeing some of the parts he plays. Many of the plays that seem most exemplarily early modern address themselves to a time of introspective role-playing between managed childhood and self-determining adulthood, like Shakespeare's *Hamlet* (1600) or Calderón's *La vida es sueño* (1635). It is hard to tell whether it is a period ideology or our own that takes acting out as youth's natural condition.

No longer children, not yet adults, young men were often included within traditional social organizations specifically as marginal figures, imitating the privileges of adulthood in lieu of possessing them. In the early sixteenth century sons of patrician Venetian families formed clubs known as the *Compagnie della Calza* (Companies of the Stocking). Long disenfranchised by Venice's gerontocracy, these young Venetian men vented their frustrations in comic scenarios staging the victory of youth over age (Figure 7.3).[29] In Paris and other French cities, bands of law students and clerks, called Basoches, mounted parades and performances that satirized judges, members of Parlements, and others who held the positions that they hoped in time to occupy.[30] The Inns of Court in London, where students in their teens and twenties trained for careers in law, also sponsored performances, sometimes taking part themselves, most famously, and disastrously, when a 1594 production of *Comedy of Errors* ended with onlookers swarming the stage.[31] This performance at Gray's Inn was part

FIGURE 7.3: Scene from Commedia dell'arte, *Two Ages*. Anonymous French master (second half of sixteenth century). Found in the collection of the State A Pushkin Museum of Fine Arts, Moscow. (Photo by Fine Art Images/Heritage Images/Getty Images.)

COMMUNITIES OF PRODUCTION

of a much longer Yuletide celebration that imagined its students as citizens of a fantastic commonwealth, sending diplomatic embassies to the Queen and to other Inns. Such role-playing recalls older traditions of festive inversion, but also enabled the students real practice in skills of courtly conduct. Notebooks kept by Inns of Court scholars bear out their reputation as eager playgoers; a poem in one of them makes fun of their fascination with 'Shakespeare's plays instead of my Lord Coke'.[32] The *Parnassus* plays (*c.* 1600), written and staged in Cambridge by students, show a deep familiarity with professional London playing, which is satirically suggested as a possible career choice for students about to leave the university.

While they might be placed at the lower margins of existing social structures, young men were also capable of forming counter-social groups of their own. Both students and apprentices mimicked and challenged established hierarchies, as indeed did players more generally. Carnival plays in German-speaking areas were often turned over to groups of young men of all social classes.[33] These plays, when they were distinct plays at all and not just pretexts for misbehaviour, were less elaborate and much less pious than the longer-form religious performances that many cities also sponsored for their serious citizens. Scala complained about the 'continual din of Florentine youth' at his plays in 1618, suggesting again a nexus of youth, playgoing, and behaving badly. English apprentices developed considerable recognition and indeed self-consciousness as a distinct class, and often expressed it with and against professional playing. On Shrove Tuesday, 1617, rioting 'prentices . . . played their parts', tearing down a playhouse, 'cutting the players' apparel all in pieces, . . . burned their playbooks and did what other mischief they could'.[34] This may have been a protest directed against rising prices for admission to the playhouse, and apprentices conventionally misbehaved on Shrove Tuesdays. But it also seems a gesture of subcultural solidarity against the different subculture of playing. In all these accounts one can make out the attempts of young men to occupy spaces and functions from which they are, for a time at least, barred – to rehearse, as it were, the social status to which they aspire, to hold the mirror up to society and apply to it their own form and pressure.

My observations in this section have largely been specific to young men. It is worth asking if, in early modern theatres, there was a comparable age for women, an intermediary period of suspended responsibility between the powerlessness of childhood and the relatively greater self-determination and responsibilities of adulthood. In some ways women making theatre seem to have moved directly from childhood to adulthood, functionally children until they entered circulation as lovers, mothers, workers and performers. A Florentine account from 1616 of a mountebank's young assistant taps the attractiveness of this missing moment of transition: 'The shapely Vettoria, dressed like a neat and trim boy, packs in large crowds with her dangerous leaps, her divine dancing, and her beautiful gaze. . . . Of course there are certain old men who keep gazing at her with their mouths open, because they want to play games with her and have a taste themselves.'[35] Like a realized Rosalind, Vettoria unsettlingly balances boyishness and womanliness, childishness and maturity, always an object of desire for the old ambiguous hunger of comically impotent, socially powerful adulthood.

MAJORITY

Adults constitute the most readily recognizable communities engaging in the production of theatre, certainly the ones that are most visibly communities of choice. These communities are not constituted so differently from those associated with youth, but they have the privilege of defining themselves as norms: while the elective communities of the young appear countercultural to the extent that they are visible at all, the varying kinds of organization and affect that govern mature communities seem to define possibilities that are settled rather than transient. For its social pre-eminence I call this stage 'majority' rather than 'adulthood'. The heading also underscores a bias that I have been unable to avoid. Established companies of players and institutions that sponsored playing leave better records than the more contingent arrangements of players and spectators who might come together for a single performance or even a season and then separate. These fugitive associations, too, are among the communities of theatre's production, perhaps even its largest in terms of sheer numbers of persons and encounters. Other associations, longer-lasting than these but with more mediated relations to performance, were just as indispensable to early modern playing: worlds within worlds of workers, many of them women, who supplied playhouses with the food and drink they vended, the costumes they wore, the structures they used, and the audiences they entertained.[36] Playing could be just as indispensable to them: in 1614 when the playing companies temporarily moved their performance north of the Thames, the watermen who provided transport across the river protested that they could no longer support their families, since more than half their business had come from people crossing the river to see plays.[37] But space does not permit more than a notice of these other communities of producers.

For many theatrical productions in the period, financial, political, and ideological support was represented as communal, a community putting on a show for itself on an occasion of civic, national, or especially of religious importance. This kind of performance, and this mode of supporting production, is sometimes mistakenly described as medieval, but in fact traditional Hocktide plays in Coventry continued sporadically into the 1590s, and hundreds of *autos sacramentales* were written by Lope de Vega and Calderòn for Easter celebrations across seventeenth-century Spain.[38] Generally, though, even productions that claimed communal belonging were undertaken at the expense of a smaller group or even an individual within that community. Across Spain, France and England, guilds, confraternities, and other societies sponsored performances not nominally for their own gain, but for the good of their parish, town or region. Performance could also be offered to a community as a kind of civic ornament, as the Este dukes periodically provided Ferrara with Ariosto's plays during Carnival.[39]

Such expressions of faith or largesse did not remove the production of these plays from financial concerns entirely. Until the final performances of the Chester plays in 1575, local authorities showed a keen awareness of their economic returns to the city.[40] Many popular forms of theatre and performance were effectively fundraisers, like church-ales or the selling of paper livery badges at Robin Hood games. The efforts of freelance players were also frequently diverted to needy local causes. What seem like the perennial conflicts between city authorities and playing companies in London may be explained as attempts by the city to encourage, or extort, the players to support hospitals and almshouses. Threats to constrain playing would silently disappear when companies offered to share their profits for the public good, aligning their interests with those of the larger community.[41] In Madrid, the first licensed *corrales*, in the Calle de la Cruz (1579) and the Calle del Principe (1582), were required to share profits with the city's hospitals, and later *corrales* were supervised by the hospitals' Protector on the Council of Castile. Eventually, in 1638, companies leased the *corrales* directly from the Council.[42] Here as much as addressing itself, a community was raising money from itself, for itself.

Some communities of production seem almost wholly elective, like the Dutch *rederijkerskamers* or chambers of rhetoric, amateur performance societies like *de Eglantier* (the Eglantine) of Amsterdam or *de Goudbloem* (the Marigold) of Antwerp that staged original shows in competitions, or learned Italian academies that produced dramas, like *gli Intronati* (the Thunderstruck) of Siena or the Accademia Olimpica of Vicenza. Machiavelli's comedies *Clizia* and probably *Mandragola* were performed for private audiences of friends, not even calling themselves an academy.[43] Such groups could range from elite scholarly academies to something like a social club, with members sharing a neighbourhood or social station (or lack thereof, in the case of groups like the *Congrega dei Rozzi* [the Rough-edged], a collective of artisan-performers outside Siena).[44] Performances by such associations deal in cultural and social capital, with both material and status rewards largely symbolic. While *rederijkerskamers* hosting a competition sustained considerable expenses to provide prizes for winning entries, and winners took pride in their victories, competitors did not find their positions in society substantially changed by the outcomes (Figure 7.4).[45] If anything, emphasis seems to have been on maintaining a sense of solidarity among competing chambers: hosts and judges ensured that every competing chamber took home some prize. Winners (which is to say, competitors) in turn donated some of their prize money to relieve the local poor.[46] As in Spain, in 1635 the governors of Amsterdam's orphanages and almshouses decided not to depend any longer on the generosity of the chambers of rhetoric and replaced existing playhouses in Amsterdam with a larger one, which they paid for and

FIGURE 7.4: Members of a chamber of rhetoric performing. Jan Steen, *The Rhetoricians* (c. 1655).

operated. The rhetoricians' performances became overtly profit-seeking, and extremely profitable, with the city's orphanages and almshouses now controlling playing and receiving the proceeds.[47]

Close financial and managerial relations among playhouses, companies of players, charitable institutions, and local governments were widespread. The Confrérie de la Passion, originally a religious charity, had been granted exclusive rights to produce plays on religious themes in Paris since 1402, excepting those performed by schools and universities. By 1548 the Confrérie had suffered mission creep from religious community to theatrical enterprise: all groups performing in the capital had to either lease the Confrérie's theatre in the Hôtel de Bourgogne or pay the Confrérie a fee.[48] An English company was fined in 1598 after contracting with the Confrérie for the Hôtel de Bourgogne when they also performed outside it.[49] Thomas Sebillot's *Art poétique française* (1548) tied theatre's decline from its excellence in antiquity to these new exchanges and investments: 'the favor of the populace that was a major ambition among the old Greeks and Romans has died away with us. . . . [We] rather put on plays to bring in cash.' The default Sebillot sees is at once moral, political, and aesthetic: 'we are more concerned with just putting [plays] on than in developing them to their full perfection.'[50] The recurring translation of public entertainment to public benefit is economic in the broadest sense: it sketches the boundaries of the communities within and among which it takes place.

Making theatre required capital, not only money but also time, space, energy and material; it could also raise capital, usually in the form of money alone. This poses the question of what kinds of exchange qualify theatre as *professional*, that is, a community of production that supported itself through performance (it was always *commercial*, arising out of exchanges of labour and goods). There are easy examples in opportunistic mountebanks, the profiteering *commedia dell'arte* troupes (who nevertheless chose names like *I Confidenti* [the Confident] or *Gli Accesi* [the Kindled] in imitation of *amateur* academies like the *Intronati*), or early Spanish troupes like Lope de Rueda's, which already by 1560 was seeking to buy property for a playing yard.[51] But what about the production of Ariosto's plays, paid for by the Este family, performed by one-time collectives of courtiers, regional musicians, and others who performed for money in other contexts?[52] Or those of the shoemaker, playwright, and committed Lutheran Hans Sachs, who besides competing as a *Meistersinger* and writing city-sponsored Carnival plays, led a playing troupe during the 1550s which staged his 'comedies' and 'tragedies,' apparently out of a sense of moral commitment?[53] What was the status of boys at Merchant Taylors' School, performing at court for what were called gifts and semi-publically to paying audiences from the guild that also supported their school? 'Professional theatre' is less a description of economic relations than of differently defined communities, or community within a community, or multiple communities within multiple communities.

In professional theatre, one community extracts resources from another community in exchange for performance. One way to determine the shape of these communities is to ask whether money raised for performance comes back to the community or leaves it. Civic communities recognized this early: towns and territories throughout Europe tried to limit what wandering players charged for their skills, lest they take too much from either individuals or the area.[54] To see where interests and identities align or diverge may be more important than to reduce relations to questions of theatrical professionalism, which do not always fit the complex ways these communities interacted.

Where on the scale of professionalization do family groups fall? Performance groups rooted in kinship – affinities born into, rather than elective – are frequent features of European theatre through the sixteenth and seventeenth centuries and well into the twentieth.[55] The earliest known fixed stage in England was erected around 1525 by John Rastell and a circle around him which included, among others, his brother-in-law Thomas More; members of the group printed and probably performed plays by themselves and others, as well as leasing costumes.[56] The greatest of the travelling *commedia* troupes of the sixteenth century, the *Gelosi*, was built around the talents of husband and wife Francesco and Isabella Andreini, especially Isabella. Although it disbanded physically at Isabella's death in 1604, virtually the Andreini family continued to perform: Francesco cultivated Isabella's legacy in print, and their son Giambattista Andreini formed his own company, called as if in response to theirs *I Fedeli* (the Faithful), which became perhaps the most celebrated of the seventeenth-century companies.[57]

Rather than seeing playing running in families, one can discern familial structures, both traditional and non-traditional, emerging from playing as the (more) determining instance. Even non-familial companies, especially those relying on young performers, could gravitate towards familial structures. Sometimes such structures were legally mandated. In Spain, actors were required to travel with their wives when on tour; if married, women actors had to be accompanied by their husbands and, if not, by their fathers.[58] Before it became usual for women to act onstage in Spain, a touring Italian *commedia* troupe with women was given special permission to play, but only provided the women were married, accompanied by their husbands, and dressed as women.[59] To participate in a theatrical community of production required, for some, the additional community of marriage.

Molière's multiple companies could be described as a family enterprise, albeit a confusing one. Molière and Madeleine Béjart founded their youthful *Illustre Théâtre* together in 1643, with two of Madeleine's siblings and six other actors. Béjart's mother and two more younger siblings (one of them, Armande, perhaps actually Madeleine's daughter) lived with the group, and Molière and Béjart may also have been romantically involved.[60] Through failures,

COMMUNITIES OF PRODUCTION 141

reorganizations, and departures, Molière and Madeleine Béjart remained the core of his troupes until her retirement. Armande Béjart grew up in their companies, became an actor in one of them, and eventually married Molière. Travelling groups of performers might also be bolstered by non-performing family members. When the Duke of Modena's company travelled to England in 1678, two-thirds of its thirty-six members were wives and children of the actors.[61] Even if they never ventured onstage, such family members' work in handling costumes, collecting fees, maintaining living spaces, even sustaining performers emotionally and knitting the group more tightly, could also be counted as professional playing.

While Molière's troupe was familial in some ways, its members were also legally contracted to each other, their obligations and their rights stipulated in writing. These voluntary communities among persons who were bound only and equally by their formal agreement are among the most significant innovations of early modern playing. The earliest surviving example is an agreement drawn up in Padua in February 1545 among eight men to join together through carnival of 1546 in a 'fraternal company . . . reciting comedies from place to place'. To maintain their 'fraternal love', the 'brothers' established articles to govern their behaviour: a leader was appointed, common property purchased (a horse, to carry props and costumes), arrangements for a cash box made (three separate keys, profits deposited daily, nothing withdrawn until the end of their agreement). The articles set penalties for leaving the company, compensation for illness or injury, and, in an unusual detail, forbid the members from playing cards together.[62] Profits and debts at the end of their term of agreement were to be divided equally. Similar contracts appear among wandering French players in Chartres in 1549, minus the stipulations about horses and cards, and even for the Troupe Royale at the Hôtel de Bourgogne in 1642.[63]

Companies founded on contract professed a different sense of their communities than those with familial models of organization: fraternal, horizontal, not without its own hierarchies but nevertheless marked by a strong sense of egalitarianism. As in the contract from Padua, such companies were often imagined as a 'brotherhood' of 'fellows'; the *Meistersinger* guilds of sixteenth-century Germany similarly made 'brotherhood' among their members a crucial goal.[64] Some English companies were constituted as joint-stock companies, with members jointly and differentially owning the value of the company's stocks of costumes, playbooks, and other equipment. While this kind of economic organization seems to have originated in 1553 with the high-risk, high-reward Merchant Adventurers, it boomed in England after mid-sixteenth century, and playing companies were at its leading edge.[65] Rather than merely dividing up a take, such companies became investment vehicles, with players, their heirs and eventually outside buyers holding different numbers and fractions of shares. 'There is nobody in the world who loves the monarchy more than actors', asserts Samuel Chappuzeau, an eyewitness French theatre historian, guardedly, in 1674, 'but they do not tolerate it among themselves: their government is in any case not wholly democratic, and in part aristocratic.'[66] Because of their sense of merit, Chappuzeau explains, actors insist on unequal shares rather than dividing everything equally. But this unequal division too rested on a notion of shared profitability. 'Both sexes share in the authority of their state', Chappuzeau continues, 'women being as useful as men, or more.'

Formation of acting companies was perhaps both most lively and most regularized in Spain. Unlike most other traditions, professional Spanish actors worked for hire – perhaps the situation most recognizable to us as 'professional' – rather than for take or a share, and renegotiated their contracts in a yearly market, when actors returned to Madrid to be recruited for the Easter *autos* as well as to sign up with new companies for the coming theatrical season.[67] While some Spanish companies were composed of actor-sharers, actors generally contracted for a fixed wage per performance and another *per diem* allowance for food.[68] The terms of contracts resembled those of Padua or Chartres, minutely specifying compensation during illness, or which parts an actor would be given. One actor was even promised that his shirts would be washed.[69] Actors did not contract with each other, though, but with the *autor*, not the author of plays but of the company itself. *Autores* and *autoras* (some were women) were something like modern producers, brokering agreements between players, owners of *corrales*, and others whose labour produced the plays during the Easter rush, and overseeing the logistics behind performance during playing season.

The models of actors working for a wage and sharers working for a cut were not incompatible or exclusive. Playing companies in both England and France also hired actors for set wages, as well as workers for other positions, like bookkeeper, tireman, or gatherer. Some of these relationships were as longstanding as those of sharers. But the two structures could also come into competition. The playhouse owner Philip Henslowe frequently entered into individual contracts with actors and others that put them in his service as wage-earners, potentially aligning their particular interests more with Henslowe's than with their companies.[70] In 1615, players accused Henslowe of intentionally breaking five companies in three years[71] – for companies 'broke' (or dissolved), as well as formed, sometimes quietly going separate ways, sometimes more dramatically. Molière's *Illustre Théâtre* lasted only a little over a year before being forced to sell its costumes, its members scattering to other provincial companies. In 1593 Pembroke's Men may have broken and been forced to pawn their costumes and possibly also to sell their playbooks; that at least has been suggested as a reason that London in 1594 saw the publication of so many new plays.[72] But breaking could be creatively destructive: both Molière's

COMMUNITIES OF PRODUCTION

company and Pembroke's Men rebounded in different forms. Early modern companies were strikingly fluid, losing players to other troupes and gaining new ones, forming and reforming as they travelled. Spanish companies broke and reconstituted every year after Carnival. In England, the Queen's Men was assembled from members of other companies in 1583, like all-stars; at Molière's death in 1673 his company first dispersed to those of the Hôtel de Bourgogne and the Théâtre du Marais, and then in 1680 re-coalesced by royal decree as the Comédie Française.[73]

In the early modern period, one of the most crucial communities of production was the ephemeral audience. Between 1500 and 1700, playgoers increasingly contracted to see performances, exchanging a set fee – 'to like or dislike at their own charge . . . as you have preposterously put to your seals already, which is your money', sneered playwright Ben Jonson – in advance of receiving a relatively predictable product, 'since', observed Cervantes with equal scorn, 'plays have become a saleable merchandise'.[74] Paying for plays let audiences buy into a performance community rather than being born to it: access to one fungible good was secured by another, rather than being linked to social condition. But playgoers were also channelled by their money and the access it purchased as performances moved from the liberty of the street, where one paid as much or as little as one wanted, to the enclosures of English playhouses, French theatres, or Spanish *corrales*, with their stepped tiers of admission prices sorting audiences by desire and ability to pay.[75] Ganassa, an Italian company leader who spent the 1570s and 1580s playing in Spain, no doubt thinking of structures like these, said he made his money 'corralling sheep'.[76] The *corral* in fact was a much more permeable space than the English playhouse, which self-consciously sheltered playgoers within its freestanding wooden O. A *corral* was more or less improvised into the space of its street, blocking off a section of a *calle* or defile and erecting a stage at one end. The windows and porches of nearby buildings might be pressed into service as boxes or alternative viewpoints, making it a novel and hybrid community of negotiated interests, ambiguously public and private.[77]

We know little about these short-lived communities of playgoers, about what they liked, what feelings or needs brought them together, or how they felt when they assembled. We know some of them had longstanding, varied interests in playgoing. The brothers Thomas and Felix Platter, for instance, separately toured Europe around 1600, and recorded what they saw in unusual detail, in particular many kinds of performance. Thomas famously visited playhouses in London, where he saw a production of *Julius Caesar*, but he also visited the Hôtel de Bourgogne, where a *farceur* improvised verses; Avignon, where he saw Italian mountebanks, pastorals in 'a mixture of Italian and Languedocean', and a 'tragedy' played in the streets; and Barcelona, where he bought a pair of castanets to send home to Basel after watching dancers perform a percussive sarabande.[78] His half-brother Felix recorded with delight seeing an actor playing St Paul have his pants set on fire by the fireworks that were meant to represent the light of grace.[79] The Platters are exceptional in many ways – learned, curious, tourists with a wide taste for new kinds of theatre. But they seem to have made another sort of community that is both elective and affective, that of aficionados of performance.

SENESCENCE

In 1613 the poet Malherbe recorded a disturbing performance by Italian players at Fontainbleau: 'Arlequin is certainly very different from what he once was, as too is Patrolin: the former is fifty-six years old, and the latter eighty-seven; these are not ages proper to the theatre, which calls for lively temperaments and measured minds, and those one rarely finds in old bodies like theirs.'[80] What becomes of old players? Some, like Giovanni Pellesini, who seems to have presented the Patrolin or Pedrolino that alarmed Malherbe and who had been associated with the character from its earliest mentions in 1576, keep playing.[81] Some, no doubt, fared better than Pellesini, like the clown Will Kemp, who left Shakespeare's company and London around 1600, apparently on a wager to dance across the Alps. Some fared worse: Molière collapsed and died after a performance of his *Imaginary Invalid* (1673). 'Shoemaker and also Poet', *Meistersinger* and playwright Hans Sachs experienced his most productive years of playwriting after he turned fifty, and he continued to compose plays and other works past his mid-seventies (Figure 7.5).

Family companies in particular sometimes travelled with older people: in 1627 one leader of a *commedia* company wrote to a patron that his performing group was accompanied by both his children and his aged mother.[82] But whereas children represent a resource, senescence is a drying-up of resourcefulness, and eventually of production itself. It is thus less a condition than a process. To become old is to lose one's place in one's community of production and fall away from it. The end of production is not simply a physical condition akin to wearing out, as Malherbe cruelly makes clear. It is not just that old men physically cannot carry on, as if the issue were merely one of decorum or even physical strength. It is that playing requires continually renewed resources, and as Malherbe coldly calculates, these become scarcer as one ages.

But detachment from one community can mean forming new communities. Richard Tarlton, the most famous player in the Queen's Men, the premier company of the 1580s and early 1590s, may have retired from the stage to run taverns in London's playing neighbourhoods.[83] Shakespeare retired far from them to his properties in Stratford. Edward Alleyn, the most prominent tragedian of the 1590s, gradually left playing to join his father-in-law Philip Henslowe in a number of entertainment-related business ventures, including

FIGURE 7.5: Hans Sachs, who identified himself as 'Shoemaker, and also Poet', at age 80. Andreas Herneysen, 1575. (Photo by Ullstein bild/ullstein bild via Getty Images.)

bear-baiting and playhouse-building. In 1619 Alleyn endowed the College of God's Gift in Dulwich, a school and charity, which continues to this day. Alleyn's past followed him more awkwardly than Tarlton's or Shakespeare's: when he married John Donne's daughter in 1623, Donne told Alleyn that he could not stay in Donne's house because he was a player.[84]

In part Pellesini had to keep playing, and English players had to either join new communities or expand their old ones, because playing did not imagine any other institutional support for them. As we have seen, contracts for *commedia* companies often included a clause about providing care in case of illness or injury, but this was clearly meant to be short-term. In 1631, actors in Spain were permitted to form a confraternity of their own, the Cofradía de la Novena, which was open to *autores*, actors, and their spouses and children. The Cofradía collected payments from working actors to care for the old and impoverished, and to pay for funerals.[85] The tirelessly upbeat Chappuzeau describes a practice among French actors of the later seventeenth century of retiring actors being paid pensions by their replacements 'sufficient to live on ... to the end of their days'. At the Hôtel de Bourgogne, he continues, when an actor died, it was customary for the company to give the next of kin a gift of a hundred *pistoles*.[86] In their wills, English players often left small keepsakes to their fellows, suggesting the deep personal bonds that could arise within companies. Shakespeare, for instance, left money to buy rings to Richard Burbage, his company's leading actor; and to John Heminges and William Condell, who brought the first folio of Shakespeare's plays into print – 'my fellows'.[87]

CHAPTER EIGHT

Repertoire and Genres

Culture and Society

FRIEDEMANN KREUDER

In his well-known article, 'Culture is Ordinary', written as he meditated on the landscapes, orchards, castles, houses, mills, gasworks and farming valleys of Welsh border lands, Raymond Williams considers the 'shape of culture' in his native country and its 'modes of change', and makes the following observation:

> We use the word culture in . . . two senses: to mean a whole way of life – the common meaning; to mean the arts and learning – the special processes of discovery and creative effort. Some writers reserve the word for one or other of these senses; I insist on both, and on the significance of their conjunction. The questions I ask about our culture are questions about our general and common purposes, yet also questions about deep personal meanings. Culture is ordinary, in every society and in every mind.[1]

Williams's twofold sense of 'culture' both as an ordinary process of finding shared meanings and values, and as the creative work of discovery and creation in domains such as the arts and learning provides a useful interpretive frame for an examination of early modern theatrical genres and repertoires. His insistence that culture works on both the social and individual levels, and through the axes of both traditional continuity and creative change also holds relevance for an age that, on the one hand, rediscovered and re-established the tradition of ancient dramatic genres and forms, and, on the other hand, creatively changed those forms in the pulse of new empirical social conditions. With his sense of the individual freely processing traditional forms and actively creating new ones, Williams avoids a deterministic approach, whether one stresses the social dimension trumping the individual or the material substructure mechanistically dictating culture, conceived as dependent superstructure. Like his teacher Gramsci, Williams avoids both deterministic extremes.

Williams's rich sense of culture as an activity produced and experienced by people of a wide socio-economic ambit nicely applies to early modern theatrical genres and repertoires, which were most successful (and economically profitable) when they were able to engage ordinary social life and the very rich popular culture of itinerant piazza and street performance, cheap print, strolling minstrels, street hawkers, popular festivals such as carnival, and much else. At this same time, early modern genres cannot be understood without studying the sustained elite and humanist process of cultural disinterment from the ancient past and rearticulation in both print and performance. Just as the fifteenth-century humanist Poggio Bracciolini resurrected Lucretius from oblivion, humanists discovered, exchanged, edited, translated and wrote commentaries on texts of Plautus, Terence, Seneca, Euripides, Vitruvius and Donatus, thereby reviving 'comedy', 'tragedy', and other classical forms. But whereas Machiavelli, Lope, Ben Jonson, Thomas Hardy and Andreas Gryphius are unthinkable without the rediscovered tradition of the ancient past, the classical forms had to connect to the forms and pressures of contemporary life. If the revived ideas about dramatic genre did not spark across into early modern cultural life, they died on the vine, or stayed within the confines of elite, academic antiquarianism, like the production of *Oedipus the King* staged within the precious, inward-facing walls of the Teatro Olimpico in Vicenza in 1585. But when the tragic buskin and 'Marlowe's mighty line' took the stages of the English amphitheatres in the late sixteenth century, something happened. Lope de Vega learned the rules and forms of classical genres, as he makes irritatingly clear in the *New Art of Making Comedies*, but then he threw away the rules in the press of the highly successful market of *corral* performance. The great Arte actor-writer Flaminio Scala argued, in an imaginary dialogue between a neoclassicist theorist and a practising actor, that the rules of drama had to be tested, as if in the (incipient) empirical sciences, before flesh-and-blood audiences.

Early modern genres emerged out of the general sociocultural conditions of the time; they can be considered as 'social actions' that fulfilled particular functions for social groups. Early modern culture pervasively combined oral, popular, modes of language and performance with the modes of written, elite culture: the latter was obviously nothing new (it has been pointed out what a 'writerly' form ancient Greek drama was) but the culture of writing surely was changed by the printing press, which humanists like Erasmus pounced on for educating a wider socio-economic sphere than had previously been reached. Just as Cervantes's great novel melds Quixote's books and Sancho's proverbs, early modern dramatic genres and the repertoires performed by acting companies amounted to a productive, if sometimes antagonistic, encounter between the oral and the written, the popular and the elite, the piazza and the book. Embracing both the oral and the written, early modern theatrical genres were omnivorous. As in the case of late-sixteenth-century Italian tragicomedy, genres were created from other genres. There was a strong tendency to mix rather than to purify genres; such productive melding occurred both in the academic's study, as with Battista Guarini's elaborate theoretical defences of tragicomedy, and in the hold of performance, as with the itinerant players who come to Elsinore to perform, in Polonius's words, 'tragical-comical-historical-pastoral'. To pitch drama beyond the confines of the humanist study was, of course, to play the marketplace, the crucible where the repertories of early modern professional companies were wrought. If those who 'live to please' must 'please to live' (Samuel Johnson), the Gelosi, the Lord Chamberlain's Men, Zan Ganassa's Madrid-based troupe, Valleran le Conte's Parisian-based but also itinerant outfit, and the early German travelling actors all employed canny commercial strategies to allow the companies to take advantage of playgoers' tastes and thus make their offerings attractive. They developed, in the white heat of market performance, both the dramatic genres of the times and actor-based repertoires of gags, witticism, physical routines, speech genres, scenes, and speeches.

RINASCIMENTO: RECEPTIONS OF ANTIQUITY AND NEW FORMS OF THEATRE IN ITALY

Elite, early modern culture in Italy understood itself as *Rinascimento*, as a rebirth, a new creation of the present from antiquity that defined itself against the supposedly 'dark' Middle Ages. The grandeur of antique culture, which from the perspective of some contemporaries could never be regained, was to be recaptured by imitation (*imitatio*). This worked through both textual and visual means: first, via fifteenth- and sixteenth-century editions of Plautus, Terence, Seneca, the Greek tragedians (mostly Euripides), and Aristotle's *Poetics*. Second, the visual picture of theatre architecture, design and painting was reconstructed through the disinterment of Vitruvius's *De architectura* and other texts, with the recent discoveries of Italian perspective painting augmenting the research into antiquity. Rome was an early centre of humanist research and, during the second half of the fifteenth century, numerous Latin comedies and tragedies were being staged in the *Accademia* founded by Pomponius Laetus. Since the inauguration of Pope Sixtus IV in 1471, productions for festive occasions in palaces or public places were also recorded also outside the academies, becoming objects of great interest. The politically motivated Latin performance of Plautus's *Poenulus* by Tommaso Inghirami in

1513 in a provisional wooden theatre at the *Piazza del Campidoglio* drew an audience of some 3,000 spectators.[2] But the motive to provide 'authentic' reconstructions of ancient theatre could be eclipsed by the desire of the Renaissance court to represent itself above anything else. The artists were at the service of the respective sovereign to whom they had to pay honours and whose fame they had to safeguard.[3] In these courts, the theatre tended to withdraw from the public sphere of the urban population into the inner space of courts, and turned into an exclusive art form.

Comedy became the centrepiece of Renaissance festive culture, especially in the Este court of Ferrara, where multiple vernacular translations of ancient comedies were performed. Ludovico Ariosto, who would later become famous as the author of the romance epic *Orlando Furioso*, played a fundamental role in inventing forms of Italian humanist comedy aiming to heighten the sense of realistic mimesis. Perhaps even more important than his first comedy *La Cassaria* in 1508 was the play *I suppositi*, which gets rid of patently Roman tags such as the slave girls and pimps of the earlier play and translates the New Comedic situation more effectively to the context of early modern Italy.[4] (*I suppositi*, translated into English by George Gascoigne as *Supposes*, provided Shakespeare with the subplot for *The Taming of the Shrew*.) In the same spirit of translation, Bernardo Dovizi in *La Calandria* (1513) takes the twin theme from Plautus's *Menaechmi* and adds the important elements of gender and transvestism, to explore problems of identity and subjectivity. Machiavelli, in a famous debate with Ariosto, argues for the use of local dialect rather than Tuscan as a way to translate comic form even more effectively to the present day. In addition to the linguistic realism of *La mandragola*, he translates into dramatic terms the instrumental rationality famously explored in *Il Principe* (1513).

Whereas Italian early modern comedy tilted towards the realistic representation of urban life, the spaces of tragedy remained imaginary: the genre was widely discussed in theory but performed much less often than comedy.[5] Humanists produced ancient tragedies in Italian translation, for example Seneca's *Phaedra*, translated into Italian by Francesco Pitti and performed in 1509 in Ferrara. The first surviving modern tragedy in five acts written in Italian, dramatizing a plot from Boccaccio's *Decameron,* was *Pamphila & Philostrato* by Antonio Camelli da Pistoia, performed in 1499 in Mantova and Ferrara, and printed in 1508. Giangiorgio Trissino's *Sophonisba* (1524) became an important vernacular model for tragedies that imitated ancient examples, but tellingly it was not performed until 1562 in Vicenza, with scenic decorations arranged by Andrea Palladio. In Machiavelli's *La mandragola*, the protagonist Lucretia defies her pure Roman namesake by consenting to sexual desire in the supposed name of 'providence'. By contrast, Trissino's Sophonisba, counted among the enemies of Rome in the Second Punic War and eventually defeated, is all virtue: faced with the forcing of her sexual will for political reasons, she discovers her own will in committing suicide with poison. But it must be said that Italian comedy was much more successful than tragedy in melding Williams's two meanings of 'culture': Machiavelli played better than Trissino.

With roots in classical pastoral and a class of rough-hewn mythological court plays dating back to the late fifteenth century, pastoral drama began to vie for neoclassical legitimization in the 1550s, placing Ferrara once again at the centre of avant-garde experimentation in Agostino Beccari's *Il sacrificio*. (Angelo Poliziano's 1480 *Orfeo*, itself a fusion of the *sacra rappresentazione*, early humanist ideas about tragedy, and classical pastoral, provides an interesting antecedent.) Again in Ferrara, Torquato Tasso's 1573 *Aminta* played the notion of 'love' as an amoral, primordial natural force against the rational order of neo-platonic *amor*. The 'natural' of Italian pastoral could be subsumed, at least in theory, by the domesticating, civilizing principles represented by the court itself. The 'civilizing process' could thus be played on the theatrical boards of the Italian court and academy.[6]

VENICE AND POPULAR THEATRE

The greater region of Venice, from which the *commedia dell'arte* emerged, was the crucible of dialect theatre, whether performed by *buffoni* such as Zuan Polo Liompardi in both the piazza and in ceremonial occasions of state, or whether scripted and published, as with the anonymous *La Veniexiana* (1535). The Paduan actor-writer Angelo Beolco (alias Ruzante), who used Paduan, Bergamask and Venetian dialects in his scripted plays, moved between court and popular culture and enjoyed great popularity in Padua and Venice during the 1520s and 1530s. Most of his plays feature the famished, degraded, desperate, but inventive persona of 'Ruzante', a displaced Paduan down on his luck (and love) but theatrically virtuosic, both linguistically and physically. As generically omnivorous as Shakespeare, Beolco absorbed popular forms such as the *bulesca* (plays about the *bravo*, or tough guy), the *villanesca* (plays regarding the *villano*, or peasant), and the *maridazzo* (polydialect plays staging wedding feasts that take a momentarily violent turn). At the same time and increasingly in the 1530s, Beolco drew on ancient New Comedy and the new humanist work of Ariosto and Machiavelli. Unlike these *commedia erudita* writers, however, the actor Beolco sporadically earned some money for his performances and thus anticipates the professional *commedia dell'arte*.[7]

The *commedia dell'arte*, based on codified but flexible character types, proposed the actor as autonomous 'author' working in a highly codified and organized system of improvisation. Like the travelling troupe visiting Elsinore, who, in Polonius's words, could perform 'tragical-comical-historical-pastoral', the Arte actors absorbed a multitude of genres, modes, postures and tones, belying their customary association with farce. They opportunistically filched both from the scripted comedy and from non-dramatic literary texts such as Boccaccio's *Decameron* and Ariosto's *Orlando furioso*. The conflict animating Arte plays results usually from the desire of young lovers who stand against the economic interests of their fathers' generation – and occasionally the misdirected erotic aspirations of the old man, given to lust after the same woman who is the object of his son's affection. This conflict, decisively if perilously mediated by the servant Zanni or his female counterpart Franceschina, achieves a temporary resolution that does nothing to abate the cyclical logic of generational conflict, the inversion of master and slave relations as well as the metamorphoses of love and identity. The several manuscript collections of scenarios, and the one collection printed at the time (Flaminio Scala's 1611 *Teatro delle favole rappresentative*)[8] include in addition to comedies pastorals, 'heroic' works, tragicomedies and even tragedies. Whether in Italy, Spain, France, the German-speaking regions, or elsewhere, the *commedia dell'arte* managed to harness culture in Williams's broadest sense: it absorbed popular, oral performance modes while still appropriating the structures and forms of scripted, humanist comedy. The actors celebrated the performativity of the human body – and the usability of humanist form – before dukes, merchants and occasionally cobblers.

THE ERA OF ELIZABETH I: POPULAR THEATRE AND HUMANISM IN ENGLAND

The Elizabethan and Jacobean theatre of Shakespeare also drew from both oral-popular and elite-literary traditions.[9] The playing practice of the popular theatre of the vernacular mystery and morality plays, replete with spectacular scenic effects, coarse humour, occasional improvisation, and direct interactions with the audience, thrived on the verbal and bodily performativity of the actors.[10] Countering this, but merging with it in the most successful cases such as the work of Marlowe, Jonson and Shakespeare, was the textually-based humanist drama, linked to classical models.

In humanist pedagogy, reading and performing Latin and vernacular drama served to train the art of rhetoric as well as the ethical development of the individual.[11] The first English-language dramas in the humanist tradition originated in the contexts of grammar schools and universities, as for example *Ralph Roister Doister* (1552), a play by the headmaster of Eton, Nicholas Udall, which combined the local vernacular tradition with plot patterns taken over from Terence and Plautus. The anonymous 1553 *Gammer Gurton's Needle* was performed at the University of Cambridge. In the domain of tragedy, Thomas Sackville and Thomas Norton's *Gorboduc*, or *Ferrex and Porrex* (1562), adapted the five-act form of Seneca – a dramatist generally of great importance to the

REPERTOIRE AND GENRES   153

humanists – to a subject matter from early English history. More independent and creative was Marlowe's engagement with Seneca, fleshing out the violence and sensationalism that had likely been closet drama in Roman times, refracted by the secondary narrations of messengers and left to the spectator's imagination. In plays such as the immensely successful *Tamberlaine* (Part I 1587/8, Part II 1588) crescendos of violence operating at both the textual and performed levels viscerally engaged Marlowe's audience, who was forced to question the ethical values of humanism.

The cultural matrix for the development of commercial theatre in London consisted precisely in Marlowe's capacity to meld the humanism of Cambridge University with the rawness of the capital's bear-baiting pit. In addition, the function of drama changed appreciably, reflecting crucial social and political shifts in Elizabethan England. According to Louis Montrose, early modern English theatre represented, and in some part helped to effect, the transition 'from a culture focused on social dynamics within the local community to one that incorporates the local within a national framework and subordinates it to the political and cultural centre'.[12] Early modern English drama responded to the pulse of both the monarchical state and paying London audiences: the latter a fluctuating, and non-controllable market. The commercial theatre, under attack from both Puritan church and municipal authority, depended on the monarchy for support. At the same time, it worked within the framework of commercial interests and performatively reflected collective interests and conflicts. The dramatic genres that developed provided the formal vehicles for these partly opposed social functions of theatre.

English professional theatre brilliantly deployed a range of genres responding to the changing pulses and tastes of its audiences. One of the first genres to dominate the public stage was the history play, riding the wave of the English victory over the Spanish Armada in 1588. Evolving from the audience's nascent national consciousness and patriotism after long conflicts with the continental powers (especially Spain), the historical plays were less concerned with the fate of individual kings than rather the societal situation, the dynamics of dynastic conflicts, such as the Wars of the Roses, and the question of the legitimacy of royal domination.

Romantic comedy, represented best by John Lyly and William Shakespeare, placed at its centre an amorous couple that can only be brought together after overcoming obstacles, such as the father's resistance, various intrigues and spatial separation. Here, the influence of Italian comedies such as *Gl'ingannati* of the Intronati academy, probably mediated by the *commedia dell'arte*, was unmistakable. English romantic comedy, following Italian plays such as Luise Pasqualigo's *Gl'intricati*, opposed an ideal sublime love to its coarse ironic counterpart: Rosalind and Orlando to Touchstone and Audrey in Shakespeare's *As You Like It*. As some romantic comedies of both Lyly and Shakespeare demonstrate, the mode of pastoral could be nicely conjoined with the genre of comedy.

In the satirical comedy of Ben Jonson, John Marston and Thomas Middleton, social reality was represented through the distorted, but revealing lens of critical exaggeration. Humoral imbalance and a degree of obsession whose intensity strained the limits of comic decorum governed these laboratories of misbehaviour. Countering the antitheatricalist claim that to view sin was to imitate it, Jonson fiercely argued for the form's moral integrity. London, outwardly rational but inwardly seething with greed and ambition, increasingly came to provide the satiric scene, and satiric comedy was absorbed into city comedy, whose most important representative was Thomas Middleton. It portrayed the conflicts between outwardly respectable bourgeois London and various overachievers and adventurers. The City of London owed its self-government, economic prosperity, and social stability to a citizen-based guild structure, but from 1600 on, this arrangement was undermined by ruthless social climbing, reckless pursuit of profit, and Puritan sectarianism.

Tragicomedy emerged in the first decade of the seventeenth century. Plays like Beaumont and Fletcher's *A King and No King* did not so much focus on the juxtaposition of comic and tragic strains (a general feature of much Elizabethan and Jacobean drama) but carefully constructed a tragedic plot almost leading to catastrophe but averted by a surprising turn of events. The continental model was Battista Guarini's late sixteenth-century pastoral tragicomedy *Il pastor fido*, enhanced by a series of theoretical apologias he wrote in defence of the hybrid genre against the conservative critic Giason Denores. When John Fletcher, in *The Faithful Shepherd* (1607), attempted to imitate closely Guarini's pastoral tragicomedy, the play failed with London audiences, and he then turned to a non-pastoral form of tragicomedy with his collaborator Beaumont. Shakespeare, whose own rural background may have helped him represent shepherds, shepherdesses and countrymen more realistically than others, was practically the only English dramatist who acted on Guarini's claim that the pastoral mode could transform tragedy into comedy, especially in his late plays.

Cultural ambivalence regarding the code of revenge informed the wildly popular genre of revenge tragedy, in which an avenger executes vigilante justice in cunning intrigue, usually against someone who has killed a member of his family. In the genre's prototype, Thomas Kyd's *The Spanish Tragedy*, revenge tragedy was shaped by the representation of violence on stage and in some cases it may have raised questions about the state's legitimization of violence. Vying cultural conceptions (ascetic, Anglican, Puritan) of love and marriage informed the genre of domestic tragedy. From the conflict between marriage and extramarital love affairs on the part of the wife develops tragic consequences, which usually end with the wife's death.

THE SPANISH THEATRE OF THE *SIGLO DE ORO*

Early modern Spanish theatre, where religious forms like the *auto sacramental* survived well beyond their counterparts in England, tended to restore the vertical perspective of heaven, earth and hell (vestigially preserved, to be sure, in the outdoor English amphitheatres) to the early modern stage.[13] In the *auto*, dramaturgical tension arose from the opposition of immanence and transcendence, which revealed the events on stage as part of a Christian history of salvation. Pedro Calderón de la Barca, in his 1645 *auto sacramental El gran teatro del mundo* (The Grand Theatre of the World), staged theatre as a quintessential symbol of the world. God, a stage director par excellence, desires to provide a spectacle of the world for himself as audience; the world is the stage, humans are the actors, and their roles are the different social classes of the king, the wise man, the beauty, the rich, the countryman and the beggar. Death calls the actors from the stage and once the play is over God hands out the dues according to their capacities of accepting, enduring, suffering and fulfilling the role in life that has been demanded from them. The Spanish theatre of the *Siglo de Oro* (The Golden Age) coincided with the last phase of the long period between the reign of Charles I (1519–56) and the Treaty of the Pyrenees between Spain and France (1659). Gold and silver coming from America during this time allowed Spain great undertakings beyond its borders and thus the expansion of its power across all of Europe. But during the long reigns of Philip III (1598–1621) and Philip IV, unambiguous signs of economic fatigue could be felt inside the empire. During this time, meanwhile, the professional theatre established itself as a phenomenon of mass culture. The three popular 'areas' – the Corral theatre, the Corpus Christi stage, and the Court theatre – yielded a large number of plays while continuously renewing the repertoire. Since the entertainment value of theatre was mainly dependent on its ability to offer something new to the audience, plays were quickly worn out and had to be replaced in time by new ones. The dramatists tried to counter the short shelf life of individual plays with phenomenal productivity. At the age of seventy-two in 1632, Lope de Vega claimed to have written 1,500 plays; Tirso de Molina wrote 400 plays in twenty years. Dramatists and actors frequently crossed lines between the three major kinds of theatre. The same authors who delivered *comedias* to the Corral theatre and *fiestas* to the Court theatre also wrote the *autos sacramentales*, which were performed before the people on the day of Corpus Christi at different city sites. The actors who had therefore been hired by the church belonged generally to troupes also playing at the *corrales*. A *comedia* usually consisted of a prologue with flatteries for the audience, an introduction of the troupe and the play, and the appeal for attention, mixed with humorous stories and wordplays. Then a mixed programme followed, which always proceeded in the same order: first act of the *comedia* – always consisting of three acts (*jornadas*) – followed by a realistic farce, caricaturing specific social types, as an intermezzo; second act of the *comedia*, rounded off by a dance performance; third act of the *comedia* with a subsequent masquerade of animal masks and other costumes, which ushered the audience out of the *corral*.

In the *comedia*, the instincts, needs and suffering of the body were subjected to the 'rule' of the free will of each individual, who was responsible for realizing both its earthly as well as its eternal identity in the kingdom of God. Many dramas, especially 'honour' plays such as Lope de Vega's *Castigo sin venganza* (1635) or Calderón's *El medico de su honra* (1637), emphasized the worldly over the heavenly mission, whereas plays like Tirso de Molina's *El condenado por desconfiado* (1615/18) stressed the latter. Various types emerged in the character system of the *comedia*, whether ideal, anti-ideal, or somewhere in the middle. The protagonist with a legacy stretching to Mozart, Shaw and beyond was the figure of Don Juan in Tirso de Molina's *comedia El burlador de Sevilla y convidado de piedra* (The Trickster of Seville and the Stone Guest, written and performed between 1619 and 1624). No code of honour obstructs or confines Don Juan's desires and erotic aspirations, who is either unable or unwilling to control his instincts for the sake of socially legitimated honour. By dishonouring numerous women – allegedly to promote his own idiosyncratic form of 'honour' – he embodies the terrible vision of appropriating the world through sexual conquest and abuses the very concept of free will.

The protagonist of Calderón's *The Constant Prince* provides the antidote to Don Juan.[14] The drama deals with an episode from Portuguese history, the Portuguese expedition to Tangier in 1437, when Moors captured Prince Ferdinando as a hostage for the city of Ceuta, as a result of which he died. Calderón transformed the historical figure into a martyr whose unshakeable belief in God enables him to bear all sufferings. In the earthly world with its changes of fortune, only complete steadfastness as a total fulfilment of the free will, embodied by martyr Fernando, could overcome the ephemerality of life and secure the individual's identity for all eternity. Contemporary cloak and dagger plays, as well as morality dramas (*comedias de costumbre*), were also dramaturgically shaped by the opposition of the body-based, affect-driven desire to appropriate the world and spiritual asceticism.

THE FOUNDING OF THE ACADÉMIE FRANÇAISE AND THE *FORMATION DE LA DOCTRINE* IN FRANCE

The consolidation and stabilization of the monarchy in the late-sixteenth and early-seventeenth centuries set the stage for Cardinal Richelieu's national interventions in politics and cultures: spheres that were closely connected in his view. Richelieu decidedly supported the interests of the absolutist king by curtailing the privileges of the provincial aristocracy. Richelieu had high aspirations in what might be called the arena of 'cultural politics'. The founding

REPERTOIRE AND GENRES

of the Académie Française during his period of dominance decisively impacted the development of French classical theatre, with its representations of the state and its elaborations of individual and civic morality.[15] The fundamental duty of the Académie Française was the consolidation of national cultural achievements, completing the work begun by the Pléiade poets almost a century before in contesting Latin and elevating French as the dominant language.[16] Because of this singular literary and linguistic orientation of its area of influence as well as its exploitation by the absolutist ruler as an instrument of monarchic culture politics, the Académie Française differed from other academies that had developed in Europe since the Renaissance.

The rediscovery of Aristotle's *Poetics* in the mid-sixteenth century led, in combination with French absolutism, to the development of a normative regular dramaturgy in the classical period. Although the critique of the academicians did not lead to significant revisions to Corneille's play during the *Querelle du Cid*, the criteria for standardization – which had been available since the commentaries of Julius Cesare Scaliger and others on the *Poetics* a century earlier – were nevertheless widely accepted in the debate's aftermath. Scaliger's earlier *Poetics* supplied the basis for new treatises such as Jean Chapelain's *Lettre sur la règle des vingt-quatre heures* (1630) and *Discours sur la poésie representative* (1635). Here, the poetic category of *vraisemblance* (verisimilitude) came intimately related to the demand for *bienséance* (decorum), which referred both to Aristotle's deliberations on the coherent composition of characters in tragedy and included also the moral beliefs of the court audience, oriented by the ideal of *honnêteté*. Furthermore, Chapelain's call for the unity of place, time and plot aimed towards a stringent dramaturgical elaboration of the subject matter. For *bienséance* was precisely what Corneille had lacked, according to his detractors. The physical violence in the duel between Rodrigue and Dom Gomez was one of the sticking points, as well as the sensual intensity of Chimène's love for Rodrigue. Shaping ensuing critical debate of the French classical period were several important theoretical treatises, chief among which (after Chapelain) was Abbé d'Aubignac's *La pratique du théâtre* (1657). The neoclassical ideas for tragedy espoused by neoclassical theorists were certainly fulfilled by the drama of Racine, who was appointed to the Académie Française in 1673.

Belying the one-sided critical discourse circling around *Le Cid*, the French theatrical repertoire was actually rather heterogeneous during the first governing phase of Louis XIV, especially considering the work of Molière. His critical intellectual ambitions and actual theatre practice stand in pronounced but productive tension. Although, unlike Shakespeare, he adhered to neoclassical dramaturgy, Molière richly absorbed the oral, popular, performance-based modes of both the French farce that had prevailed for over a century at the Hôtel de Bourgogne and the *commedia dell'arte* troupes with which he shared the stage during his long years of provincial touring. After returning to Paris in 1658, he channelled oral-performative modalities into regular five-act comedies, all the while drawing on Terence and other figures studied in his humanist education. Like the *commedia dell'arte* actor-authors, he synthesized oral and literary modalities, but he went far beyond them in forging a satisfactory and enduring dramatic structure, with an almost pitch-perfect sense of how to capture the 'improvisation effect' on the page.

CRISIS AND SELF-ASSERTION: FORMS OF THEATRE IN GERMANY

During the period covered in this volume, the Holy Roman Empire slowly splintered into many petty states that acted mostly autonomously with regard to their cultural politics. Theatre of the German-speaking regions was consequently less unified than that of the emerging nation-states of England, Spain, and France. But the absence of political unity could make the German states more open to international influences, drawing on the examples of other countries in addition to following the humanist imitation of ancient paradigms.[17]

The ancient poetic theories of Horace and Aristotle as well as comic and tragic Roman drama, were frequent points of reference. A key theoretical text was Martin Opitz' *Buch von der Deutschen Poeterey* (Book of German Poetry, 1624). Following Jaques' often-cited monologue in Shakespeare's *As You Like It* (1599/1600) and Sigismundo's famous philosophical speech in the third act of Calderón's *La vida es sueno* (1635), the great Silesian poets emphasized the essentially theatrical character of the world. In the key scene of his first tragic drama *Leo Armenius* (1650), Andreas Gryphius contrasted the *Schauplatz der Eitelkeit* ('scene of vanity') to the paradisial hereafter. The famous dedication preface of Daniel Casper von Lohenstein's *Sophonisbe* (1680) elaborated explicitly on the idea that the world is a theatre and man only a performer. This sceptical and pessimistic worldview reflected the devastations, epidemics and famines of the Thirty Years' War, as well as the destruction wreaked on the continent overall. A large number of plays featured peace or war as subject matters, such as Johann Rist's *Friedenswünschendes Teutschland* (Peace-Desiring Germany, 1647). In addition, many historical dramas, such as Lohenstein's *Cleopatra* (1661) or Jakob Bidermann's *Belisarius* (1607), addressed the crises of the Holy Roman Empire that would eventually lead to the Thirty Years' War. Martyr plays, whether Catholic or Protestant, proposed exemplary conduct from a Christian perspective. Crucially important also to theatre of the German-speaking regions in this period was the Jesuit theatre, which seems to have emerged from the central role given to rhetorical instruction in its schools. The plots of the Jesuit plays follow familiar moral paths, offsetting virtues and vices, believers and heretics, martyrs and tyrants, heroes and sinners.

Authors of the Silesian tragic drama, such as Gryphius and Lohenstein, also addressed historical-political, biblical or mythical themes. The form was supposed to inure one against the horrors of the time, inculcate steadfastness by showcasing martyrdom (cf. Gryphius's *Catharina von Georgien*, 1657), or offer consolation in the face of worldly horrors while advocating politically prudent conduct (cf. Lohenstein's *Cleopatra*, 1661). The unities of place and time were more or less accurately observed, as was decorum of character. The plot focused on verbal argument, relying heavily on declamation. In comparison with other theatrical forms of the time, sensual effects occupied a secondary role. Silesian prose comedy, similar to tragedy in its educative aspirations, only cast members of the lower class as comic figures. The comedies warned against moral decline and the disregard of rules, aiming to socially discipline the societal order. They highlighted the illusory nature of the world and the vanity of all things worldly, deconstructing false pretences and poses. Influences were multiple: the humanist drama of Nicodemus Frischlin; the performances of Terence and Plautus at gymnasia; the *Meistersinger* drama by Hans Sachs and Jakob Ayrer; and the *commedia dell'arte* and other itinerant theatre.

Travelling theatre troupes increasingly performed in Germany from the end of the sixteenth century. In cities, courts, and markets, they established a commercial, impermanent theatre. Across the Empire, first Italian theatre companies, then English and finally also French troupes were active. The first German theatre troupes existed from the end of the Thirty Years' War onwards. The travelling theatre subordinated the spoken text to stage action, and rhetoric to the body. The plays were written in simple prose and afforded ample opportunities for improvisation and impromptu interludes. Such theatre offered the opportunity to adopt accessible plays and codified acting techniques from the country of origin. The passionate and sensual presentation of affects and bloody actions held centre stage. The plays were only successful when the original scripts were radically cut and tailored down to playable scenes. The travelling theatre promiscuously mixed various theatrical genres and modes: comic opera, burlesques, farce, comedy, mythological plays, and tragedies. Many comedic and tragic dramas often had a simple and stereotypical structure (erotic intrigues, political entanglement, festivities). Texts by Calderón, Lope de Vega, Molière, Marlowe and by Shakespeare were adapted by the itinerant German troupes. In particular, the travelling companies' theatre reflected on the micro level of its dramaturgical structure, offsetting the performativity of popular effects against the textual models of elite humanist culture – the very dialectic of a transnational cultural dynamics, and one nicely embracing Williams's full sense of 'culture'.

Because of a common humanist inheritance across geolinguistic lines, whether observed in the breach or the observance, the genre 'system' of different early modern theatres was remarkably coherent. Tragedy and comedy carried classical legitimization, in an age when theatre was attacked for being a low and scurrilous art, and the possibilities for hybridization across this binary division were almost infinite. With Italy leading the way, a fertile relationship existed between theory and practice, the former as often invoked to justify the latter (as in the case of the Guarini–Denores quarrel) as in its own right. As Polonius' riff on 'tragical-comical-historical-pastoral' suggests, genres were created from other genres. Humanist and neo-classical ideas could insulate dramatists and theatre producers from engaging a wider public, as they seem to have done in the *Querelle du Cid*. But they were crucial in giving shape and form, under the demand and excitement of new urban audiences, to the ordinary ways of life that, for Raymond Williams, constitute a vital dimension of 'culture'.

CHAPTER NINE

Technologies of Performance

From Mystery Plays to the Italian Order

BLAIR HOXBY

For the feast of the Annunciation in 1439, the Florentine Filippo Brunelleschi staged a drama in the nave of Santa Annunziata that employed ingenious machinery (*ingegni*) set up on two stages, one located above the wooden tribune that surmounted the entrance portal and the other on the stone *tramezzo* that separated the nave from the presbytery. These playing spaces delimited the space for performance, a space that comprised both the players and the laity. The lay audience first beheld the prophets debating on the *tramezzo*; they next turned back toward the tribune to behold the Eternal surrounded by the glory of rotating heavens; then, after following the flight of an angel over their heads, they once again faced the *tramezzo*, where they beheld the Annunciation (Figure 9.1).[1] In its use of multiple stages, its appropriation of found structures for its playing space, and its co-involvement of *dramatis personae* and audience, Brunelleschi's *sacra rappresentazione* exhibited a mastery of traditional dramaturgical techniques that theatre historians often describe as 'medieval'. Yet its sophisticated *ingegni*, which were greeted as a wonder and preserved for more than a century, also forecast the theatre of machines that would be one of the great developments of the Renaissance and the Baroque.

If we glance ahead to a scene that Gian Lorenzo Bernini's student Niccolò Menghini installed in the Gesù to mark the Forty Hours' Devotion, we sense what a difference two centuries can make, for by 1646 it seemed natural to

FIGURE 9.1: Hypothetical reconstruction of the *ingegni* designed by Filippo Brunelleschi for Santa Annunziata, 1439. Model constructed by Cesare Lisi (Florence, 1975). Property of the Amministrazione Provinciale, today Città Metropolitana di Firenze.

produce a frontal spectacle with theatrical lighting perceived through the equivalent of a proscenium arch (Figure 9.2). Congregants were invited to see 'the pillar of a cloud' by which the Lord guided the Israelites in their flight from Egypt (Exodus 13.21–22) as the antitype of the Eucharist (brilliantly illuminated

TECHNOLOGIES OF PERFORMANCE

FIGURE 9.2: Apparatus for a Forty Hours' Devotion at the Chiesa del Gesù on 6 April 1646, designed by Niccolò Menghini.

in a theatrical glory) that had protected the Jesuits as they crossed a Europe ravaged by the Thirty Years' War to offer prayers for the health of Pope Innocent X.[2] The effect of such perspective scenes was, according to Joseph Furttenbach the Elder, to overwhelm the spectator with wonders until he scarcely knew if he was in the world or out of it.[3]

Between Brunelleschi's representation of 1439 and Menghini's spectacle of 1646, technologies of performance were radically transformed. For during those centuries there emerged a humanist dramaturgy that spurned the use of stage mansions that could simultaneously represent places far removed from one another. And that development in turn fostered the invention of a new theatrical order that divided the stage from the auditorium and privileged the eye over the ear. What's more, although the Catholic Church remained a patron of the arts, it no longer monopolized them. For, once the Protestant Reformation made monarchs the arbiters of religion and the guarantors of peace, secular rulers attracted much of the talent and energy that had hitherto flowed to the church. Now secular princes and academies often patronized the latest advances in theatre architecture, scenography and machines. Not the least of these was the construction of permanent theatres – buildings not seen since the fall of the Roman empire. Early modern technologies of performance drew on so many arts and sciences and were put to such diverse ideological uses that they seem to epitomize all the contradictions of the era. Yet in retrospect, we can see that most of the 'advances' in technologies of performance, whose effects were felt throughout Europe by the eighteenth century, originated in Italy. England, Spain, and France supported semi-autonomous dramatic traditions whose staging practices did not follow Italy's in lock-step and whose 'medieval' survivals remained strong. Perhaps for that reason, they produced dramatists (Shakespeare, Calderón, Corneille) whom we still value as poets of genius. But if our ambition is to trace the progress from medieval to Enlightenment technologies of performance, we must spend much of our journey in Italy. For, by the late seventeenth century, what had once been recognized as the 'Italian Order' had simply become the modern theatre.

SCENIC UNITY

Whether staged on a neutral, circular *platea* representing the cosmos, on a series of fixed scaffolds erected at key locations in a cityscape, or on pageant wagons like those used in Toledo, Barcelona, York, and Coventry, medieval plays often made use of multiple playing spaces whose relationship was allegorical rather than topographic. Thus, in the *Castle of Perseverance* (*c.* 1400–25), a bed for the birth of the human soul was located at the centre of a circular *platea* by a castle, while five mansions were located at the periphery of the circle: God to the east, the World to the west, the Flesh to the south,

TECHNOLOGIES OF PERFORMANCE 165

Belial to the north, and Greed to the northeast, between Belial and God (Figure 9.3). The setting of *Perseverance* asked its spectators to see the arena before them as both the world and a spiritual cosmos corresponding to the world. It furthermore suggested that the temporal struggle of Mankind was just a chapter in a great mystical combat between the forces of good and evil that would only be decided at Doomsday.[4] On the other hand, the Lucerne Passion Play, whose layout was recorded in 1583, transformed the entire cityscape into a historico-spiritual cosmos, with heaven placed at the east end of the city, hell at the west, and the key sites of providential history arranged not chronologically or geographically but typologically. The spectators could therefore compare sites in the theatricalized cityscape just as they were taught to compare one 'place' (or passage) to another in the Bible.[5]

Vestiges of such staging techniques persisted in Europe for centuries. For example, the Hôtel de Bourgogne in Paris employed the *décor simultané* until Cardinal Richelieu reformed the theatre in the 1630s. Until then, as T. E. Lawrenson explains, a stage could symbolize multiple places at once. Actors simply had to position themselves in front of an item of decor that suggested the setting before moving downstage; when new actors positioned themselves near a different item of decor, the setting of the downstage action shifted accordingly.[6] The staging of Spanish *autos sacramentales* to celebrate the Feast of Corpus Christi was even more traditional. Two or four pageant wagons drawn by oxen might draw up on either side of a scaffold erected outside a church. These might represent the House of Doubt and the House of Faith, or the Path of Virtue and the Path to Hell. The design of these wagons was influenced by the latest developments in stage machinery, but the logic of their arrangement remained allegorical or cosmological.[7] We might say the same even of Shakespeare's Globe, where the area below the stage was known as 'hell', the roof that covered the players was referred to as the 'heaven' or 'heavens', and the stage, by extension, could be invoked as earth. Thus, as Tiffany Stern notes, when Titus concludes that 'sith there's no justice in earth nor hell, / We will solicit heaven' (*Titus Andronicus* 4.3.50–1), and when Hamlet exclaims, 'O all you host of heaven! O earth! What else? / And shall I couple hell?' (*Hamlet* 1.5.92–3), they are metatheatrically invoking the architecture of the Globe.[8] The persistence of such 'medieval' technologies of performance in the seventeenth century should not be underestimated.

But the advent of a new theatrical order in Italy did eventually overshadow them. What was this new order? The first set inspired by the requirements of classical dramaturgy may have been a painted scene devised in 1483 by Cardinal Riario for a comedy produced by the Accademici Pomponiani and commemorated in Sulpizio da Veroli's edition of Vitruvius's treatise on Roman architecture.[9] Three years later, Plautus's *Menaechmi* was recited in Ferrara on what the ducal chroniclers describe as 'a stage shaped like a city made out of planks and

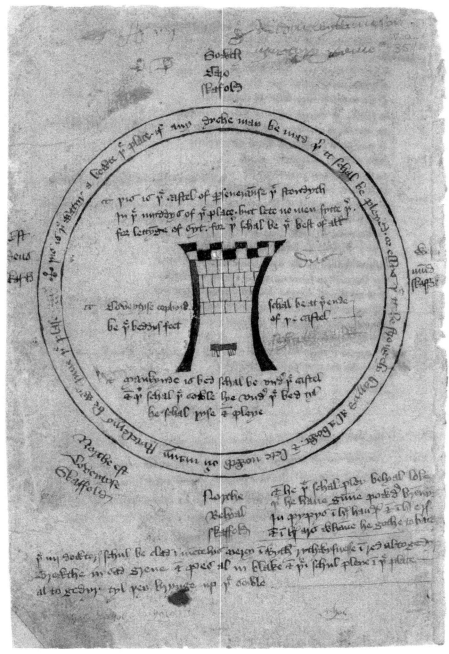

FIGURE 9.3: Diagram for a performance of *The Castle of Perseverance* (c. 1400–25) in Folger MS V.a.354. By permission of the Folger Shakespeare Library. North is at the bottom of the diagram.

painted' with 'five houses with battlements, each with its own door and window'.[10] Theatre historians have imagined this scene in different ways: as a stage that preserved the basic layout of a medieval stage with mansions; as a scene with curtained houses like those shown in the illustrated edition of Terence published in Lyon in 1493; or (less probable) as a perspective scene *avant la lettre*. But whether or not it was portrayed in perspective, the scene was intended to represent a single city street and to form a unified picture. The *città ferrarese* can thus be interpreted as a transitional stage between the simultaneous representation of multiple settings whose collocation was allegorical rather than topographical and the fully-fledged perspective set.[11] For a 1508 production of Ariosto's *Cassaria* in Ferrara, Pellegrino da Udine transformed this cityscape into a painted backcloth that contemporaries called a 'perspective' (*prospettiva*).[12] By 1542, Vasari, building on the innovations of Girolomo Genga and Baldassare Peruzzi (Figure 9.4), had made the stage perspective continuous for a production of Pietro Aretino's *Talanta* by placing

FIGURE 9.4: Baldassare Peruzzi. Theatrical perspective with the symbolic monuments of Rome, A291. Gabinetto dei Disegni e delle Stampe, Uffizi, Florence, Italy. Photo: Scala/Art Resource, NY.

wings along two uninterrupted diagonal lines that converged on a point at an infinite distance, thus creating the illusion of a street of great depth.[13]

It may be no accident that perspective sets were first introduced for the production of the *commedia erudita* of humanists, for in his well-known preface to *Andria*, the fourth-century Roman grammarian Donatus said that comic and tragic writers began *in media res* because they wanted to hold to 'an orb and circle of their art'.[14] Humanists in turn linked this ideal to Aristotle's observation that 'tragedy endeavors to keep as far as possible within a single circuit of the sun' (*Poetics* 5.1449b12–15).[15] Whereas for much of the twentieth century theatre historians invoked Lodovico Castelvetro to explain that Renaissance theorists fretted that the audience of a play would grow incredulous unless there was an exact correspondence between the time elapsed in performance and the time supposed to have passed in the fiction, many of Castelvetro's contemporaries appealed, instead, to the need to impose an artificial order on the sprawl of history. In a revisionist account of the 'artificial day', David Riggs suggests that the impetus behind this change of emphasis may have been the epistemic shift from the symbolic cosmos of the Middle Ages, which lent its own coherence to a dramatic pageant like the Corpus Christi festival, to a universe of infinite extent and indefinite duration, a universe that spoke in the language of mathematics.[16] Ludovico Zorzi adds that the centralization of political and cultural power in the hands of despots such as the Medici may have made the vogue of perspective inevitable, for geometry reveals the proportion in inequalities and the logic of a single point of view.[17]

The theatre decoration of the *cinquecento* supports the contention that the dramatic unities were not the product of a naive aspiration to representational realism but a means of subduing the recalcitrant matter of history to the order of design. For a production of Antonio Landi's *Il commodo* (1539), Bastiano da San Gallo introduced an artificial sun to underline the play's respect for the unity of time (Figure 9.5).[18] As Vasari recounts, he arranged a lantern behind all of the houses and a sun 'made of a crystal sphere full of distilled water, behind which were two flaming torches that made it so resplendent that it rendered luminous the entire sky of the stage'.[19] Operated by a small windlass, the sun appeared to ascend at the beginning of the comedy and to descend by its conclusion. Rather than stress the power of Bastiano's device to produce an illusion of reality, the official record of the event underlines its service to the artificial order of the poet: 'One saw a Sun rise little by little in the Sky of the Stage which, gently progressing, gave notice act by act of the hours of the *imagined* [*finto*] day' (my italics).[20] The passage of time also furnished the thread of the six *intermezzi* intercalated into the comedy.[21] When Vasari imitated Aristotle's artificial sun for a production of Aretino's *Talanta* in 1542, he amplified the theme of time's passage on the ceiling of the theatre, which was decorated with large panels depicting the four stages of day, each surrounded by six smaller panels depicting

FIGURE 9.5: Hypothetical reconstruction of the stage with sun machine erected in the courtyard of the Palazzo Medici in Florence in 1539. Photo R. Bencini. Property of the Amministrazione Provinciale, today Città Metropolitana di Firenze.

the hours appropriate to it. Such a decorative programme is consistent with Ernst Cassirer's observation that although the Renaissance acknowledged the need for 'fixed points and centres', it treated the choice of those points as belonging to 'the freedom proper to the mind' of the observer or artist.[22]

If we cared to distinguish Renaissance from Baroque scenography, we might say that in the Baroque era artists were no longer content to structure the world, but instead wished to dramatize both the act of structuring and the struggle of interpretation. Bernini's private theatrical representations are a case in point. A year after the 1637 flood of the Tiber River, he staged a play in which boats passed across the stage on real water. When the levee suddenly broke, the water gushed toward the audience, only to be stopped at the last instant by another barrier that rose up to dam it. In another play, an actor carrying a torch 'accidentally' set fire to the scenery. The audience scrambled for the exit only to find that, at the height of the confusion, the conflagration had vanished and a beautiful garden had appeared on stage. On yet another occasion, Bernini staged a production that involved two theatres with two audiences. It commenced with two actors standing back-to-back reciting a prologue to their respective audiences. Then a curtain was raised up from the floor between the two actors, and the play commenced. At the conclusion of the play, the curtain dropped, and 'the audience saw the other audience leaving the other theatre in splendid coaches by the light of torches and the moon shining through clouds.'[23]

Bernini's stage plays affirm that, far from being predicated on a naive realism, the Italian theatrical order assumed that the recalcitrant facts of nature and history had to be ordered; but by the 1630s, Bernini had made the additional discoveries that the lines dividing the real from the artificial, the mundane from the heavenly, and the corporeal from the spiritual were fluid and that persuading audiences to transgress them could induce intense responses of wonder, rapture, surprise, chagrin and reflection.

MOVEABLE SCENES AND MACHINES

Sacre rappresentazioni, mysteries and Corpus Christi plays made use of stage machinery whose origins have often been obscured by the depredations of history but whose secrets were certainly transmitted to Renaissance machinists. At the same time, the escalation of humanist studies lent a fresh impetus to the development of scenic devices. For in ancient authorities, scholars found tantalizing evidence that seemed to authorize a theatre of changeable scenes and wondrous machines. It appeared that at some point in antiquity theatres had employed a *scaena ductilis*: a large, painted screen that could be removed to reveal a new scene.[24] In Greek and Roman theatres, side scenes called *periaktoi* had flanked the smaller entrances to the right and left of the *porta regia*, or central entrance. These were constructed as prisms with three decorated faces. Vitruvius explained that 'when the play is to be changed, or when gods enter to the accompaniment of sudden claps of thunder, these may revolve and present a place differently decorated.'[25] Pollux added that they could be used to change the scene within the same city or to move the action to an entirely new location, but that they were chiefly useful 'for bringing Things forward from the Port, Sea-gods, or whatever else was too unwieldy for the Vehicle to bear'.[26] Classical authorities also attested to the use of an *ekkyklema*, a platform that either rolled or rotated out from the *skene* to reveal the inside of a palace – often strewn with corpses. They described a *mechane* (or crane) that could be used to stage heavenly ascents or descents and a *theologeion* whence gods could make their pronouncements. In the reconstructions of ancient theatrical *apparati* produced by the Jesuits Martin Delrio and Tarquinio Galluzzi, Furies rose up from the 'lowest steps', spirits emerged from 'the stairs of Charon', water gods were poured onto the stage using a revolving device, gods were suspended in mid-air using one type of crane, mortals were raised from the earth using another, heroes were transformed into gods using a revolving machine, scenes of violence were revealed using a moveable platform, lightning struck, thunder rolled, and an 'automaton' performed unnamed wonders 'driven nearly by its own power'.[27]

Illustrations explaining scenic devices such as those in Daniel Barbaro's edition of Vitruvius (1556) both supplied blueprints for future use and promoted experimentation with rotating stages, turning prisms, sliding flats, and flying machines. According to Egnazio Danti, Bastiano da San Gallo may have been the first scenographer to use *periaktoi*, but Danti provides more details of a later Florentine production of 1569 in which the first scene represented the bridge at Santa Trinita, the second the gardens of the Villa d'Arcetri, and the third the square d'Alberti.[28] The first sets that used *periaktoi* ran into difficulties because they used contiguous prisms that allowed no side entrances. Nicola Sabbattini's *Pratica di fabricar scene e machine ne' teatri* (1638) and Joseph Furttenbach's *Architectura recreationis* (1640; see Figure 9.6) illustrated a system that solved that problem. Still, even their system required one or two men beneath the stage floor to turn each prism. Coaching so many stagehands to work in silent unison must have been no easy feat. As Sabbattini confessed, it was common to have a ringer pick a fight in the back of the hall, raise a false alarm, or sound a trumpet in order to draw attention away from the stage while the change was made.[29]

The need for such ruses must have encouraged the gradual change to moveable flat wings. Although these may have been used as early as 1589 by the Medici's theatre designer and scenographer Bernardo Buontalenti, their existence is clearly documented in Giovan Battista Aleotti's Teatro Farnese in

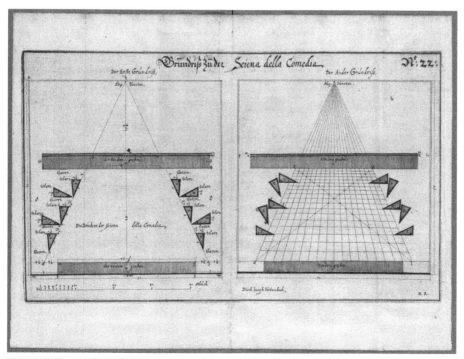

FIGURE 9.6: Scheme of *periaktoi* in Joseph Furttenbach's *Architectura recreationis* (1640). TS 239 117 F. By kind permission of Houghton Library, Harvard University.

Parma, constructed in 1618 and inaugurated in 1628.[30] Yet even in the Teatro Farnese, such wings ran on rails or grooves, requiring one stagehand per wing and the same sort of rigidly disciplined crew necessary to operate *periaktoi*. Giacomo Torelli significantly improved this system. In order to obtain centralized control of the wings, Torelli cut through the stage floor, running the wings on trolleys that were connected by ropes to a single drum. When this was set in motion by a counterweight, all eight pairs of wings changed simultaneously. As Per Bjurström observes,

> Torelli's invention was of more than technical importance. He had made possible just that instant of change, of uncertainty and transition, that was to become one of the most attractive attributes of the baroque stage – a moment's suspense while the clarity of the set dissolves, and then the sudden appearance of a new conception. The audience was allowed to share the actual moment of change, and experienced the transformation as an imaginative stimulus just because it could not be grasped clearly by the intellect.[31]

Torelli's scenography shared this rhythm of disruption, uncertainty, and sudden revelation of order in common with the figured dances that so often played a role in the masques, *ballets de cour*, and theatrical festivals of Renaissance princes.[32] That the moment of transition was itself a theatrical event is underlined by the fact that, under Torelli's direction, most scene changes took place *within* acts, not between acts when the audience was distracted.

It may seem surprising that the theatre of the early modern period should lavish such care and expense on technical matters of stagecraft when Aristotle had declared that *opsis* (spectacle) 'though an attraction, is the least artistic of all the parts [of tragedy], and has least to do with the art of poetry' (*Poetics* 6.1450b16–18). But early modern readers were quick to note that Aristotle himself conceded that *opsis* could arouse tragic fear and pity (*Poetics* 14.1453b1). Surveying the extant tragedy of the ancients, Castelvetro observed that the action of some of them could 'be communicated to the audience by little more than the language', but that of others could 'be mounted only with a great variety of costumes, much expense, and elaborate stage sets'. In the *Eumenides*, for example, the chorus of Furies had to 'appear in eerie transformations', while in *Prometheus Bound* the suffering Titan had to 'be chained to a replica of Mount Caucasus' and 'visited by a number of different deities'. Against the authority of Aristotle, Castelvetro maintained staunchly that stage spectacle should not 'be spurned because it is the work of an art other than that of poetry or because it entails great expense or because the poet is an artist of higher rank than the costumier. 'The one relevant consideration', he said, making a concession to Horace's *Ars Poetica* (ll. 185–8), was 'whether a proposed piteous and fear-inspiring spectacle' could be 'staged realistically'.[33]

TECHNOLOGIES OF PERFORMANCE 173

An anonymous treatise attributed to the theatrical producer (*corago*) Pierfrancesco Rinuccini lists forty-two spectacular stage effects that a competent machinist should be able to produce.[34] These include celestial choirs suspended in the heavens; deities descending through the air in chariots; Lucifer's fall in the company of his rebel angels; underworld scenes; furies rising from the depths; characters being transformed into monsters, animals, or trees; city walls collapsing amid military assaults; earthquakes; and tempests. How these visual effects could be arranged in a sequence is demonstrated by the stage directions of Ben Jonson and Inigo Jones. For example, toward the end of *Chloridia*, performed by Queen Henrietta Maria and her ladies in 1631, the directions read, '*Which* [dance] *done, the farther prospect of the scene changeth into air, with a low landscape in part covered by clouds. And in that instant, the heaven opening, Juno and Iris are seen, and above them many airy spirits, sitting in the clouds*'. After a song, we read, '*Here out of the earth ariseth a hill, and on top of it, a globe, on which Fame is seen standing with her trumpet in hand . . . at which, Fame begins to mount, and moving her wings, flieth up to the heaven*'. After a dialogue exchange between Fame, the chorus, and other allegorical figures, '*Fame being hidden in the clouds, the hill sinks, and the heaven closeth.*'[35]

Some special effects were not beyond the reach of London's popular theatres. We read, for example, that at a performance of Marlowe's *Doctor Faustus* at the Fortune, 'a man may behold shagge-hayr'd Deuills runne roaring over the Stages with squibs in their mouths, while Drummers make Thunder in the Tyring-house, and the twelve-penny Hirelings make artificial Lightning in their Heavens.'[36] Yet in open-air amphitheatres, spectacular effects such as fireworks guided along strings to simulate lightning could not efface the recalcitrant presence of the theatre itself, with its painted ceiling, pillars, unchanging stage background, and universal lighting: they could only overlay it.[37]

The Italian Order, which first appeared in England in the masques designed by Inigo Jones, promised a more thoroughgoing visual illusion. In order to create the impression of a sky while allowing communication with the stage floor, the Italian Order sometimes used draped silk heavens but typically employed bow-shaped boards hung lower and lower as the stage receded (just as the stage floor was raked up and the wings were raked in toward a common vanishing point). The boards closest to the audience were painted in cruder azure and white, while the clouds receding to the back of the stage were gradually softened, melded into each other, and tinted with more orange.[38] Additional clouds – used to introduce deities or conceal persons – could be manipulated by using drums, ropes and pulleys to move them up or down and even to make them swirl and grow (Figures 9.7 and 9.8).[39]

A mountain many times the height of the sub-stage could be elevated by using spindles to raise a series of nested boxes covered by canvas. A placid sea

FIGURE 9.7: Scene featuring an entrance upon clouds. San Salvatore, Venice, 1670s. Bibliothèque nationale de France.

could be produced by sliding boards painted with waves, while the fiercer waves of a stormy sea could be produced by spinning a series of rotating, wavy cylinders painted blue and black with silver caps.[40] When a character was to be transformed into a rock, tree or animal, he or she could stand behind a painted cloth which was raised up from the stage floor or even employ a trick costume that could transform his or her appearance in an instant if, for example, he turned his back to the audience or she pulled her skirt up over her head.

TECHNOLOGIES OF PERFORMANCE 175

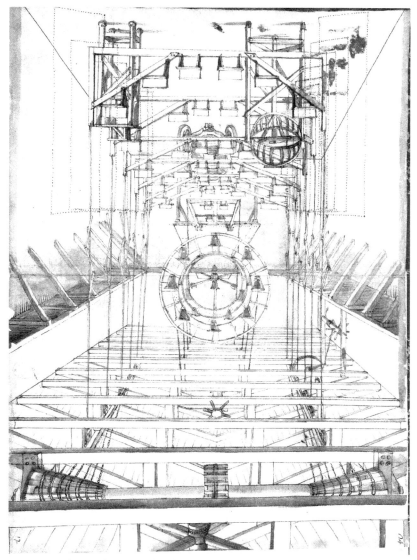

FIGURE 9.8: The machinery behind the entrance upon clouds shown in Figure 9.7. San Salvatore, Venice, 1670s. Bibliothèque nationale de France.

Hell scenes could be represented by opening the back stage and setting fires in pits placed in front and behind the actors. Flames could be made to appear from the floor of the main stage by using traps to raise and lower pots filled with Greek resin, fuelled by torches, and covered with perforated paper (Figure 9.9). Conflagrations could be produced by soaking the scenery in aqua vitae and setting it alight. Sets that were meant to collapse during a siege or an

FIGURE 9.9: Jean Berain, design for the appearance of demons among flames. Bibliothèque nationale de France.

earthquake were built unstably and supported by iron rods: When the time arrived 'to present the ruins, all the bars at one instant' could be slid down 'towards the stage floor' so that 'all the pieces of the houses [were] overturned and [represented] ruins'.[41] The effects of a thunderstorm could be simulated by rolling large stone balls across the floor above the audience, by twirling thin ruler-like strips of wood on the end of strings to simulate the howling of the wind, by throwing sulphur out from above the heavens and setting it alight, and by shooting squibs down wires set at the back of the scene.[42] How many of these effects could be combined in one spectacular finale is suggested by Jean Berain's design for the *tragédie en musique, Armide* (Paris, 1686), in which demons hover over Armida's enchanted palace, the buildings collapse amid flames, and she herself exits through the sky in a flying chariot (Figure 9.10).[43]

If the introduction of perspective scenery and the elaboration of the dramatic unities can be convincingly tied to cultural developments that we are inclined to label rational and modern – from city planning, to the centralization of authority, to the elaboration of a mechanical universe – many stage spectacles invoked systems of belief that defy this narrative of modernization: demonology, alchemy, magic, meteorology, climatology. These ancient arts and sciences suggested that selves were not sovereign and autonomous but open to influences from airs and waters, spirits and demons; that tempests were caused by the powers of darkness who inhabited the middle atmosphere; and that language,

FIGURE 9.10: Jean Berain, finale of Philippe Quinault and Jean-Baptiste Lully's *tragédie en musique Armide*, 1686. Centre historique des Archives nationales, Paris. COTE 0[1]*3238, f° 57.

178   A CULTURAL HISTORY OF THEATRE IN THE EARLY MODERN AGE

talismans, dance and song could manipulate the occult resemblances that pervaded the universe, empowering the initiated to harness the virtue of the stars through sympathetic magic. It is impossible to understand the court masque without reference to these beliefs, but even plays such as *Macbeth* (with its witches who 'Hover through the fog and filthy air' [1.1.12]) and *The Tempest* (with its aerial spirit who flames amazement with his 'fire and cracks / Of sulphurous roarings' during the shipwreck at sea [1.2.203–4]) are best interpreted in light of them. Because arts and sciences do not develop in lock-step, historical change is rarely if ever marked by the displacement of one ruling episteme by another. That is nowhere more apparent than in the technologies of performance, where the latest scientific innovations may be deployed to realize a scene whose power, despite speaking to the political occasion, depends on the audience's knowledge of an ancient, occult belief system.

LIGHTING

In the amphitheatres of London and the *corrales* of Madrid, acting troupes performed in the even illumination of the afternoon sun. When a character entered with a candle, the stage property was enough to suggest that the scene – say, Othello's murder of Desdemona – was set in darkness. The presence of torches on stage would suffice to indicate that the action was taking place outside at night. Even the indoor, private theatres of London relied primarily on the diffused illumination of the sunlight entering windows set high in the walls.[44]

Scenographers working with princely budgets in indoor theatres could achieve more striking lighting effects. Sebastiano Serlio recommended that the stage be illuminated from the middle with a hanging fixture; that a vase of water with a floating piece of burning camphor be placed above that; that the painted scenes be lit by 'a large number of candles . . . placed leaning at the scene'; and that all the windows of the stage set be illuminated with coloured lights, an effect achieved by placing lamps behind glass containers filled with coloured liquids.[45] Nicola Sabbattini maintained that perspective scenes looked best when illuminated from one side, while Jean Dubreuil emphasized that when using a series of flat frames or wings 'the first frame should have the least light, the next should be lighter, and the last should have the strongest light' in order to promote an impression of distance.[46] One way to light the back of the scene was to place numerous oil lamps in a pit dividing the main stage from the back scene. When scenographers wished to produce a particularly brilliant source of illumination – say, the sun – they might place a torch behind a glass container filled with liquid and backed by a barber's basin. Stars could be created by using lamps or candles backed by tinsel reflectors.

Unless care was taken to ventilate the stage, the smoke produced by so many candles and lamps could 'produce so effective a screen that before the second act [was] done the actors [would] seem to be not men but shadows, while the spectators, as if blinded, [would], without realizing the cause, get the impression that they [were] losing their sight'. Leone De Sommi's solution was to open as many windows as possible below the proscenium so that the air could rise up through holes bored in the roof behind the scenery.[47] The leaping of dancers on stage could also shake the stage lights, so many architects advised that steps be taken to anchor them to posts or beams that were independent of the stage floor.

Although Renaissance audiences must have been accustomed to watching spectacles in well-illuminated halls, scenographers did articulate the advantages of a darkened auditorium. De Sommi, who worked at the court of the Gonzaga in Mantua from 1556 to 1592, explained through his mouthpiece Veridico that, whereas he might place 250 torches in a hall of the same size for other occasions, he would place only twelve candelabra behind the backs of the audience during a theatrical performance because 'a man who stands in the shade sees much more distinctly an object illuminated from afar'.[48] Joseph Furttenbach the Elder, who learned his craft from the famous Parigi of Florence, concurred: 'It were better if no windows were put at the sides of the audience, so that the spectators, left in darkness like night, would turn their attention to the daylight on the stage.'[49]

De Sommi insisted that the purpose of stage lighting was not simply to illuminate the set and make the expressions of the actors clearly visible to the audience; it was to set the mood. He favoured the use of bonfires and torches on the streets, rooftops and towers, not only of his comic but of his tragic sets because

> nearly all tragedies open in a happy strain; and consequently it will not be unfitting to arouse the mind, so far as we may, to this happiness, although disasters and deaths are to ensue later. I remember once I had to produce a tragedy of this kind. During all the time when the episodes were happy in mood I had the stage brightly illuminated, but so soon as the first unhappy incident occurred – the unexpected death of the queen – while the chorus was engaged in lamenting that the sun could bear to look down on such evil, I contrived . . . that . . . most of the stage lights not used for the perspective were darkened or extinguished. This created a profound impression of horror among the spectators.[50]

How such an effect could be created Sabbattini explains: metal canisters suspended from pulleys were dropped all at once around the lamps or candles, hiding their flames without extinguishing them.[51]

THE DIGNITY OF PERMANENCE

'Among all things made by hand of man', writes Serlio, 'few in my opinion bring greater contentment to the eye and satisfaction to the spirit than the unveiling to our view of a stage setting.'[52] Yet until the late sixteenth century, most spectacles were staged in temporary venues, and the word 'theatre' (*teatro*) had not yet acquired its modern sense: a circular arena erected to behold an equestrian ballet might be referred to as a *teatro*, while what we now call the Uffizi Theatre of the Medici might be referred to as the *sala delle commedie* (hall for plays).[53] Although Ariosto seems to have overseen the construction of a permanent perspective scene in Ferrara around 1531, it was destroyed by a fire the next year.[54] London's The Theatre (1576) and Vicenzo's Teatro Olimpico (1580–85) fared better. But the model for modern theatres was really established by the Teatro Farnese that Aleotti designed for Runuccio I Farnese, Duke of Parma, in 1618 (Figure 9.11). Aleotti drew on two traditions: the tiered, open-air theatres built for aristocratic audiences of Renaissance tournaments; and the temporary wooden theatres built by Vasari and Bernardo Buontalenti to stage the erudite comedies and spectacular intermezzi of the Medici. Aleotti brought the *porta regia* of Andrea Palladio's Teatro Olimpico

FIGURE 9.11: Farnese Theatre of the National Gallery in the Pilotta Palace, originally designed by Giovanni Battista Aleotti for Runuccio I Farnese, Duke of Parma, in 1618 and inaugurated in 1628. Reconstructed after bomb damage in the Second World War. Creative RM/Atlantide Phototravel, Getty Images.

forward to the front of the stage, greatly expanding it and transforming it into a proscenium arch – an innovation that may also have been suggested by the prominent role of triumphal arches and framed portals in both Renaissance street theatre and the visual arts.[55] He moved Palladio's side entrances down to the level of the *cavea*, transforming them into triumphal arches through which horses and chariots could make their entrance. And he deepened both the seating area and the stage, leaving room for perspective scenes with moveable wings. This arrangement was perfectly suited to entertainments that combined the traditional *tournament à theme* with the new art form that Florence and Rome had introduced at the turn of the seventeenth century, opera. The large, flat *cavea* could be used for balls, equestrian ballets, and even (when flooded) mock naval battles; and, when left unoccupied, it improved the theatre's acoustics.[56] Most subsequent theatres – especially the opera houses built in Venice – would make use of the *cavea* for seating and would build the box seats that Aleotti designed but never built, but with the Teatro Farnese the Italian Order had emerged in a clearly recognisable form.

In some theatrical centres such as Paris, symmetrical scenes drawn in central perspective and adorned with stage machinery continued to be the norm until the French Revolution. But by the 1690s, some scenographers such as Fernando Bibiena and Filippo Juvurra were also experimenting with an alternative visual order by foregoing spectacular machine effects in favour of perspective scenes that were drawn at an angle oblique to the sight lines of the audiences. By the late seventeenth century, courts and public opera houses were finding it difficult to pay both for the extravagant fees of celebrity singers and for the costly machine effects that could introduce deities to the stage. What's more, the one-point perspective favoured by rulers with aspirations to absolute rule was not well suited to the political sensibilities of all cities. Scenes drawn in oblique perspective did not create such an evident hierarchy.[57]

John Locke's sensationalist psychology also encouraged the idea that greatness, or, as Joseph Addison described it, the 'largeness of a whole View, considered as one entire Piece', challenged the cognitive and affective capacities of viewers, flinging them into a 'pleasing Astonishment', producing a 'delightful Stillness and Amazement in the Soul', and soliciting the subsequent expiation of the eye and action of mind that was one of the sources of men's delight in the mimetic arts.[58] Whereas scenographers in the seventeenth century had striven to evoke wonder with rapid scene changes and miraculous stage metamorphoses, some of their heirs in the early eighteenth century began to place their faith in the suggestive power of extent. Their scenes did not impress a sharp and striking image on the mind; they invited the imagination to play. As Esteban (also known as Stefano) de Arteaga explained in his account of opera seria (1783), the chastened and regularized opera championed by Pietro Metastasio:

since the secret of the fine arts is to present things so that the imagination does not stop where the senses stop, but that there is also something left to be imagined which the eye does not see and the ear does not hear, so the departure from perspectives running to a central vanishing point and thus constituting, so to speak, the limit of visual and imaginative power, was like opening up an immense path to the busy, restless imagination of those beholding the scene from a greater distance.[59]

In such scenes, staircases spiral to imperceptible heights, steps descend to hidden depths, and absent presences lurk around the corner. As the tragic action unfolded in these grand settings, the souls of the stage persons became associated in the minds of the spectators with the sublimity of their surroundings, and the scene, by the same laws of association, became imbued with the *pathos* of the events that had transpired before it. This was an art of cumulative suggestion and affect that, as it reinvested the stage with an aura of mystery, initiated a new chapter in the history of technologies of performance.

CHAPTER TEN

Knowledge Transmission

Theatre at the Crossroads of Concept, Medium and Practice

ELLEN MACKAY

PROLOGUE: TOWARDS A CULTURAL HISTORY OF THEATRICAL KNOWLEDGE TRANSMISSION

This chapter considers how theatrical practices, ideas and memories were created and passed down in the period lasting from 1400 to 1650. Because knowledge is not just information, but also the impression that it makes, its transmission is often a murky business. The concept of the theatre varied strongly under the fluctuating force and pressure of the Renaissance's defining movements, such as the rise of humanism and its idealization of classical dramatic theory, the spread of Protestantism and its suspicious take on artifice and showmanship, the strengthening of mercantilism and its stimulation of an entertainment economy, and the first stirrings of statism and colonialism, both of which used the stage to sow a sovereign agenda. The aim of what follows is not to liberate the theatre from this turbid climate, but to study the ways in which it was metabolized amid such cultural churn. Viewed from this vantage, even canonical events in the annals of the Renaissance stage are bound to take on a less familiar cast.

A case in point is the judgement on *Le Cid*, which rejected the play for being a 'shock' to the public's sensibilities.[1] By striking out against Corneille's unity-breaking, runaway hit, the Académie Française sought to wrest control of legitimate theatre knowledge away from popular opinion and into the hands of an elite, governing body. Right from Chapelain's opening decree, 'it is all but impossible to give pleasure to anyone by disorder and confusion', the unruly street entertainments of jugglers, ballad-singers, charlatans, clowns, acrobats and mountebanks were written out of France's sanctioned national tradition. Yet notwithstanding the assertion that only 'regular' drama was fit for the authorized stage, popular performance traditions held strong, even in high places. Some of Paris's most beloved farceurs, like Gros Guillaume (a flour-faced glutton and naïf), Turlupin (a braggart), and Gaultier-Garguille (a pinched old miser) moved indiscriminately between the Pont Neuf's charlatan stalls and the professional stage, with Gros Guillaume serving as the director of the *Comediens du Roi* from 1612 to his death in 1634 (Figures 10.1, 10.2 and 10.3). No less a cynosure of the French stage than Molière grew up just down the street from Tabarin, the celebrated jack-pudding or mountebank's assistant, and he stole some of his best gags from the street performer's repertoire, as well as from travelling *commedia dell'arte* troupes he met during his years of provincial touring. As Molière's experience demonstrates, knowledge of the theatre in the early to mid-seventeenth century strayed well outside the lines of its official definition.

More fundamentally, definitional boundaries were inherently blurred by a Renaissance culture in which theatre and performance pervaded the offstage world. For instance, Gros Guillaume allegedly developed his clown persona while working as a baker's boy, until his gift for hawking – and eating – became a vendible delicacy in its own right. Gros Guillaume's successor, Guillot-Gorju, trained as a physician and shuttled between stage quack and doctor. As their mixed careers demonstrate, theatre was not only a form of labour the public paid for, but a register or staging ground of professional virtuosity. In other domains, its role was no less foundational. The festal rituals that marked the annual calendar, from the wintertime carnivalesque rites of Boy Bishop's Day to the midsummer fireworks of St John's Eve, meant that theatre was not just a special kind of event, but the common expression of holiday time. Encyclopaedic works like Jean Bodin's *Universae naturae theatrum* (*The Theatre of Nature*, 1596) and Pierre Boaistuau's *Théâtre du Monde* (*Theatre of the World*, 1558) rendered the theatre not just the venue for drama's performance, but the horizon across which the whole pageant of human knowledge and divine works took place.[2] While the Renaissance may have been the moment in which the secular, commercial stage emerged in a distinct institutional form, the period's conception of the theatre remained embedded in the practice of everyday life.

Consequently, knowledge of the Renaissance theatre was not a fixed thing that could be acquired and stored like a coin in a vault, but a mode of cultural expression that was hard to untangle from fundamental habits of thought and action. To handle this complexity, the chapter that follows unfolds in three parts. The first two, 'Teaching Theatre' and 'Remembering Theatre', address the stage and its understanding directly, via objects and scenes of deliberate

FIGURE 10.1: Gros Guillaume, street performer of the Pont Neuf and actor in the *Troupe Royale*. From a series of seventeenth-century engravings based on the portraits of Gregoire Huret (1606–70). Courtesy Lilly Library, Indiana University, Bloomington, Indiana.

FIGURE 10.2: Turlupin, street performer of the Pont Neuf and actor in the *Troupe Royale*. From a series of seventeenth-century engravings based on the portraits of Gregoire Huret (1606–70). Courtesy Lilly Library, Indiana University, Bloomington, Indiana.

FIGURE 10.3: Gautier Garguille, street performer of the Pont Neuf and actor in the *Troupe Royale*. From a series of seventeenth-century engravings based on the portraits of Gregoire Huret (1606–70). Courtesy Lilly Library, Indiana University, Bloomington, Indiana.

188   A CULTURAL HISTORY OF THEATRE IN THE EARLY MODERN AGE

knowledge transfer. Part three, 'Teaching and Remembering with Theatre', takes up occasions in which cultural knowledge was produced and disseminated by theatrical means to illustrate how the theatre was understood to act as a medium for ideas and beliefs to be displayed, tested and spoofed.

TEACHING THEATRE

Since people generally like to know what they are paying for, the fact that theatre emerged as a saleable commodity in the Renaissance might seem to grant it a firm knowledge base. Yet oddly, Renaissance theatre acquired the status of a commercial profession without developing any unifying traits beyond the ability to charge admission. Some standardization was imposed by civic regulations that stipulated when and where performances could be held, what kind of material was out of bounds, and which theatrical forms were most legitimate. For instance, a 1599 decree from the Duke of Mantua granted authority to Tristano Martinelli, the first Arlecchino and an established member of the ducally-sponsored Arte companies, to regulate a wide range of popular performers, including:

> mercenary actors, jugglers, acrobats who walk the tightrope, those who present demonstrations and edifices and the like, and charlatans who put up benches in the piazzas in order to sell oils, unguents, salves, antidotes against poison, perfume packages, musk water, civet, musk, stories and other printed pamphlets, animal claws, and those who put up signs to advertise treatment, and similar types of people.[3]

However, this same regulatory system helped ensure the survival of the arts it constrained, since like Molière, Martinelli absorbed the gags, moves and lore of the charlatan performers he was licensed to control.

Where theatre and its legislation were thinner on the ground, performers could tap the market without bothering to master any such skills or trades. Observing an English troupe performing in Germany in 1592, the traveller Fynes Morrison noted that despite 'having neither a Complete number of Actors, nor any good Apparell, nor any ornament of the Stage', the ragtail performers were beloved by the German public: 'both men and women flocked wonderfully to see their gesture and Action', while 'not understanding a word'.[4] Yet in Münster some three years earlier, another company – probably Will Kemp's – is remembered in the City Chronicle for its expansive range of entertainments, including musicianship ('they had with them many different instruments'), choreography ('they danced many new and strange dances') and a bilingual clown.[5] What could count as theatre therefore ran a broad gamut, from unadorned action on a makeshift stage to flair and novelty in a variety of

KNOWLEDGE TRANSMISSION

arts. In fact, so unfixed was the understanding of what the professional theatre did that English antitheatricalists often had a hard time identifying what they were against. Philip Stubbes lumped the stage's offences in with those of 'powling [plundering] lawyers', 'horrible whoredome' and 'pride in dubblets and hose', while Stephen Gosson took his stand against the stage's sheer 'varietie of pleasure', including 'garish apparel, maskes, vaulting, tumbling, daunsing of jigges, galliardes, morisces [Morris dances], hobbihorses, and showing of judgeling castes [shows featuring the juggling of clubs or bowls]'.[6]

This hodgepodge condition is a fault that playwrights liked to lay at the feet of audiences. In his address 'to the Reader' of *The White Devil*, Webster describes the formal perfection of drama corrupted by unskilled spectators who didn't know enough to know what they should want:

> should a man present to such an auditory, the most sententious tragedy that ever was written, observing all the critical laws as height of style, and gravity of person, . . . yet after all this divine rapture, O *dura messorum ilia*, the breath that comes from the incapable multitude is able to poison it (13–22).[7]

Miguel de Cervantes lodges a similar complaint when he reports that notwithstanding his success as a novelist, his plays never managed to please Spanish spectators. His grievance at the 'darkness' of 'opinion' that left his plays unperformed is explicit in his decision to publish them anyway, as *Ocho comedias y ocho entremeses nuevos, nunca representados* (Eight Plays and Eight Interludes Never Before Performed, 1615), a title that seems to tout their failure to find an audience as a sign of his works' merit.[8] Though playwrights were far from impartial chroniclers of their poor receptions, it is clear that connoisseurship of the theatre did not mean the same thing to theatre practitioners as it did to theatre consumers.

Beyond the vagaries of taste, one reason for such unfixed and wide-ranging expectations is that Renaissance theatrical practice found few outlets in print. The important exceptions were stage design, richly illustrated in Sebastiano Serlio's and Nicola Sabbatini's guidebooks (1545 and 1638, respectively), and commentaries on Aristotle's *Poetics*. But these were works that derived from a rather narrow stripe of theatrical classicism. The practices and philosophies behind the evolving, contemporary theatre lacked such documentation. Even Lope de Vega's *New Art of Writing Plays* (1609), which seemed to promise an account of his hugely popular, non-Aristotelian dramaturgy, was merely a verse imitation of Horace's *Ars Poetica* – another repetition of classical aesthetic values, and not a declaration of current ones.

Formal schooling in the new art of the stage was likewise non-existent, leaving practitioners to cobble together their craft from training in other lines of work. For playwrights, the academic drama included in the university curriculum provided an analogy, if not a model, of the professional stage. Many then proceeded to the law, a profession suited to those talented in rhetoric and debate; among the dramatic poets who took this path were Ludovico Ariosto, Pierre Corneille, Pedro Calderón de la Barca, John Webster, John Marston and Jean-Baptiste Poquelin, better known as Molière. Actors, on the other hand, often rose from trade professions, like Gros Guillaume from the bakery booth. However, these spheres of theatrical expertise were not always held distinct. Many of the best playwrights of the period were also noted players, including Lope de Rueda (a gold-beater by trade), Ben Jonson (a bricklayer) and William Shakespeare (the son of a glover), while some of the best players were lauded for their writing, including Isabella Andreini, the renowned *prima donna* of the Gelosi troupe of *commedia dell'arte*, and Richard Tarlton, Queen Elizabeth's favourite jester and the rumoured inspiration for the stage yokel Bottom in *A Midsummer Night's Dream*. As their cases proved, academic training was not a prerequisite to dramatic success. Indeed, the most successful German playwright of the sixteenth century, Hans Sachs (1494–1576), is said to have been limited to an output of 'only' 6,000 or so plays, poems, tracts and meistersongs because he remained a shoemaker all his life.

It is perhaps not surprising to find that in this uninstructive environment, theatre was commonly depicted as a skill inborn. Jesting – a wellspring of secular comedy – was held so far from performance as to be its very opposite, an unfiltered and uncorrupted state of nature. Celebrated fools like Will Sommers (*c.* 1510–50) and Claus Narr (1486–1530) were plucked from rustic origins and deposited respectively in the households of Henry VIII and the Electors of Saxony as tonics to the false flattery of courtly life. Though it is difficult to assess the accuracy of such diagnoses, their abundant lore describes both men as 'natural' fools: owing to cognitive difference, lacking in guile or art. The nicknames applied to other entertainers like il Rosso (the jester of Pope Leo X) and Gros Guillaume similarly tie the knack for fooling to the physical traits of the performer, making comedy the exploitation of an innate condition.

This *sui generis* understanding of performance further mystified theatrical ability as a gift bestowed, not a skill acquired. But signs of its pursuit still peek out from the historical record. An epitaph for Tarlton, written three decades after his death, remembers him as the 'lord of mirth' who once sought to 'learn' of others plying the same trade; once he achieved comic greatness, his mentors then became the apprentices 'of whom they taught'.[9] If Sommers and Narr are naturally funny, emulation is what makes Tarlton and his descendants exemplars of stage 'naturalness'. His rube disposition is recognized as a persona carefully crafted and put on, much like the 'cloth shoes', the 'suit of russet', the 'buttoned cap', and the 'tabor and pipe' with which he was routinely depicted. Such a vivid and expressive costume helped 'proclaim his status', as Richard Helgerson writes, as a practitioner of theatrical art rather than a person of rustic artlessness.[10]

Tarlton's attire exemplifies a crucial means of acquiring and transmitting roles in the Renaissance: by literally standing in the shoes of others. The process was apt, if risky, at a moment in which identity could travel from the outside in. As Stubbes writes in his denunciation of women's masculine fashions: 'to weare the Apparel of another sex' is 'to adulterate the veritie of his own kind'.[11] On the flip side of the same coin is Cesare Ripa, who wrote in his hugely popular emblem book *Iconologia* (1599) how it was fitting for women to wear the 'pianelle alte' or 'chopines' (high platform shoes currently fashionable) because 'gravitas in moving is appropriate for women', and perambulating in heels required them to take the careful measure of every step[12] (Figure 10.4). For Ripa, the shoes symbolized the Renaissance ideal of decorum, the suiting of an idea to its proper style of expression. But they also demonstrate that an adage popularized by Erasmus, 'vestis virum facit', or 'clothes makes the man', was a vital principle of Renaissance acting: just as women could take on a more feminine disposition by putting on elevated footwear, so actors could take on characters by adopting their outward shapes and forms.[13] As M. A. Katritzky argues, the predominantly visual records of *commedia dell'arte* – a largely

FIGURE 10.4: A velvet chopine designed to elevate and encumber a woman of quality or means. This style of footwear, imported from the Near East, was a fashion that began in Venice and Spain and spread through Renaissance Europe. Image copyright © Bata Shoe Museum, Toronto, Canada (photo: Hal Roth).

scriptless, if exuberantly citational theatrical form – indicate how strongly the tradition inhered in the masks and poses of its stock types. Learning the part was thus a process of conforming one's body to its characteristic shapes and motions. The intimacy of observation and gymnastic prowess required for this art help explain why *commedia* parts often travelled down family lines, much as circus skills run in families today. Discourses, gags, poses, attitudes and sheer muscle memory were passed down from father to son, and mother to daughter.

For professional actors outside the *commedia* tradition, the more common way of taking on a role was to memorize it from the handwritten part or scroll on which it was transcribed (Figure 10.5). Both forms were designed to be cheap and efficient methods of theatrical knowledge transmission. Because they contained nothing but a character's speeches written one after the next, separated only by short, unattributed cues (usually only two or three words), they incurred a minimum of work for the scribe and a minimal cost to the company. And because they offered no evidence of the play's broader content, they also safeguarded the work from unscrupulous printers or rival companies. Still, however pragmatic the reason for this limited apportioning of dramatic information, the performer's understanding of the theatre, and the vision of the theatre he or she disseminated in turn to the public, was necessarily influenced by it.

Especially notable was the antisocial view of character that a part's redacted format conveyed. Parts left wholly unknown to the actor his or her non-speaking life, to say nothing of the lives of the other *personae* that peopled a given dramatic world. They also did not contain any of the participatory action called for by a play, such as the choreography of dances or fights or the lyrics or musical settings of songs. (Instead, abbreviated lists of staging information including entrances, exits, and musical cues were relegated to a document called the plot that was hung for easy consultation backstage.) It might seem, then, that the effect of this method of theatrical knowledge transmission was to reduce a play to no more than the sum of its parts. This supposition is supported by the fact that the repertory system of the secular, professional stage allowed for only limited rehearsal. Once roles were independently learned, it seems to have been common to run a show a single time before putting it before an audience.[14] Under such constraints it is likely that actors, uncertain of all but their respective lines, would have felt constrained to listen for their cues rather than fill in the scene with action. Consequently, plays would have been defined by the declamation of speeches rather than the interaction of characters.

But it is also true that the part represented the side of the theatrical event that was most fleeting and incidental to the theatrical repertory. Plays came and went, but the quotidian event of performance endured. According to this view, the conventional patterns of stage performance, from the *pasos* that divided up the acts of Spanish drama, to the jig danced after the English play's end, went unrecorded not because they were less important but because their importance

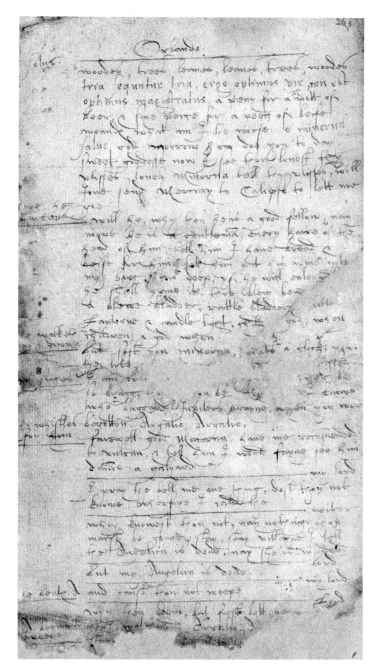

FIGURE 10.5: A page from Edward Alleyn's part of Orlando in Robert Greene's play *Orlando Furioso* (approximately 1591). No doubt because they did not make for great reading, parts are very rare. This one is the sole known survivor from the Elizabethan stage. Dulwich College MS 1f263r and MS 1f264r. Copyright David Cooper. With kind permission of the Governors of Dulwich College, London.

went without saying. Hence dancing, musicianship, clowning – features of theatrical production developed and performed across seasons and years – could be a production's most virtuosic and memorable achievements, as the Münster City chronicle demonstrates.

Moreover, the notion that the theatre took shape from the solitary study of individual parts or roles neglects the fact that, as Tiffany Stern argues, memorization seems sometimes to have happened under the guidance of an 'instructor' who may well have shaped the style of a character's performance.[15] The prevalence of this practice is debatable, but in light of the uncertain literacy rates of players, it could not have been insignificant. Margaret Greer's discussion of the contractual records of Diego Martinez de Mora and his daughter raises the possibility that in Spain, where actresses were not expected to know how to read, the construction of a production out of layers of performance, under conditions similar to directorial instruction or collective devising, may have been pervasive.[16] The result is a professional theatre poised somewhere between unwritten habit and scripted variation, whose knowledge basis cannot securely be located in any one domain.

REMEMBERING THEATRE

If learning theatre in the Renaissance was a process of bringing others' words and gestures to life, preserving theatre was quite the opposite. Michel de Certeau has discussed how the 'writing of history' always necessitates a kind of 'death' or 'rupture' to turn scenes of life into 'a form of knowledge'.[17] For theatre to be preserved for cultural use, it had to be transformed from a live event into a more perdurable form.[18] A helpfully self-conscious example of this effort was the memorial – the object expressly designed to hold something or someone in collective memory. This chapter section examines the knowledge of the Renaissance theatre conveyed by various commemorative objects, including books, medals, and monuments, in order to illuminate the ways the kaleidoscopic world of performance was translated into enduring, collective, and accessible forms of knowledge.

Doubtless the best remembered figure of the Renaissance stage is William Shakespeare. Yet even though his tomb and memorial bust have made Stratford's Holy Trinity Church the prime pilgrimage site in the cult of his idolatry, his gravestone, with its rustic curse – 'Blese be the man that spares these stones / And curst be he that moves my bones' – has been disparaged as a poor index of his genius. Instead, the folio edition of Shakespeare's *Workes* (1623) was the thing devised to serve, in Ben Jonson's famous phrase, as the playwright's 'monument without a tomb'.[19]

Jonson's claim was apt. The emergence of the printed play effected a profound distinction in kind and number between the theatrical remains of any

KNOWLEDGE TRANSMISSION   195

previous period of theatre history and those of the Renaissance. Though plays
were not always deemed books worth keeping – Thomas Bodley's initial
exclusion of them from the library that bears his name at Oxford is an infamous,
if perhaps overemphasized, example of the 'very unworthy mat[t]ers' playbooks
were thought both to be and to take for their subjects[20] – they conserved to an
unprecedented extent the work of the early modern stage. In some cases, the
saving action of printing houses can seem almost heroic. In the Preface to his
Ocho Comedias, Cervantes wrote that when it was clear that no theatre
company would produce his plays, he 'dumped them in a trunk and . . .
condemned them to oblivion'; the secondary market for published drama was
all that kept them from that fate.[21]

Comments like those of Cervantes make print's value to the remembrance of
the Renaissance stage seem self-evident. By copying a text that existed only in
the author's handwritten draft (called 'foul papers') and/or in the prompter's
script (a 'fair' or cleaned-up version of the play transcribed for the company's
ownership), printing houses proliferated a precarious object, conserving it for
broad and long use. Yet such an account paints a misleading picture of drama in
manuscript, which could be quite resilient, as long-running mystery cycles and
civic plays demonstrate. Margaret Greer points out the 'survival of at least one
hundred autograph or partly autograph manuscripts of the principal dramatists'
of the Spanish Golden Age, and the preservation of 'some three thousand
manuscripts dating from the last decades of the sixteenth century to the early
years of the eighteenth'.[22] On the other hand, *zibaldoni*, the notebooks into
which *commedia dell'arte* performers transcribed their verbal and physical
routines, survived only in small numbers, but their poor retention made no dent
on the endurance of this robust performance form. Print, it turns out, was less
the medium of theatre's rescue from oblivion than the business that transformed
performance into a commodity that could and should be widely kept.

One effect was the elevation of the dramatist to a new position of prominence.
In her study of the 'entangled histories of print and the modern stage', Julie
Peters points out that before the Gutenberg revolution, playtexts were not
germane to theatrical production: 'Travelling entertainers had to invent their
material or find it where they could, in stories from great authors, in jokes and
songs heard along the way, in books like the collections of *sermons joyeux*
[parodic and burlesque sermons]'.[23] Much like the later *commedia dell'arte*
tradition, the pre-Renaissance stage was based on a physical repertoire, made
up of routines, styles, gags and poses. Only when printers sought plays to feed
the appetites of a new class of leisure readers did plays shift in the understanding
of an increasingly literate public to become authored works, devised by poets
instead of produced by companies. The sway exerted by this format is especially
vivid when set against the non-adoption of others. For instance, Flaminio
Scala's magisterial collection of *commedia* scenarios, *Il teatro delle favole*

rappresentative (1611), provides a tantalizing indication of what a different written record of Renaissance theatre might have looked like, one with an emphasis on the troupe's repertory of actions rather than each character's individual speeches. But the weak sales of Scala's work suggest a reading public disposed to value dialogue over stage business. Among the reasons for this preference was the resurgence of the classical tradition. The humanist recovery and dissemination of Seneca, Terence and Plautus in new translations helped to secure the ascendency of the printed play by making it formally indistinct from the venerated drama of the ancients.

Print's facility for recuperating, retaining, and retailing dramatic text was exploited by new works too. An intriguing tendency of Renaissance dramatists was the exaggerated account they offered of their own output. Contemporaries scoffed at Alexandre Hardy's boast that as France's first professional playwright, he wrote 500 works, of which only thirty-four survive. By comparison, Thomas Heywood seems almost modest in his claim that he had 'a hand, or at least a maine finger' in 'two hundred and twenty' plays, of which there remain about thirty. Lope de Vega is perhaps the most startling example; in 1632 he estimated he had written 1,500 plays, of which 450 are extant. In some measure, these disparities reflect the wider culture's willingness to leave the theatre unremembered, for unquestionably, plays were allowed to disappear. In the English tradition alone, at least a thousand lost plays have been identified.[24] But in some measure, playwrights inflated the value of their labour by exaggerating the threat of scarcity. As Cervantes demonstrated when he described rescuing his drama from certain 'oblivion', the printed play shone bright as a beacon of theatrical memory when cast against the shadow of potential loss. One reason for the playbook's perceived retentive force was dramatists' deliberate orchestration of this chiaroscuro effect.

Yet the playbook was in many respects a poor retainer of theatrical memory. Reissued by a third party for a quick profit, sometimes without the author's support or input, the printed play was stripped of the history of its development – it left the reader no way of tracking the deletions, additions, revisions and alternative takes that arose during the compositional process, or issued from censorship, or emerged in rehearsal and performance, sometimes over decades. Its usefulness in the dissemination of theatrical knowledge therefore did not derive from its accurate reconstruction of the extended scene of dramatic writing, nor did it reflect the scene or colour of performance, with its extemporal byplay, interludes, songs and jigs. By transforming the variability of actors' actions and speech into type inked and pressed onto its pages, the published play imposed a cohesive narrative structure and predictive value upon theatrical performance that derived not from the stage's affordances, but from print's. Consequently, while the book exerted an extraordinary shaping force on the idea of Renaissance theatre, that idea was one that left the history and

KNOWLEDGE TRANSMISSION

community of the theatre's devising conspicuously unremembered. The Shakespeare Folio exemplifies this lopsidedness; in Jonson's elegy, Shakespeare stands alone as the 'Soule of the Age! / The applause! delight! the wonder of our Stage!'

A second example of theatrical memorialization, dedicated to Isabella Andreini, the celebrated member of the *Compagnia dei Comici Gelosi*, construes the theatre's legacy quite differently. Whereas for Jonson, the Folio's plays exalted the author's singular poetic gift, Isabella's commemoration established 'a generative archetype', as Robert Henke has written, for the whole population to follow.[25] In the wake of her untimely death following the miscarriage of their eighth child, Isabella's husband, Francesco Andreini, chose to dedicate himself to memorializing his wife and scene partner, upending in the process pervasive assumptions about the immorality of actresses, the negligibility of women's contributions to the theatre, and the cultural value of a life lived on the stage. Remarkable in the epitaph he composed for her monument is his decision to list her pre-eminence in 'Theatric Art' as her last and culminating claim to salvation:

Isabella Andreini, *of* Pavia, *a Lady remarkable for Virtue, Honour, and Conjugal Fidelity; Eloquent and Ingenious, Religious, and Devout; A Friend to the Muses, and Head of the Theatric Art; lies Here, in expectation of the Resurrection.*[26]

Not unlike John Heminge and Henry Condell, the members of the King's Men who readied Shakespeare's (near) complete works for print, Andreini secured Isabella's memory by publishing her 'Lettere' and 'Contrasti', the monologues and dialogues she had devised in different characters' voices. But importantly, Francesco emphasized that the compositions should be extrapolated for general use to show 'to future actors the true way of composing and performing'. Her writings therefore functioned less as a record of what she had achieved than as a paradigm for the prima donna's ideal way of being. The fact that an 'Isabella' inamorata role was developed in her honour, adding her distinctive combination of skills and traits to the *commedia dell'arte* types, demonstrates the success of this agenda.

Importantly, though, the influence of this paradigm extended beyond theatrical circles. Other Isabellas bred in the actress's image included girl children christened with her name and medals stamped with her portrait, proving her shaping effect not only on the *commedia dell'arte*, but on femininity more broadly construed, performed and felt. As an instance of theatrical memory-making, Isabella therefore remains hard to summarize. While Shakespeare's Folio supplanted the corpse of the playwright with a corpus of drama, allegedly preserving verbatim 'what he hath left us',[27] Isabella's legacy operated in a more intimate, embodied and mutable register, accessed in the casual play of fingers over the coin impressed with her profile, or in the play of feeling evoked by a child's name. One way of characterizing her mnemonic profile is as a mending of the rupture that de Certeau takes as the condition of history. Isabella Andreini may have been conferred to her monument 'with a pomp that could not have been exceeded if she had been a princess',[28] but she was also woven into the fabric of everyday life, her patterning of womanly conduct exemplary of the difficulty of confining the theatre to a fixed and monolithic record of achievement.

A final memorial, for Till Eulenspiegel, seems to take this lesson as its comic point. A trickster figure from Germany's medieval oral tradition, Eulenspiegel's escapades were first recorded in print in Johannes Grüninger's 1510 book *Ein kurtzweilig lesen von Dyl Ulenspiegel* and spread in chapbooks from Denmark to Italy. Jacob Burckhardt has called him the mythic prototype of the Renaissance court jester for his skill at yoking satire and scatology, a talent that is written into his name. In High German, Eulenspiegel means 'owl mirror', a rebus of reflectiveness and wisdom, and in Low German, 'wipe my arse'.[29]

As befits a folkloric, picaresque hero, Eulenspiegel's biography is both implausible and thin: after roaming across much of central Europe, committing outrageous shenanigans at the expense of tradesmen, aristocrats and even the pope, he is said to have perished of the plague in Mölln, near Hamburg, around 1350, where he was buried bottom-up thanks to a posthumous bit of buffoonery involving the slip of one of his casket-bearing ropes. Yet the fictionality of this history did not prevent the town of Mölln from erecting a grave for him. In a pioneering instance of performance heritage tourism, a tomb was found or built sometime before 1504 to commemorate Eulenspiegel and a festival was created in his honour; passing through in 1591, Fynes Moryson noted that 'the Townsmen yeerly keepe a feast' for the 'famous Jester' and 'shew the apparell he was wont to weare'. By then the 'monument' had to be secured by a 'grate' to keep it from being 'carried away peece-meale' by pilgrims who believed that its fragments would cure the toothache.[30]

It could be said that Eulenspiegel's greatest prank was this sanctified treatment he received after his 'death'. But especially intriguing is what people thought they were doing when they upheld it. That the notional remains of a folkloric jester and mocker of popes could be entitled to the same sort of veneration and endowed with the same sort of healing power as the relics of a saint suggests a surprisingly serious respect for the theatre's spirit of subversion. One understanding of performance commemorated in the Renaissance was thus its parodic, disruptive force. Central to its festal makeup was the antic disposition that still rises from the grave of Eulenspiegel in the punning invitation to 'wipe my arse'.

TEACHING AND REMEMBERING WITH THEATRE

These several memorials show the theatre to be a restless phenomenon, hard to confine to the artefacts that preserve and transmit it. What differs among the forms of remembrance taken by William Shakespeare, Isabella Andreini, and Till Eulenspiegel is the degree to which they embrace this restlessness. Print transformed plays into a collectible commodity, leaving the recollection of theatrical achievement dependent on the 'capacities' of 'purses', not 'heads'; at least, so said Heminge and Condell before they addressed Shakespeare's 'gentle readers' with the solicitation, 'whatever you do, Buy.'[31] By contrast, the more talismanic mementos of a famous lover (Isabella) and a folk-hero fool (Eulenspiegel) construe the memory of performance interactively and iteratively spread between individual objects, bodies and minds. This last section takes up the implications of this alternately fixed and fluid style of theatrical knowledge transmission by switching directions to consider what happened when performance was used to transmit cultural information. Particularly when leveraged to inculcate new knowledge or belief, the stage oscillated between seeming like a dangerous and stubborn habit, a dazzling force of political persuasion, and an unstable platform.

Performance's power to shape the popular consciousness was perhaps most strongly expressed by Protestant reformers, who sought to extricate religion from what they believed was its excessively theatrical scaffolding. The recollective cues that were extirpated from the sacrament of Communion, that quintessential mnemonic rite ('Do this in remembrance of me' [Luke 22.19]), exemplify the theatricality of Christian memory in pre-Reformation Europe, including the display of sumptuous sights (altarpieces, rood screens, ornate clerical garb), the wafting of fragrance (incense), the playing of music (hymns, the sacering bell), and the exchange of gesture (the celebrant's elevation of the host, the congregation's genuflection). To Protestants, the repeated, embodied performance of Communion was proof that 'Popish priests and Jesuites' had 'turned the Sacrament of Christs body and blood into a Masseplay'.[32] By stripping the altars of such venerable rites, they claimed to be ridding the service of a pagan, festal spirit utterly incompatible with the artless truth of Christian faith. For Catholics too, eradicating false belief meant going after its performed expression. An account of the evangelizing of America during the second voyage of Columbus celebrates the toppling of local altars, about which the 'Indians' were said to dance like frenzied Bacchanals, in order to clear the way for true faith to take hold (Figure 10.6).

Diana Taylor has argued that European colonialism can be broadly characterized by this invalidation of embodied, performed forms of knowledge production in order to consolidate authority in written matter like proprietary maps and legal edicts.[33] For Taylor, the priority that historians have tended to grant archival muniments over the repertoire of performance-based culture is

FIGURE 10.6: Benedictine monks toppling an idol in Haiti during Columbus's second voyage. The attempt to eradicate 'false' belief at the site of its embodied performance provokes an immediate, violent response. From *Nova Typis Transacta Navigatio* [*A New Account of the Navigation*] by Caspar Plautius, writing pseudonymously as Honorio Philopono, engravings by Wolfgang Kilian, 1621. Courtesy Lilly Library, Indiana University, Bloomington, Indiana.

in part the legacy of the age of Conquest. Yet as she notes, it is also true that colonial powers made elaborate use of spectacle performance to stage their own supremacy. Overtly theatrical forms including the royal entry and the *auto sacramental* were deployed to enact the transfer of American lands, resources and peoples into European hands. A foundational example that marked an awkward start to Western-style drama in North America is Marc Lescarbot's *The Theatre of Neptune in New France* (1606), the first play written and performed by colonists on colonial territory. In this nautical spectacle, which Lescarbot claimed was performed in mid-November in what is now the Bay of Fundy, the few French mariners who had survived the scurvy epidemic of the previous winter were conscripted to enact a mythologized version of their own voyage in which first Neptune and his Tritons, and then the 'Indians' of the Port-Royal settlement, gave their blessing to France's takeover.

To be sure, the words that Lescarbot put in the mouths of the Mi'kmaq, such as, 'De la part des peuples Sauvages / Qui environnent ces païs / Nous venons rendre les homages / Deuz aux sacrées Fleur-de-lis' [On behalf of the savage peoples / Who inhabit these countries / We come to render homage / Due to the sacred Fleur-de-lis], exemplify the prejudice of colonial historiography, revising the mutual confusions of first contact into a record of divinely sanctioned,

KNOWLEDGE TRANSMISSION

docile submission.[34] But Lescarbot's 'Theatre', appended though it was to the first *History of New France* (1609), did not simply orchestrate the occasion for a scribal culture to exalt its achievements. For one thing, its playscript seems destined to bring out the gap between the printed text of the event and its single performance, since even readers who had never set foot in Canada must have noticed that the author's stately vision would have been impossible to realize on a hardscrabble imperial outpost. For another, the spectacle tradition was known to be a problematic conduit of knowledge in the Renaissance. In his study of spectator responses in sixteenth-century Florence, Konrad Eisenbichler has demonstrated that contemporary European audiences generally failed 'to note the content' of spectacle entertainments and lingered instead on the 'scenery, machinery', and 'extravagance of the event'.[35] Ben Jonson, famous for both his royal masques and his falling out with his collaborator, the architect and designer Inigo Jones, developed an idiom for this problem. In the preface to *Hymenaei* (1606), he complained that whereas the poet's contribution to the masque was its 'soule' or 'inward part', 'grounded upon *antiquitie,* and solid *learnings*', the 'outward celebration' or 'body' of the 'shew', with its 'short-liv'd' pleasures, was too often 'sensually preferr'd'. The result, he said, was a form destined to be 'utterly forgotten', its magnificence stupefying rather than edifying to the beholder.

Of course, to some extent, stupefaction was the point of what Jonson called 'the Spectacles of State'.[36] Elaborately staged water pageants that sprang up in the sixteenth and early seventeenth centuries across the rival courts of Western Europe index the use of theatrical shock and awe for political ends. Beyond Lescarbot's example, there were entertainments of this sort staged in Fontainebleu for the baptism of François II in 1543; at Edinburgh's Holyrood Palace in 1562 to celebrate the wedding of Mary Stuart's half-brother, John Fleming, and Elizabeth Ross; at Florence's Pitti Palace for the wedding of Christine of Lorraine and Ferdinando de' Medici in 1589; at Elvetham, the Earl of Hertford's estate in Hampshire, for the entertainment of Elizabeth I in 1591; and in the French Alps at Lake Mont Cenis for the wedding tour of Marie Christine de Bourbon and Victor Amédée of Savoy in 1619.[37] Among the most astonishing iterations of this genre was the 1550 royal entry of Henri II and Catherine de' Medici into Rouen, which featured fireworks, sea gods, gladiators, unicorns, elephants, and a Brazilian village built into an artificial island in the Seine with 300 naked 'savages' on it, fifty of whom were indigenous Brazilians and 250 of whom were Norman sailors made to look like indigenous Brazilians. Apparently the King took great pleasure in this human exhibition; he even alighted on the isle to hunt specially stocked parakeets and monkeys before its residents broke out in a skirmish and set fire to their lodges. But what exactly Henri saw in it, and what exactly it was devised to show, was then and remains now largely indecipherable.[38]

If scenes like the one in Rouen were sure to dazzle, the patronage of and participation in such confused productions could make royalty seem undignified, as when a witness to a comparable scene of imperial minstrelsy expressed dismay at its countenancing. At the 1605 performance of Inigo Jones's and Ben Jonson's *Masque of Blackness,* in which Queen Anne and her retinue performed in blackface, Sir Dudley Carleton recoiled from the racist shock of seeing the finest ladies in the land transformed into a 'Troop of lean-cheek'd Moors', their painted skin immodestly exposed, their forms indistinguishable ('they were hard to be known').[39] Carleton's testimony proves how readily a pageant of cultural supremacy could slide into a scenario in which the monarchy garbled its message and lost its distinction. As Jonson quipped in exasperation at the unintelligibility of Jones's mythical-cosmological-allegorical conceits, 'Tis true / Court Hieroglyphicks!'[40] Yet their popularity was no joke; the perceived degradation of the office of the monarch caused by Stuart fondness for masques fuelled the Puritan revolution. In some measure, the misfire of his Spectacles of State contributed to the death on the scaffold of Charles I.

Still, where Renaissance spectacle entertainments most directly showed the strain they put on their informational use was in scenes of New World cultural inculcation, where the stakes of clear transmission were especially high. Among several Christianizing plays the Franciscan missionary Motolinía describes in his *Historia de los Indios de Nueva España* (History of the Indians in New Spain, 1541) the Corpus Christi performance in Nahuatl of *The Siege of Jerusalem* (1539), set on the enormous plaza of the city of Tlaxcala, is a particularly 'dazzling and enigmatic' example.[41] Performed by an entirely indigenous cast to celebrate a recent anti-Muslim alliance between France and Spain, the play consisted of an extended battle between the Christians and the Moors with the latter eventually surrendering in defeat. At a glance, the purpose of this play was extraordinarily explicit since it concluded in a collective baptism. Its 'Moors', cast on the wrong side of a holy war, ended the play on the right one thanks to their real-world conversion. But Motolinía also reported that the Moorish Sultan and his commandant were costumed to look like the Conquistadors Hernan Cortés and Pedro de Alvarado. He offers no comment on this surprising twist, but as scholars including Susan Castillo and Patricia Ybarra have concluded, by inserting Cortés's defeat into a teleology of holy victory, the performance made a 'conundrum' of the destiny it represented, turning Spain's heroes into infidels and presenting their drubbing as the path to eternal bliss.[42] Like *The Theatre of Neptune, The Siege of Jerusalem* thus demonstrated the unfirm control colonial powers exerted over their performance of conquest. They seem not to have noticed, or not known how to check, the theatre's capacity for irony, parody and doublespeak – the same knack so vividly commemorated by the obscene quibble of Eulenspiegel's grave.

KNOWLEDGE TRANSMISSION

Both at its centres of power and at their margins, the Renaissance was rich in expressions of this idea that theatre could jam the signal it was meant to transmit. As Bottom's disastrous court performance in *A Midsummer Night's Dream* proved, plays were even built on the premise that the stage's most solemn occasions could and would turn ridiculous. Yet institutions of power still seized on the theatre's capacity to endure in collective memory, perhaps because they knew first-hand the difficulty of extinguishing performed forms of knowledge production. One of the most fantastical expressions of the theatre's mnemonic hold on its public came from Giulio Camillo. According to his 1550 treatise, Camillo invented and built a one-person Vitruvian playhouse that served as the storage and retrieval system for the whole history of Western thought. The concept is not so strange if humanist mnemonic systems are taken into account. As set forth in the oratorical treatises of Cicero and Quintillian, memory was an art whose practitioners were taught to distribute information across the architecture of a specific site, often a palace or theatre. This location would then secure a private memory within a clear organizing scheme. Camillo's innovation was to externalize this process, rendering cultural memory universally accessible. As internet commentators on his apocryphal contraption never tire of pointing out, Camillo's *Ideo del Teatro*, or *Idea of the Theatre*, thereby turned the Renaissance stage into the equivalent of a Google search.

At the time of his death (also 1550), sceptics of Camillo's project outnumbered believers. Erasmus denounced the theatre as pseudo-occult hokum, and the total lack of any evidence that it was ever built kept Camillo's name from appearing in the annals of the Renaissance stage. Yet there is some truth to the notion that the dream of a universal artificial memory was born with his treatise. Though Camillo did not invent the present information age, his inspirational, Jules Verne-like relation to it attests to the dazzling double-sidedness of the Renaissance idea of the theatre. Its stage is at once the paradigm of knowledge transmission at its most accessible and far-reaching as well as a 'charlatan' invention, no more (or less) yielding than the elixirs mountebanked by Tabarin on the Pont Neuf.[43]

NOTES

Introduction: Early Modern Theatre

1. Forgacs and Nowell-Smith 1985, 25, qtd. by Green 2008, 25.
2. As will become clear, my understanding of culture follows the discussion of Williams 1977, 11–20 and *passim*.
3. Burckhardt 1990.
4. Ginzburg 1980.
5. A caveat must be entered here, because of the insightful way that the *Theatre Histories* of McConachie et al. deal with various cultural issues, such as the rise of print culture during our period, in its discussion of early modern theatre and performance. See McConachie, Nellhaus, Sorgenfrei and Underiner 2016.
6. For information about this group, see http://obvil.paris-sorbonne.fr/projets/la-haine-du-theatre.
7. Williams, in fact, wrote considerably on drama, mostly modern, and was a Professor of Drama at Cambridge University.
8. See the chapters 'Base and Superstructure' and 'Determination' in Williams 1977, 75–82 and 83–94. Williams' brand of cultural Marxism that resists a simplistic substructure–superstructure relation draws in part from Antonio Gramsci's writings on culture. See Gramsci 1971, 323–4, to which Green 2008, 49 refers.
9. Williams 1977, 128–35.
10. Williams 1977, 121–7.
11. Rioux and Sirinelli 1997, 31.
12. See Roger Chartier's discussion of Febvre's concept in Chartier 1988, 24.
13. Cohen 1985.
14. Henke 2015.
15. Korda 2011.
16. Chastel 1991, 180–206.
17. Henke 2002, 202.

18. See 'Deep Play: Notes on the Balinese Cock Fight', in Geertz 1973, 412–53.
19. Darnton 1984, 412–53.
20. Kindermann 1957–74, Vol. 2, 205–6.
21. Henke 1997b.
22. Bakhtin 1984.
23. See 'The Problem of Speech Genres', in Bakhtin 1986.
24. Williams 1977, 13.
25. Williams 1977, 15.
26. Burckhardt 1979, 31–5.
27. Besides the work of Febvre discussed here, see Bloch 1973, Aries 1996, and the work of Jacques Le Goff and George Duby.
28. Febvre 1982.
29. Green 2008, 28–9.
30. Lovejoy 1970.
31. Darnton 1984, 78.
32. Orgel 1996, 1.
33. Braudel 1972–73.
34. Williams 1977, 83–9. For a study on the idea of 'exchange' in early modern theatre, see Henke and Nicholson 2008.
35. Burke 2008.
36. Burke 2009.
37. Gambelli 1993.
38. For the polydialectal fecundity of Venice, see Cortelazzo 1989.
39. For Pickelhering as an English-German-Dutch hybrid, see Schindler 2001, 73–99.
40. Greenblatt et al. 2009.

Chapter One: Institutional Frameworks

1. Gramsci 1971, 323–4; Williams 1977, 83–9.
2. Williams 1977, 128–35.
3. Anderson 1974, 21. The overview of backgrounds to European early modern theatre is indebted to the work of Anderson and of Cohen 1985.
4. Anderson 1974, 18.
5. Cohen 1985, 83.
6. Szönyi 1989, 104.
7. For more on Shrovetide plays in German lands, see Ehrstine 2002.
8. For the text of the play and contextual information, see Aubailly 1978.
9. Harvey 1941.
10. Ferrone 1993.
11. White 1993; Pettegree 2005, 89–91.
12. Elton 1953.
13. Harris 2000, 117–47; Gonzalez Echevarria and Pupo-Walker 1996, 1: 260–85. A *coral* theatre was established in Mexico City in 1597, playing a repertory of *autos* and *comedias* similar to those in Spain.
14. Williams 1990, 28; Limon 1985.

NOTES 207

15. Powell 2000, 3–14.
16. Cohen 1985, 166.
17. This focus on the urban companies may distort the total picture, but our knowledge of the structure and workings of regional and provincial companies is very limited. They may or may not have used such a model.
18. In fact, senior English actors, taking on apprentices, took them on insofar as the senior actors were also members of guilds, not into any acting confraternity, there being none.
19. Walker 1931, 97–105.
20. Walker 1931, 100. Later companies had varying numbers of sharers, but this initial number is striking.
21. A detailed and illuminating discussion of the complex current in this regulation appears in Roberts 1994, 29–55.
22. Jesuit dramatic enterprise is too extensive to detail here. See, for Brazil, Gonzalez Echevarria and Pupo-Walker 1996, 3: 105–8, regarding the remarkable plays of José de Anchieta (1534–97), and also McCabe 1983. McCabe estimates that some 100,000 plays were produced on Jesuit stages in the period 1650–1700.
23. This was John Ogilby's Theatre in Werburgh Street, Dublin, which had a box for Lord Deputy Strafford with whom Ogilby had come to Ireland. As early as 1601, Lord Deputy Mountjoy, following a similar logic, had had *Gorboduc* staged in Dublin Castle.
24. Who also issued *ukase* edicts banning the *skomorokhi* in 1648 and 1657.
25. Buccheri 2014, 29–58.
26. Lancashire 2009, 36–65.
27. Groves 2015, 55–85.

Chapter Two: Social Functions

Many thanks to Marissa Greenberg for her feedback on earlier drafts of this essay.

1. 2.7.139–43. Quotations from Shakespeare's plays are from Evans et al. 1997. Subsequent citations will be in the body of the text.
2. For the sake of concision, I focus primarily on the visual and aural senses, which early modern writers, following classical authorities, believed to be of the highest order. However, smell, taste, and touch also influenced playgoer experiences and, as we shall see, were strikingly entwined with sight and sound.
3. For a transnational approach to this fascinating subject, see Henke 2015.
4. Gurr 2004, 59.
5. On women as performers, see McManus 2002; Brown and Parolin 2005; Katritzky 2007; Parolin 2012; and Kerr 2015. On female playgoers, see Howard 1994; Whitney 2006, 201–40; McKendrick 1989, 179–82, 192–4; and Wiley 1972, 207–11. On women as labourers in the theatre industry, see Korda 2011.
6. Henke 1997a, 212.
7. Beaumont and Fletcher 1647, sig. Gggggggg4v. Spelling and punctuation in quotations from all primary sources have been modernized to accord with the other volumes in the *Cultural History of Theatre* series.

8. Shergold 1967, 537.
9. Qtd. in Howarth 1997, 241. For the French, see Tallemant des Réaux 1834–5, 6: 23. Sitting onstage became popular in France only after the success of Corneille's *Le Cid* in 1637, but the practice was widespread in England well before then. See Gurr 2004, 34–7.
10. Wiley 1972, 220–1.
11. Shergold 1967, 538.
12. Shergold 1967, 538.
13. Wiley 1972, 214.
14. Bentley 1991, 150.
15. Fox 2000, 18.
16. For studies of audience reception in contemporary performance, see Bennett 1997; and Kennedy 2009. On reader-response theory and the influence of written accounts, such as newspaper reviews, on playgoer expectations, see Carlson 1990, 10–25.
17. For a complementary approach to more recent theatre, see Bennett 1997, which 'concentrate[s] on the cultural conditions that make theatre and an audience member's experience of it possible' (vii), rather than individual variations in spectator response.
18. Lindberg 1976; Gent 1995; Wilson 1995; Clark 2007.
19. Smith 1999, 101–6. See also Folkerth 2002; and Bloom 2007.
20. Pro. 35–6 in Dekker 1953–61, 3: 121–2, qtd. in Smith 1999, 224.
21. Ottonelli 1655, qtd. in Kerr 2015, 32.
22. From Garzoni's *La piazza universale*, qtd. in Henke 2014, 486.
23. Lea 1934, 354, qtd. in Katritzky 2005b, 128.
24. Stubbes 1583, sig. L8r.
25. Stubbes 1583, sig. L8r.
26. Stubbes 1583, sig. L8v.
27. Crosse 1603, sig. P2v.
28. The description is from a 1570 funeral oration by actor Adriano Valerini (Marotti and Romei 1991, 36, qtd. in Henke 2014, 486). I have written on the term 'ravish' in Lin 2012, 121.
29. Duffy 1990. On the cult of images in medieval Europe, see also Belting 1994.
30. Rubin 1991, 153; Scribner 2001; Duffy 2005, 95–102.
31. Brathwaite 1620, sig. A6r.
32. Egerton 1623, sig. A8r.
33. Stubbes 1583, sig. L8r.
34. Huygens 1982, 55, qtd. in Hunt 2010, 217.
35. Muir 2007, 129–53.
36. On inverting subject and object, see Grazia et al. 1996.
37. Hutton 1996, 278–85.
38. Bergeron 2011, 147.
39. Greenberg 2015b.
40. Acosta 1604, 493 [sig. Ii8r].
41. Ogilby 1671, sig. Hh4v.
42. *Oxford English Dictionary Online*, 2nd ed. (1989), s.v. 'splendour, *n.*' (defs. 1a, 2), published online December 2015, http://www.oed.com/view/Entry/187140.

NOTES 209

43. British Library C 18 e 2 / 74, qtd. in Stern 2006, 65.
44. Goulart 1607, 39 [sig. D4r].
45. Alter 1990.
46. On *admiratio* and *catharsis*, see Herrick 1947; Rubidge 1998; and Greenberg 2015a, 76–107.
47. See McManus 2002. On the influence of professional actresses on court performances, see Gough 2005.
48. The text, which exists in a pamphlet apparently by Aurelian Tounshend, is transcribed in Orgel 1971, 149–50.
49. Goulart 1607, 39 [sig. D4r].
50. The terms 'New World' and 'Old World' have their own imperial history, of course. I use them here specifically to highlight interconnections between European and American audience dynamics.
51. Bradford 1622, sig. H1v.
52. Bradford 1622, sig. H3v.
53. The dialogic relationship between indigenous and colonial experiences of wonder was discussed most seminally in Greenblatt 1991.
54. The incident was subsequently memorialized in Nathaniel Hawthorne's 1837 short story 'The Maypole of Merry Mount', included in his *Twice-Told Tales*, and in Robert Lowell's 1968 play *Endecott and the Red Cross*. See Drinnon 1980; Struna 1996, 48.
55. Morton 1637, sig. R2v.
56. Morton 1637, sig. R3v.
57. Morton 1637, sig. R3v.
58. Spelman 1613/1910, 1: cxiv, qtd. in Hirsch 2013, 145.
59. Hirsch 2013, 143–5.
60. Butler 1993.

Chapter Three: Sexuality and Gender

1. Teresa of Avila 1988, 210. On the theatrical qualities of Bernini's Cornaro Chapel, see Tamburini, 2012, 25–30.
2. Laqueur 1992 stresses the persistence of the Galenic 'one sex, two genders' model, but authors such as Hillman and Mazzio 1997 and Billing 2008 have persuasively challenged this thesis. On the complex questions related to this topic, also see Sawday 1996; Park 2006; and Crawford 2007.
3. See Butler 1990, esp. 135–9.
4. See Jones and Stallybrass 2001, 1–37.
5. Saslow 1996, 171.
6. Beaujoyeaulx 1982, 37v.
7. See Gough 2005, 208–10.
8. McManus 2002, 117.
9. Britland 2006, 33.
10. Franko 2015, 56–67. Grotesque, 'monstrous', and hermaphroditic bodies were recurrent features in early modern theatre, especially in the context of masques and pageants at court.

11. Petit de Julleville 1886, 423–5.
12. See the studies by Davis 1975, 97–124; Le Roy Ladurie 1980; and Burke 2009, 178–204.
13. Enders 2011, 9–12.
14. Gibson 1981, 427–8.
15. Picot and Nyrop 1880, 97–113.
16. Picot and Nyrop 1880, 103.
17. Enders 2011, 107–43.
18. On the Charivari, see Le Goff and Schmitt 1981, as well as the outstanding chapters in Davis 1975, 97–151.
19. See Klapisch-Zuber 1981, 149–64; and Ingram 1988.
20. Sisson 1936, 129–30.
21. Sisson 1936, 101.
22. High-quality studies of this subject include those by Newman 1991; Paster 2004; and Park 2006.
23. Here I follow the analysis made by Charles Carlton, in his 'Widow's Tale' article (Carlton 1978).
24. On this rich, complex topic, see the introduction and various chapters in Matthews-Grieco 2014.
25. See Tigner 2012, 180.
26. Reprinted in Gurr 2004, 230.
27. Reprinted in Gurr 2004, 229.
28. On this phenomenon, see Aretino 1984, 244–5, and Garber 1992, 86–8.
29. Orgel 1996, 25–30 and 38–41.
30. Taylor 1630, 106.
31. On Tullia's double career as courtesan and poet/philosopher, see Hairston 2014, 'Introduction'.
32. Nashe 1972, 115.
33. Alberto, cited in Taviani 1969, 231.
34. See Barbara Fuchs, 'Diversifying the Classics: Bringing the *Comedia* to L.A. Audiences', a paper given at the Renaissance Society of America annual meeting, Boston 2016.
35. Ferrone 1993, 13–14.
36. See Scott 2010, 1–37 and Kerr 2015, 3–35.
37. Garzoni 1996, 1182–3.
38. Valerini 1570, 33.
39. Puteanus, in MacNeil 2003, 94; Du Ryer and Tasso in Taviani and Schino 1982, 342 and 122.
40. MacNeil 2003, 58–61.
41. Andreini 2005, 30.
42. Ruggiero 2006, 285.
43. On the influence of *Gl'ingannati* on *commedia dell'arte* repertoires, see Andrews 1993, 97–102; on the simultaneously hetero/homoerotic qualities of Lelia's kiss with Isabella, see Giannetti 2009, 49–61; and on the diffuse interest in and discourses of female same-sex relations in the period, see Traub 2002. The play is also the original source for Shakespeare's *Twelfth Night*.

NOTES   211

44. Stallybrass 1992, 77.
45. Howard 1998.
46. Orgel 1996, 153.
47. Weaver 2002, 49–51, and the chapter by Sharon Aronson-Lehavi on 'Sexuality and Gender' in vol. 2 of *A Cultural History of Theatre*.
48. Arenal and Schlau 1989, 239.
49. Weaver 2002, 49–51.
50. Weaver 2002, 197.
51. See Greer 1997, 135–49.
52. Kallendorf 2007, 36.
53. Heise 1992, 365–72
54. Leims, cited in Ortolani 1995, 155–6.
55. Ortolani 1995, 162–76.
56. Ortolani 1995, 171.

Chapter Four: The Environment of Theatre

1. Carlson 1989, 7.
2. Mumford 1961, 277; qtd. in Carlson 1989, 19.
3. Fairholt 1843, I, ix.
4. See Strong 1984; Smuts 2007, 219–23.
5. Smuts 1989, 74.
6. Carlson 1989, 22.
7. Marks 1998, 133–41.
8. Limon 1985; Williams 1990, vol. 1.
9. Moryson 1967, 304. For a discussion of Moryson, see Bosman 2004, 567. See also Katritzky 2008.
10. See the *Frankfurt Stadtarchiv, Ratssupplikationen* 1619, cited in Katritzky 2008, 43.
11. On the travels of the *commedia dell'arte* troupes, see Henke 2008.
12. Qtd. from the Tudor chronicler Hall in Anglo 1969, 22.
13. On Renaissance comedy as an avant-garde form, see Clubb 1995, 108–10.
14. Carlson 1989, 25.
15. Evangelista 1984, 50–1.
16. Henke 2013, 462.
17. Evangelista 1984, 51–2.
18. Withington 2005, 45.
19. Cartwright 1999, 13–14.
20. Marlow 2013, 8.
21. Nelson 1994, chs 2 and 3.
22. Marlow 2013, 88.
23. Orgel 1975, 14.
24. Orgel 1975, 14.
25. Holinshed 1808, 934.
26. Heijden and Boheemen 2006, 253.
27. Bosman 2004, 567–70.

28. Wilson 1969, 132.
29. McCabe 1983, xi.
30. Orgel 1975, 2 (original emphasis).
31. Greer 2000.
32. Platter 1892, 392–3.
33. Wickham et al. 2000, 86.
34. Mullaney 1988, 30.
35. Dillon 2000.
36. Wickham et al. 2000, 402.
37. Newman 2007.
38. Howard 2007, 163.

Chapter Five: Circulation

1. J. H. Elliott in a review of books on the rediscovery of America in *The New York Review of Books* 40: 12 (24 June 1993): 38; cited in Parr 1995, 18.
2. For a detailed discussion of Torres Naharro's *Comedia Tinellaria*, see Gillet 1943, 509–14. For a discussion of the international gathering in *Cymbeline* 1.5, see Billing 2014, 131–54.
3. McKendrick 1989, 27–9.
4. Artioli and Grazioli 2005, C1362.
5. Artioli and Grazioli 2005, L364.
6. Archduchess Cecilia Renata (Habsburg) in a letter to her brother Archduke Leopold Wilhelm; Artioli and Grazioli 2005, C1355.
7. Butler 2015.
8. For a detailed discussion of the 1568 marriage in Munich and the presence of Italian actors featuring Orlando di Lasso and the ensuing making of the famous frescoes at Castle Trausnitz in Landshut, see Katritzky 2006, 44–58; the other weddings are referred to in Henke and Nicholson 2008: 10–11.
9. Wikland 1962; Limon 1985, 3. For the Netherlands and Germany, see Schrickx 1986; Katritzky 2005a.
10. Spohr 2009.
11. Drábek and Katritzky 2016, 1529.
12. Limon 1985, 109–10.
13. MacLean and McMillin 1998.
14. For friendship albums, see Katritzky 2007, 61–72.
15. Hýzrle z Chodů, Jindřich 1979.
16. '*Tyrann und Märtyrer sind im Barock die Janushäupter des Gekrönten.*' Benjamin 1974, 249.
17. Cohen 1985.
18. Honigmann 1982. See also Honigmann and Brock 1993.
19. See Schrickx 1986; the case of travelling actor Robert Browne is discussed in Brand and Rudin 2011, and in Katritzky 2012, 139–40.
20. For further instances of English comedians' commercial activities on the Continent, see Katritzky 2012, 139–42.

NOTES

213

21. Drábek 2015, 7–18. See also Hyman 2011, and Rudin 1976, 2–11.
22. See Dubská 2012.
23. For England, see Beier 1985.
24. See Black and Gravestock 2006.
25. Ferrone 1993, 50–88.
26. This metaphor has been brilliantly explored and literally documented by Jean-Christophe Agnew in Agnew 1986.
27. For a detailed analysis, see Veltrusky 1985.
28. See in particular Katritzky 2007, 167–9.
29. Scherl and Rudin 2014, 666–70.
30. Katritzky 2007, 1.
31. Henke 2002, 200.
32. Henke 2002, 200.
33. Henke 2008, 26–8. Willem Schrickx's article on Italian actors in Antwerp in 1576 is cited in Henke.
34. McNeill 1974, 114–15.
35. See Drábek 2015, 13–16.
36. Limon 1985, 42–3.
37. For more details, see Drábek and Katritzky 2016.
38. For a suggestive account, see Huxley 1941.
39. Korda 2011.
40. Cerasano 2004; Edmond 2004; Parr 2004.
41. Qtd. in Gurr 2009, 27–8.
42. Grant 2011, 311–13.
43. See also Ravelhofer 2002, 287–323.
44. For a detailed discussion, including the commercial context, see Muggli 1992, 323–40.
45. See Parr 1995.
46. For a detailed account, see Neill 2010; Vitkus 2003, 107–62.
47. See McManus 2012.
48. Such as the Lutheran Ondřej Klatovský's Czech–German popular manual of 1540; see Štědroň 2002, 171–89.
49. Kumpera 1992, 247–98. See also Monroe 1900.
50. See Wetmore 2010, namely Joohee Park's and Angela Yarber's essays (29–44 and 67–74, respectively).
51. McKendrick 1989, 50–1, 276 n. 21.
52. Okoń 1970, 190. For more on Joseph Simons, see McCabe 1983, ch. 12. English translations of Simons's tragedies are available in Simons 1989.
53. Havlíčková 2014, 205–16.
54. See Christian Neuhuber's and Bärbel Rudin's contributions to Havlíčková and Neuhuber 2014. For the renown of *The Virgin Martyr* (and William Rowley's *A Shoemaker: A Gentleman*) in continental Europe, see Rudin 1980, 95–113.
55. Fülöp-Miller 1930, 411.
56. Fülöp-Miller 1930, 412. For recent research, see Nicole T. Hughes's (Columbia University) PhD thesis 'A Theater of the Americas: Dramatic Creation and Historical Imagination, 1500–1640', analysing the Jesuit mission in Hispanic America. For a

detailed discussion of the Jesuit performative events at Goa, India, see Katritzky 2014.

57. Fülöp-Miller 1930, 412.
58. Jowett 2011.
59. See in particular Wells Slights 1981.
60. See for instance Altman 1978.
61. Waith 1952, 37–8. See also Hoy 1996.
62. For a detailed discussion of *Leo Armenius*, see Szarota 1967.
63. Podlaha 1901.
64. Parente 1987, 198–208. See also Parente 1984, 525–51.
65. Schlueter 2012, 283–90
66. For an elaboration of Shakespeare as the inventor of the modern self, see Bloom 1998. For a detailed discussion of the transnational perspectives in Shakespeare, see Wofford 2008.
67. Granda 1969.

Chapter Six: Interpretations

1. Petrarca 2006, 99 and 101.
2. Petrarca 1999, 86–90.
3. Pico della Mirandola 1997, 11–13.
4. Machiavelli 1993, 139–40.
5. Machiavelli 1993, 178.
6. All citations are from Erasmus 1965, 152.
7. Euringer 2000, 61.
8. See Schnarr 2002.
9. Alberti 1998, 94.
10. Alberti 1998, 94.
11. Alberti 1998, 268.
12. Prisciani 1992, 39. '[. . .] cusì li Atheniesi prima, tal aggreste principio revolgendo in spectaculo urbano, lo chiamoreno theatro, cioè visorio, nel quale, stando grandissimo turba da la longa ancora senza impedimento alcuno vedesse et potesse anche esser visto.' (Trans. S. Hulfeld.)
13. Wiles 2011 provides a historical long-term study of this relationship.
14. See Cassiani 2007.
15. Cruciani 1983, 222–5.
16. A further testimony on the subject is the somewhat obscure but enthusiastic *Trattato di architettura* (*c*. 1464) by Antonio Averlino Filarete. See Ruffini 1983, 23–60. Ruffini's book sharpens the understanding of how important this utopian period of the humanist theatre discourse is to comprehending the development of the so-called 'Renaissance theatre'.
17. See the Machiavelli chapter in Wiles 2011, 48–74.
18. For documentation of the Medici theatre festivals, see Nagler 1964. For a critical commentary on the evolution of the 'teatro all'italiana', see Zorzi 1977.
19. See Deborre 1996, 80–1.

NOTES

20. Ehrstine 2002, 31–41.
21. The *Térence des ducs* is available in Gallica, the digital library of the Bibliothèque nationale de France, see http://gallica.bnf.fr/ark:/12148/btv1b8458135g/f14 and commented in Wikipedia, see fr.wikipedia.org/wiki/Térence_des_ducs.
22. See Allegri 1988, 59–109; Casagrande and Vecchio 1989.
23. See Victor 2014, 708.
24. Ingegneri 1989, 26–31.
25. Carlson 1993, 38.
26. See the related chapters in Carlson 1993, 37–89.
27. Vega Carpio 1914, 36.
28. Vega Carpio 1914, 23.
29. Aquin 1993, 344. 'Non utendo aliquibus illicitis verbis vel factis ad ludum, et non adhibendo ludum negotiis et temporibus indebitis.' The English translation follows the 1947 edition, available under dhspriory.org/thomas/summa/SS/SS168.html.
30. Qtd. in Carlson 1993, 23.
31. Barish 1985, 80–131; Reyff 1998, 15–69.
32. Platter 1968, 123.
33. Platter 1968, 305–8. See Katritzky 1998.
34. Platter 1968, 347–9.
35. Platter 1968, 585–7.
36. Platter 1968, 791.
37. Platter 1968, 792.
38. Cervantes 2004, 113–20; Mancing 2004, 549–51.
39. See Taviani 1969, LXXXIII–CV.
40. Edited and annotated in Ojeda Calvo 2007 and Marotti and Romei 1994, 344–433.
41. Edited and annotated by Hugh Roberts and Annette Tomarken in Bruscambille 2012.
42. For the latter, see Thompson 2009.
43. These remarks are based on Gerda Baumbach's approach to the early modern acting styles, see Baumbach 2012, 246–57.
44. Shakespeare 1982, 120 and 152.
45. Vitse 2003, 721.
46. Cotarelo 1904, 421–4.
47. Arellano 2012, 143–6.

Chapter Seven: Communities of Production

1. Except when I cite published translations, translations are my own.
2. Taylor 2007.
3. Binz 1899, 461–2.
4. Richards and Richards 1990, 256ff.
5. Limon 1985.
6. Brandt 2008, 59.
7. Wright 2008.
8. Gosson 1582; Howarth 1997, 245, quoting Subigny's *La Folle querelle*.

9. Weimann 1996.
10. Chambers 1923, 2: 292–3, misidentifying Louis as Louis XIV.
11. Henke 1997a, 212.
12. Shergold 1967, 529–30.
13. Howarth 1997, 179.
14. Parente 1987, 30–6; Shapiro 1977, 3–4; Valentin 2001, 197–200.
15. Shapiro 1977, 3.
16. On Laetus, Smith 1988, 3–5.
17. On Melanchthon, Parente 1987, 21–2; on *Ratio*, Valentin 2001, 50.
18. Jesuit education, Schnitzler 1952; on Beza, Howarth 1997, 28.
19. Montaigne 1957, 131.
20. On Merchant Taylors' boys, Shapiro 1977, 14, and Shapiro 2009, 131.
21. Brandt 1993, 47.
22. Wickham, et al. 2000, 264–7; Shapiro 1977, 20–4.
23. Deierkauf-Holsboer 1968, 1: 75–6.
24. Kathman 2004, 5–6.
25. Foakes 2002, 282–3.
26. Kathman 2004, 4.
27. Howarth 1997, 21.
28. Kathman 2004.
29. Jordan 2014.
30. Bean 2007.
31. Bland 1968, 31–2.
32. Nelson 2009, 289.
33. Simon 2008, 27, 32–3.
34. Teague 2009, 253–4.
35. Henke 2002, 88–9.
36. Jones and Stallybrass 2001; Korda 2011.
37. Taylor 1614, 204–5.
38. McKendrick 1989, 238–50.
39. Luca 1981, 18–25.
40. Mills 1998.
41. Ingram 1992, 134–49.
42. McKendrick 1989, 178–9.
43. Bettelli 1971.
44. On the *Rozzi*, see Tylus 2012.
45. Waite 2000.
46. Brandt 1993, 345–8.
47. Brandt 1993, 349, 356–7.
48. Howarth 1997, 11–20.
49. Yates 1967: 83–95; Howarth 1997, 15–17. The leader of the English company is reported as Jehan Schais by Yates and as Jean Thays by Howarth.
50. Howarth 1997, 23.
51. On *commedia* companies, Richards and Richards 1990, 59; on Lope de Rueda, McKendrick 1989, 43.

NOTES 217

52. Brand 2006, 47.
53. Bernstein 1993, 88.
54. Brandt 2008, 57; Howarth 1997, 13–15.
55. Bratton 2003, 171–8.
56. Giles-Watson 2013, 171–84.
57. Richards and Richards 1990, 61–8.
58. Shergold 1967, 518–19; McKendrick 1989, 186.
59. Shergold 1967, 507–8; McKendrick 1989, 49.
60. Scott 2000, 48–55.
61. Richards and Richards 1990, 265–6.
62. Cocco 1915, 57–8; two contracts are translated in Richards and Richards 1990, 44–6.
63. Howarth 1997, 65–6, 127.
64. Sammler 1967, 34–6.
65. On joint-stock companies in general, see Ingram 1999; on the change from common property to joint-stock, Harris 2002 and Turner 2016.
66. Chappuzeau 1674, 146–7.
67. Shergold 1967, 525.
68. Shergold 1967, 506, 526.
69. Shergold 1967, 506, 527; McKendrick 1989, 184–91.
70. Turner 2016.
71. Foakes 2002, xxxvi.n1.
72. Foakes 2002, 280.
73. Trollope 1905, 225–7.
74. Jonson, 'Induction', *Bartholomew Fair* (1614); Cervantes, ch. 48, *Don Quixote* (1605).
75. Thomas Platter notes variable pricing in London (Binz 1899, 459), Paris (Howarth 1997, 45), and Barcelona (Katritzky 2012, 138).
76. Qtd. by McKendrick 1989, 47.
77. Allen 1983.
78. Binz 1899, 458; Howarth 1997, 45, 74–5; Esses 1992, 741; Katritzky 2012.
79. Simon 2008, 30.
80. Malherbe 1862–69, 3: 337; cited by Richards and Richards 1990, 272, translation modified.
81. Storey 1978, 15–16.
82. Richards and Richards 1990, 126.
83. Thomson 1997.
84. Cerasano 2005.
85. Shergold 1967, 523–5.
86. Chappuzeau 1674, 142–4.
87. Honigmann and Brock 1993, 107.

Chapter Eight: Repertoire and Genres

1. From Raymond Williams, 'Culture is Ordinary', collected in Gray and McGuigan 1993, 6.

2. Lorenzo and Giuliano de Medici were being awarded honorary citizenship on the occasion.
3. Cf. here and for a further overview, Winkler 2015.
4. Henke and Nicholson 2014, 30.
5. Lohse 2015, 53–68.
6. Regarding the modelling of ideals of behaviour at court over the course of civilization, see Elias 1976 and 1994.
7. Henke 2002.
8. Scala 2008.
9. Cf. Richter 2012, 215–23.
10. Weiß 2000, 48–71.
11. Cartwright 1999.
12. Montrose 1996, 23.
13. Cf. Pörtl 1985; Fischer-Lichte 1990, 154–86.
14. A play made famous in 1967 by Jerzy Grotowski's legendary production. Grotowski transformed the protagonist's martyrdom into a model of the ascetic-athletic actor.
15. Cf. Pfahl 2012, 244–50.
16. Stackelberg 1996, 50.
17. Niefanger 2012, 230–43.

Chapter Nine: Technologies of Performance

1. Zorzi 1977, 72–3.
2. Weil 1974, 234–5; Dell'Arco and Carandini 1977–78, 1: 150–2.
3. Hewitt 1958, 190.
4. For more on theatre's allegorical use of space, see Hoxby 2010.
5. On medieval staging, see Chambers 1903; Wickham 1959; Southerne 1973; Meredith and Tailby 1983; and Weigert 2013.
6. Lawrenson 1986, esp. 117–18. Also see Rigal 1901, 263–4; Holsboer 1933, 109.
7. McKendrick 1989, esp. 240, 245–9.
8. Stern 2013, 17. Also see Cooper 2010.
9. Vitruvius 1486, dedication.
10. Zambotti and *Diario ferrarese,* qtd. in Pirrotta and Povoledo 1982, 302.
11. Nicoll 1966, 70–2; Zorzi 1977, 19–24; Pirrotta and Povoledo 1982, 299–310, esp. 306–7.
12. Zorzi 1977, 92. For a fuller account of the development of perspective scenography, see Marotti 1974, 167ff.
13. Zorzi 1977, 98–100; Attolino 1988, 113–17; D'Amico 1991; Pallen 1999, 20–7, 93–9.
14. Donatus 1902, 1: 38, qtd. in Riggs 1975, 161.
15. All translations of the *Poetics* are taken from Bywater 1909. On the fusion of Horatian and Aristotelian literary criticism, see Herrick 1946; Weinberg 1963; García Berrio 1977–80.
16. Riggs 1975.

NOTES

17. Zorzi 1977, 64–5.
18. Nagler 1964, 9–12.
19. Pallen 1999, 78.
20. P. F. Giambullari, *Apparato et feste nelle nozze dello Illustrissimo Signor Duca di Firenze e della Duchessa sua Consorte* (Florence, 1589), in Mamone 1981, 96, trans. in Pallen 1999, 30.
21. Attolino 1988, 145.
22. Cassirer 1963, 177.
23. Lavin 1980, 1: 150–1 (qtd. on 150). Also see Montanari 2004, esp. 308–14. For the most recent account of Bernini's theatrical activities, see Tamburini 2012.
24. Vitruvius 1914, 5.6.8; Bieber 1961, 74.
25. Vitruvius 1914, 5.6.8.
26. Pollux 1775, 9.
27. Delrio 1593–95, 18–19 (my trans.); Galluzzi 1621, 271–2. Galluzzi follows Delrio very closely. For more on Delrio, see Machielsen 2015, with earlier bibliography. For more on Galluzzi, see Fumaroli 1996, 138–70 and Hoxby 2015, 243–6, with earlier bibliography.
28. Da Vignola 1583, 92, trans. in Kernodle 1937, appendix 1, xv.
29. Hewitt 1958, 98–9.
30. On Buontalenti's theatre, see esp. Zorzi and Sperenzi 2001. On Aleotti's, see Mamczarz 1988 and Ronconi et al. 1992, both extensively illustrated.
31. Bjurström 1961, 110. On Torelli, also see Milesi 2000, with numerous illustrations.
32. See Greene 1994 and 2001; Hoxby 2007b.
33. Castelvetro 1978–79, 1: 385, trans. in Castelvetro 1984, 149.
34. Rinuccini 1983, 116–23.
35. Orgel and Strong 1973, 2: 421–2.
36. Melton 1620, 31, qtd. in Gwilym Jones 2013, 34.
37. Stern 2013, 12.
38. Sabbattini in Hewitt 1958, 146–8.
39. Hewitt 1958, 153–69; on clouds more generally, see Buccheri 2014.
40. Hewitt 1958, 130–42, 239–41.
41. Hewitt 1958, 110.
42. Hewitt 1958, 35–6, 111, 170–2, 229–31.
43. See Hoxby 2007a for antecedents.
44. Graves 2009.
45. Hewitt 1958, 28–9, 34–5.
46. Hewitt 1958, 59–61; Kernodle 1937, appendix VII, lxvi.
47. De Sommi, *Dialogues on Stage Affairs*, trans. in Nicoll 1966, 274–5.
48. De Sommi, *Dialogues on Stage Affairs*, trans. in Nicoll 1966, 275.
49. Hewitt 1958, 206.
50. De Sommi, *Dialogues on Stage Affairs*, trans. in Nicoll 1966, 274.
51. Hewitt 1958, 111–13.
52. Serlio in Hewitt 1958, 24–5.
53. Anderson 1991, 7.
54. Anderson 1991, 12.

220   NOTES

55. Kernodle 1944.
56. Mamczarz 1988.
57. Kernodle 1944, 170. On the *scena per angelo*, see Mayor 1945; Ferrero 1970; and Forment 2009. On the association of single-point perspective with absolutism, see Orgel 1975.
58. No. 412, 23 June 1712 in Addison 1965, 3: 540.
59. Arteaga 1783–88, 1: 332–3. Mayor 1945, 24, and Forment 2009, 31, both quote and translate the passage.

Chapter Ten: Knowledge Transmission

1. 'Il choque les principales règles du Poème Dramatique', Searles 1916, 1.
2. For a comprehensive history of this phenomenon, see West 2002.
3. Qtd. and trans. in Henke 2002, 159.
4. Hughes 1903, 304.
5. Qtd. in Brandt 1993, 28: 46.
6. Stubbes 1583, sigs. Kr, G[vii]r, Eiir; Gosson, sig. Cr.
7. Webster 1960, 3. Editor J. R. Brown translates the Latin apothegm as 'O strong stomachs of harvesters' (from Horace, alluding to the love of garlic among the lower sort).
8. 'Prologue to the Reader', *Ocho Comedias*, n.p., http://entretenida.outofthewings. org/text/diversion/princeps/prologue.html.
9. Davies 1617, sigs. K[6]r=NK[6]v.
10. Helgerson 1992, 216.
11. Stubbes 1583, sig. F[v]v.
12. Ripa 1765, 137; qtd. in Laughran and Vianello 2011, 273.
13. Erasmus 2001, 60.
14. Stern 2000, 64.
15. Stern 2009, 507.
16. Greer 2012, 107.
17. Certeau 1988, 1. Alice Rayner (2006) begins her second chapter of *Ghosts: Death's Double and the Phenomena of Theatre* with this passage.
18. The theatre's tracelessness is theorized by Phelan (1993).
19. Jonson 1623, sig. A3v.
20. Qtd. in Erne 2013, 194.
21. Cervantes 2016, Prologue, *Ocho Comedias*, http://entretenida.outofthewings.org/text/diversion/princeps/prologue.html
22. Greer 2012, 102.
23. Peters 2003, 2, 15.
24. Steggle 2015, 2.
25. Henke 2002, 176.
26. Epitaph translated in Bayle 1734, 328. I thank Pamela Allen Brown for sharing her extensive knowledge of Isabella Andreini's legacy with me.
27. Jonson 1623, sig. A3v.
28. Doran 1868, 2: 313.

NOTES

29. Burckhardt 2002, 109.
30. Walz 1927, 466.
31. Condell and Heminge 1623b, sig. A3r.
32. Prynne 1633, sig. P4v.
33. Taylor 2003, 18.
34. Lescarbot 2006, 54, 78.
35. Eisenbichler 2008, 269.
36. 'An Expostulation with Inigo Jones', Herford, Simpson and Simpson 1925–52, 8:403.
37. Each of these occasions and many others are detailed in Shewring 2013, *Waterborne Pageants*.
38. See Wintroub 1998, 469.
39. Qtd. in Jonson 1925–53, X: 448.
40. 'An Expostulation with Inigo Jones', Herford, Simpson and Simpson 1925–52, 8:403–4.
41. Castillo 2006, 46.
42. Castillo 2006, 48; Ybarra 2009, 42.
43. Bernheimer 1956, 226.

BIBLIOGRAPHY

Acosta, José de. 1604. *The naturall and morall historie of the East and West Indies . . . ,* trans. Edward Grimeston. London.

Addison, Joseph. 1965. *The Spectator*, ed. D. Bond. 5 vols. Oxford: Clarendon Press.

Agnew, Jean-Christophe. 1986. *Worlds Apart: The Market and the Theater in Anglo-American Thought, 1550–1750*. Cambridge: Cambridge University Press.

Alberti, Leon Battista. 1998. *On the Art of Building in Ten Books*, trans. Joseph Rykwert. Cambridge, MA: MIT Press.

Allegri, Luigi. 1988. *Teatro e Spettacolo nel Medioevo*. Roma-Bari: Laterza.

Allen, John J. 1983. *The Reconstruction of a Spanish Golden Age Playhouse: El Corral del Principe*. Gainesville, FL: University of Florida Press.

Alter, Jean. 1990. *A Sociosemiotic Theory of Theatre*. Philadelphia: University of Pennsylvania Press.

Altman, Joel B. 1978. *The Tudor Play of Mind: Rhetorical Inquiry and the Development of Elizabethan Drama*. Berkeley, CA: University of California Press.

Anderson, Michael. 1991. 'The Changing Scene: Plays and Playhouses in the Italian Renaissance'. Rpt. in *European Theatre Performance Practice, 1580–1750*, ed. Robert Henke and M. A. Katritzky, 3–32. Farnham, UK: Ashgate Press, 2014.

Anderson, Perry. 1974. *Lineages of the Absolutist State*. London: Verso Books.

Andreini, Isabella. 2005. *Selected Poems of Isabella Andreini*, ed. Anne MacNeil and James Wyatt Cook. Lanham, MD: Scarecrow.

Andrews, Richard. 1993. *Scripts and Scenarios: The Performance of Comedy in Renaissance Italy*. Cambridge: Cambridge University Press.

Anglo, Sydney. 1969. *Spectacle, Pageantry, and Early Tudor Policy*. Oxford: Clarendon.

Aquin, Thomas von. 1993. *Maßhaltung (2. Teil)*, kommentiert von Josef Groner OP. Graz: Pustet.

Arellano, Ignacio. 2012. *Historia del teatro español del siglo XVII*. Quinta edición. Madrid: Cátedra.

Arenal, Electa, and Stacey Schlau, eds. 1989. *Untold Sisters: Hispanic Nuns in Their Own Works*. Albuquerque, NM: University of New Mexico Press.

Aretino, Pietro. 1984. *Ragionamento. Dialogo*, ed. Nino Borsellino. Milan: Garzanti.

Ariès, Philippe. 1996. *Centuries of Childhood*, trans. R. Baldick. London: Pimlico.

Arteaga, Esteban de. 1783–88. *Le rivoluzioni del teatro musicale italiano dalla sua origine fino al presente*. 3 vols. Bologna: Stamperi'a di C. Trenti.

Artioli, U., and C. Grazioli, eds. 2005. *I Gonzaga e l'Impero: itinerari dello spettacolo: con una selezione di materiali dall'archivio informatico Herla (1560–1630)*. Florence: Le Lettere.

Attolino, Giovanni. 1988. *Teatro e spettacolo nel Rinascimento*. Bari: Editori Laterza.

Aubailly, Jean-Claude. 1978. *Deux jeux de carnaval de la fin du moyen age*. Paris: Droz.

Bakhtin, M. M. 1984. *Rabelais and His World*, trans. H. Iswolsky. Bloomington, IN: Indiana University Press.

Bakhtin, M. M. 1986. *Speech Genres and Other Late Essays*, trans. Vern W. McGee, ed Caryl Emerson and Michael Holquist. Austin, TX: University of Texas Press.

Barbieri, Nicolò. 1634/1971. *La Supplica: Discorso famigliare a quelli che trattano de' comici*. Milan: Il Polifilo.

Barish, Jonas. 1985. *The Antitheatrical Prejudice*. Berkeley, CA: University of California Press.

Baumbach, Gerda. 2012. *Schauspieler: Historische Anthropologie des Akteurs*. Band 1: Schauspielstile. Leipzig: Universitätsverlag.

Bayle, Peter. 1734. *The Dictionary Historical and Critical*. 2nd edn. London.

Bean, Sara. 2007. *Laughing Matters: Farce and the Making of Absolutism in France*. Ithaca, NY: Cornell University Press.

Beaujoyeulx, Balthazar de. 1982. *Le Balet Comique*, ed. Margaret M. McGowan. Binghamton, NY: Center for Medieval and Early Renaissance Studies.

Beaumont, Francis, and John Fletcher. 1647. *Comedies and Tragedies*. London.

Beier, A. L. 1985. *Masterless Men: The Vagrancy Problem in England 1560–1640*. London: Methuen.

Belting, Hans. 1994. *Likeness and Presence: A History of the Image before the Era of Art*, trans. Edmund Jephcott. Chicago, IL: University of Chicago Press.

Benjamin, Walter. 1974. 'Trauerspiel und Tragödie'. In *Gesammelte Schriften* 1.1, 249. Frankfurt: Suhrkamp.

Bennett, Susan. 1997. *Theatre Audiences: A Theory of Production and Reception*. 2nd edn. London: Routledge.

Bentley, Eric. 1991. *The Life of the Drama*. New York: Applause Books.

Bergeron, David M. 2011. 'Charismatic Audience: A 1559 Pageant'. In *Imagining the Audience in Early Modern Drama, 1558–1642*, ed. Jennifer A. Low and Nova Myhill, 135–149. New York: Palgrave Macmillan.

Bernheimer, Richard. 1956. 'Theatrum Mundi'. *Art Bulletin* 38: 225–247.

Bernstein, Eckhard. 1993. *Hans Sachs: mit Selbstzeugnissen und Bilddokumenten*. Hamburg: Rowohlt.

Bettelli, Sergio. 1971. 'When did Machiavelli write *Mandragola?*' *Renaissance Quarterly* 24: 317–326.

Bieber, Margarete. 1961. *The History of Greek and Roman Theater*. Princeton, NJ: Princeton University Press.

Billing, Christian. 2008. *Masculinities, Corporality and the English Stage, 1580–1635*. Farnham, UK: Ashgate Press.

Billing, Christian M. 2014. 'Forms of Fashion: Material Fabrics, National Characteristics, and the Dramaturgy of Difference on the Early Modern English Stage'. In *Transnational*

BIBLIOGRAPHY

Mobilities in Early Modern Theatre, ed. Robert Henke and Eric Nicholson, 131–154. Farnham, UK: Ashgate Press.

Binz, Gustav. 1899. 'Londoner Theater und Schauspiele im Jahre 1599'. *Anglia* 22: 456–464.

Bjurström, Per. 1961. *Giacomo Torelli and Baroque Stage Design*. Stockholm: Nationalmuseum Stockholm.

Black, Christopher, and Pamela Gravestock, eds. 2006. *Early Modern Confraternities in Europe and the Americas: International and Interdisciplinary Perspectives*. Aldershot: Ashgate Press.

Bland, Desmond, ed. 1968. *Gesta Grayorum*. Liverpool: Liverpool University Press.

Bloch, Marc. 1973. *The Royal Touch: Sacred Monarchy and Scrofula in England and France*, trans. J. E. Anderson. London: Routledge.

Bloom, Gina. 2007. *Voice in Motion: Staging Gender, Shaping Sound in Early Modern England*. Philadelphia: University of Pennsylvania Press.

Bloom, Harold. 1998. *Shakespeare: The Invention of the Human*. New York: Riverhead Books.

Boaistuau, Pierre. 1588. *Théâtre du Monde*. Paris.

Bodin, Jean. 1596. *Universae naturae theatrum*. Paris.

Bosman, Anston. 2004. 'Renaissance Intertheatre and the Staging of Nobody'. *ELH* 71 (3): 559–583.

Bradford, William. 1622. *A relation or iournall of the beginning and proceedings of the English plantation setled at Plimoth in New England*. London.

Brand, Peter. 2006. 'Ariosto and Ferrara'. In *A History of Italian Theatre*, ed. Joseph Farrell and Paolo Puppa, 44–50. Cambridge: Cambridge University Press.

Brand, Peter, and Bärbel Rudin. 2010. 'Der englische Komödiant Robert Browne (1563–c. 1621)'. *Daphnis* 39: 1–134.

Brandt, George W., ed. 1993. *German and Dutch Theatre 1600–1848*, comp. and trans. George W. Brandt and Wiebe Hogendoorn. Cambridge: Cambridge University Press.

Brandt, George. 2008. 'German Baroque Theatre and Strolling Players, 1550–1750'. In *A History of German Theatre*, ed. Simon Williams and Maik Hamburger, 38–64. Cambridge: Cambridge University Press.

Brathwaite, Richard. 1620. *Essaies vpon the fiue senses*. London.

Bratton, Jackie. 2003. *New Readings in Theatre History*. Cambridge: Cambridge University Press.

Braudel, Fernand. 1972–73. *The Mediterranean and the Mediterranean World in the Age of Philip II*, trans. Siân Reynolds. 2 vols. New York: Harper and Row.

Britland, Karen. 2006. *Drama at the Courts of Queen Henrietta Maria*. Cambridge: Cambridge University Press.

Brown, Pamela Allen, and Peter Parolin, eds. 2005. *Women Players in England, 1500–1660: Beyond the All-Male Stage*. Aldershot: Ashgate Press.

Bruscambille [Gracieux, Jean]. 2012. *Œuvres complètes: Les Fantaisies, Les Nouvelles et plasiantes Imaginations, Facecieuses Paradoxes, Les plaisantes Paradoxes, Pamphlets*, ed. Hugh Roberts and Annette Tomarken. Paris: Honoré Champion Éditeur.

Buccheri, Alessandra. 2014. *The Spectacle of Clouds, 1439–1650: Italian Art and Theatre*. Burlington, VT: Ashgate Press.

Burckhardt, Jacob. 1979. *Reflections on History*. Indianapolis: Liberty Classics.

Burckhardt, Jacob. 1990. *The Civilization of the Renaissance in Italy*, trans. S. G. C. Middlemore. London: Penguin.

Burckhardt, Jacob. 2002. *The Civilization of the Renaissance in Italy*. New York: The Modern Library.

Burke, Peter. 2008. *What is Cultural History?* 2nd edn. Cambridge: Polity.

Burke, Peter. 2009. *Popular Culture in Early Modern Europe*. 3rd edn. Aldershot: Ashgate Press.

Butler, Judith. 1990. *Gender Trouble: Feminism and the Subversion of Identity*. London: Routledge.

Butler, Judith. 1993. *Bodies That Matter: On the Discursive Limits of 'Sex'*. New York: Routledge.

Butler, Martin. 2015. 'The Court Masque'. *The Cambridge Edition of the Works of Ben Jonson Online*.

Bywater, Ingram. 1909. *Aristotle on the Art of Poetry*. Oxford: Clarendon Press.

Carlson, Marvin. 1989. *Places of Performance: The Semiotics of Theatre Architecture*. Ithaca, NY: Cornell University Press.

Carlson, Marvin. 1990. *Theatre Semiotics: Signs of Life*. Bloomington, IN: Indiana University Press.

Carlson, Marvin. 1993. *Theories of the Theatre: A Historical and Critical Survey from the Greeks to the Present*. Expanded Edition. Ithaca, NY: Cornell University Press.

Carlton, Charles. 1978. 'The Widow's Tale: Male Myths and Female Reality in 16th and 17th Century England'. *Albion* X: 118–129.

Cartwright, Kent. 1999. *Theatre and Humanism: English Drama in the Sixteenth Century*. Cambridge: Cambridge University Press.

Casagrande, Carla, and Silvana Vecchio. 1989. 'L'interdizione del giullare nel vocabolario clericale del XII e XIII secolo'. In *Il teatro medievale*, ed. Johann Drumbl, 317–368. Bologna: Il Mulino.

Cassiani, Chiara, ed. 2007. *Pomponio Leto e la prima Accademia Romana*. Giornata di Studi (Roma, 2 dicembre 2005). Roma: Roma nel Rinascimento.

Cassirer, Ernst. 1963. *The Individual and the Cosmos in Renaissance Philosophy*, trans. Mario Domandi. New York: Harper and Row.

Castelvetro, Ludovico. 1978–79. *Poetica d'Aristotele vulgarizzata e sposta* (1570, 1576), ed. Werther Romani. 2 vols. Rome–Bari: Gius. Laterza & Figli.

Castelvetro, Ludovico. 1984. *Castelvetro on the Art of Poetry: An Abridged Translation*, trans. A. Bongiorno. Binghampton, NY: Medieval and Renaissance Texts and Studies.

Castillo, Susan. 2006. *Colonial Encounters in New World Writing, 1500–1786: Performing America*. London: Routledge.

Cerasano, S. P. 2004. 'Alleyn, Edward (1566–1626)'. *Oxford Dictionary of National Biography*. Oxford University Press. Online ed., Jan. 2008.

Cerasano, S. P. 2005. 'Edward Alleyn, the New Model Actor, and the Rise of Celebrity in the 1590s'. *Medieval and Renaissance Drama in England* 18: 47–58.

Certeau, Michel de. 1988. *The Writing of History*, trans. Tom Conley. New York: Columbia University Press.

Cervantes, Miguel de. 2004. *Pedro, the Great Pretender*, trans. Philip Osment. London: Oberon Books.

Cervantes, Miguel de. 2016. *Ocho Comedias,* trans. John O'Neill. In *La entretenida by Miguel de Cervantes: A Digital, Annotated Edition and an English Translation (The Diversion)*. King's College, London. http://entretenida.outofthewings.org/text/diversion/princeps/prologue.html.

Chambers, E. K. 1903. *The Mediaeval Stage*. 2 vols. Oxford: Clarendon Press.

Chambers, E. K. 1923. *The Elizabethan Stage*. 4 vols. Oxford: Clarendon Press.

BIBLIOGRAPHY

Chappuzeau, Samuel. 1674. *Le Théâtre François*. Lyon: Michel Mayer.

Chartier, Roger. 1988. *Cultural History: Between Practices and Representations*. Ithaca, NY: Cornell University Press.

Chastel, André. 1991. 'The Artist'. In *Renaissance Characters*, ed. Eugenio Garin; trans. Lydia G. Cochrane. Chicago, IL: University of Chicago Press.

Clark, Stuart. 2007. *Vanities of the Eye: Vision in Early Modern European Culture*. Oxford: Oxford University Press.

Clubb, Louise George. 1995. 'Italian Renaissance Theatre'. In *The Oxford Illustrated History of the Theatre*, ed. John Russell Brown. Oxford: Oxford University Press.

Cocco, Ester. 1915. 'Una compagnia comica della prima metà de secolo XVI'. *Giornale storico della letteratura italiana* 65: 55–70.

Cohen, Walter. 1985. *Drama of a Nation: Public Theater in Renaissance England and Spain*. Ithaca, NY: Cornell University Press.

Condell, Henry, and John Heminge. 1623a. 'Catalogue'. In *Mr. William Shakespeare's Comedies, Histories, & Tragedies*. London.

Condell, Henry, and John Heminge. 1623b. 'To the great Variety of Readers'. In *Mr. William Shakespeare's Comedies, Histories, & Tragedies*. London.

Cooper, Helen. 2010. *Shakespeare and the Medieval World*. Arden Critical Companions. London: A & C Black.

Cortelazzo, Manlio. 1989. *Venezia, Il Levante, e il mare*. Pisa: Pacini.

Cotarelo y Mori, Emilio. 1904. *Bibliografía de las controversias sobre la licitud del teatro en España*. Madrid: Revista de Archivos, Bibliotecas y Museos.

Crawford, Katherine. 2007. *European Sexualities, 1400–1800*. Cambridge: Cambridge University Press.

Crosse, Henry. 1603. *Vertues common-vvealth: or The high-way to honour . . . .* London.

Cruciani, Fabrizio. 1983. *Teatro nel Rinascimento: Roma 1450–1550*. Roma: Bulzoni.

D'Amico, Jack. 1991. 'Drama and the Court in "La Calandria."' *Theatre Journal* 43 (1): 93–106.

Darnton, Robert. 1984. *The Great Cat Massacre and Other Episodes in French Cultural History*. New York: Basic Books.

Davies, John. 1617. *Wit's Bedlam*. London.

Da Vignola, Giacomo Barozzi. 1583. *Le Due regole della prospettiva pratica*.

Davis, Natalie Zemon. 1975. *Society and Culture in Early Modern France*. Palo Alto: Stanford University Press.

Deborre, Ingeborg. 1996. *Palladios Teatro Olimpico in Vicenza: Die Inszenierung einer lokalen Aristokratie unter venezianischer Herrschaft*. Marburg: Jonas.

Deierkauf-Holsboer, S. Wilma. 1968. *Le Théâtre de l'Hôtel de Bourgogne I: 1548–1635*. Paris: A-G. Nizet.

Dekker, Thomas. 1953–61. *The Dramatic Works*, ed. Fredson Bowers. 4 vols. Cambridge: Cambridge University Press.

Dell'Arco, Maurizio Fagiolo and Silvia Carandini. 1977–8. *L'effimero barocco: strutture della festa nella Roma del '600*. 2 vols. Rome: Bulzoni.

Delrio, Martin Antonio. 1593–95. *Martini Antonii Delrii ex Societate Iesu Syntagma tragoediae latinae: in tres partes distinctum*. Antwerp: ex Officina Plantiniana, apud Viduam [et] Ioannem Moretum.

Dillon, Janette. 2000. *Theatre, Court and City, 1595–1610*. Cambridge: Cambridge University Press.

Donatus, Aelius. 1902. *Aeli Donati qvod fertvr commentum Terenti accedvnt Evgraphi commentvm et scholia Bembina*, ed. Paulus Wessner. 3 vols. Leipzig: Teubner.

Doran, John. 1868. *Saints and Sinners, or In Church and About It*. 2 vols. London: Hurst and Blackett.

Drábek, Pavel. 2015. '"His Motion is no Italian Motion but Made in London": The Early Modern Roots of Czech Puppet Theatre'. *Theatralia* 18 (2) (Autumn): 7–18.

Drábek, Pavel, and M. A. Katritzky. 2016. 'Shakespearean Players in Early Modern Europe'. In *Cambridge Guide to the Worlds of Shakespeare*, ed. Bruce R. Smith, 1529. 2 vols. Cambridge: Cambridge University Press.

Drinnon, Richard. 1980. 'The Maypole of Merry Mount: Thomas Morton and the Puritan Patriarchs'. *The Massachusetts Review* 21 (2): 382–410.

Dubská, Alice. 2012. *The Travels of the Puppeteers Brat and Pratte Through Europe in the Eighteenth and Nineteenth Centuries*. Praha: NAMU.

Duffy, Eamon. 1990. 'Devotion to the Crucifix and Related Images in England on the Eve of the Reformation'. In *Bilder und Bildersturm im Spätmittelalter und in der frühen Neuzeit*, ed. Bob Scribner, 21–36. Wiesbaden: Harrassowitz.

Duffy, Eamon. 2005. *The Stripping of the Altars: Traditional Religion in England, c. 1400–c. 1580*. 2nd edn. New Haven, CT: Yale University Press.

Edmond, Mary. 2004. 'Davenant, Sir William (1606–1668)'. *Oxford Dictionary of National Biography*. Oxford University Press. Online ed., Oct. 2009.

Egerton, Stephen. 1623. *The boring of the eare contayning a plaine and profitable discourse by way of dialogue . . . .* London.

Ehrstine, Glenn. 2002. *Theatre, Culture, and Community in Reformation Bern: 1523–1555*. Leiden: Brill.

Eisenbichler, Konrad. 2008. 'How Bartolomeo Saw a Play'. In *Renaissance in the Streets, Schools and Studies: Essays in Honour of Paul F. Grendler*, ed. Konrad Eisenbichler and Nicholas Terpstra, 259–278. Toronto: Centre for Reformation and Renaissance Studies.

Elias, Norbert. 1976. *Über den Prozess der Zivilisation. Soziogenetische und psychogenetische Untersuchungen*. 2 vols. Frankfurt / Main: Suhrkamp.

Elias, Norbert. 1994. *The Civilizing Process*, trans. E. Jephcott. Rev. ed. Oxford: Blackwell.

Elton, Geoffrey. 1953. *The Tudor Revolution in Government*. Cambridge: Cambridge University Press.

Enders, Jody. 2011. *'The Farce of the Fart' and Other Ribaldries: Twelve Medieval French Plays in Modern English*. Philadelphia: University of Pennsylvania Press.

Erasmus, Desiderius. 1965. *The Education of a Christian Prince*, trans. and ed. Lester K. Born. New York: Octagon Books.

Erasmus, Desiderus. 2001. *The Adages of Erasmus,* ed. William Barker. Toronto: University of Toronto Press.

Erne, Lukas. 2013. *Shakespeare and the Book Trade*. Cambridge: Cambridge University Press.

Esses, Maurice. 1992. *Dance and Instrumental* Diferencias *in Spain During the 17th and Early 18th Centuries*. Stuyvesant, NY: Pendragon Press.

Euringer, Martin. 2000. *Zuschauer des Welttheaters: Lebensrolle, Theatermetapher und gelingendes Selbst in der Frühen Neuzeit*. Darmstadt: Wissenschaftliche Buchgesellschaft.

Evangelista, Annamaria. 1984. 'Le compagnie dei Comici dell'Arte nel teatrino di Baldracca a Firenze: notizie dagli epistolari (1575–1653)'. *Quaderni di Teatro* 24: 50–72.

Evans, G. Blakemore et al., eds. 1997. *The Riverside Shakespeare*. 2nd edn. Boston, MA: Houghton Mifflin.

BIBLIOGRAPHY

Fairholt, Frederick W. 1843. *Lord Mayor's Pageants being Collections Towards a History of these Annual Celebrations*. London: Percy Society.

Febvre, Lucien. 1982. *The Problem of Unbelief in the Sixteenth Century: The Religion of Rabelais*, trans. B. Gottlieb. Cambridge, MA / London: Harvard University Press.

Feldman, Martha, and Bonnie Gordon, eds. 2006. *The Courtesan's Arts: Cross-Cultural Perspectives*. Oxford: Oxford University Press.

Ferrero, Mercedes Viale. 1970. *Filippo Juvarra scenografo e architetto teatrale*. Torino: Edizioni d'Arte Fratelli Pozzo.

Ferrone, Siro. 1993. *Attori mercanti corsari: La commedia dell'arte in Europe tra Cinque e Seicento*. Turin: Einaudi.

Fischer-Lichte, Erika. 1990. *Geschichte des Dramas: Epochen der Identität auf dem Theater von der Antike bis zur Gegenwart*. Vol. 1. Tübingen: Francke.

Foakes, R. A., ed. 2002. *Henslowe's Diary*. Cambridge: Cambridge University Press.

Folkerth, Wes. 2002. *The Sound of Shakespeare*. London: Routledge.

Forgacs, David, and Geoffrey Nowell-Smith, eds. 1985. *Antonio Gramsci: Selections from Cultural Writings*. Cambridge, MA: Harvard University Press.

Forment, Bruno. 2009. 'Trimming Scenic Invention: Oblique Perspective as Poetics of Discipline'. *Music in Art* 34 (1/2): 31–43.

Fox, Adam. 2000. *Oral and Literate Culture in England, 1500–1700*. Oxford: Clarendon.

Franko, Mark. 2015. *Dance as Text: Ideologies of the Baroque Body*. 2nd edn. Oxford: Oxford University Press.

Fülöp-Miller, René. 1930. *Power and Secret of the Jesuits* (1926), trans. F. S. Flint and D. F. Tait. New York: The Viking Press.

Fumaroli, Marc. 1996. *Héros et orateurs. Rhétoriques et dramaturgie cornéliennes*. Geneva: Droz.

Galluzzi, Tarquinio. 1621. *Tarqvinii Gallutii Sabini e Societate Iesv Virgilianae vindicationes & commentarij tres de tragoedia, comoedia, elegia*. Rome: Alessandro Zannetti.

Gambelli, Delia. 1993. *Arlecchino a Parigi. Dall'inferno all corte del Re Sole*. Rome: Bulzoni.

Garber, Marjorie. 1992. *Vested Interests: Cross-Dressing and Cultural Anxiety*. New York: Routledge.

García Berrio, Antonio. 1977–80. *Formacion de la teoria literaria moderna: la topica horaciana en Europa*. 2 vols. Madrid: CUPSA.

Garzoni, Tommaso. 1996. *La piazza universale di tutte le professioni del mondo, nobili e ignobili*, ed. Paolo Cherchi and Beatrice Collina. 2 vols. Turin: Einaudi.

Geertz, Clifford. 1973. *The Interpretation of Cultures*. New York: Basic Books.

Gent, Lucy. 1995. '"The Rash Gazer": Economies of Vision in Britain, 1550–1660'. In *Albion's Classicism: The Visual Arts in Britain, 1550–1660*, ed. Lucy Gent, 377–393. New Haven, CT: Yale University Press.

Giannetti, Laura. 2009. *Lelia's Kiss: Imagining Gender, Sex, and Marriage in Italian Renaissance Comedy*. Toronto: University of Toronto Press.

Gibson, Walter. 1981. 'Artists and *Rederijkers* in the Age of Bruegel'. *Art Bulletin* 63 (4): 426–446.

Giles-Watson, Maura. 2013. 'John Rastell's London Stage: Reconstructing Repertory and Collaborative Practice'. *Early Theatre* 16: 171–184.

Gillet, Joseph E, ed. 1943. *Propalladia and Other Works of Bartolomé de Torres Naharro*. Bryn Mawr, PA: University of Pennsylvania Press.

Ginzburg, Carlo. 1980. *The Cheese and the Worms: The Cosmos of a Sixteenth-Century Miller*, trans. J. and A. Tedeschi. London: Routledge and Kegan Paul.

Gonzalez Echevarria, Roberto, and Enrique Pupo-Walker, eds. 1996. *The Cambridge History of Latin American Literature*, 3 vols. Cambridge: Cambridge University Press.

Gosson, Stephen. 1582. *Playes confuted in fiue actions*. London.

Gough, Melinda. 2005. 'Courtly *Comédiantes:* Henrietta Maria and Amateur Women's Stage Plays in France and England'. In *Women Players in England, 1500–1660: Beyond the All-Male Stage,* ed. Pamela Allen Brown and Peter Parolin, 193–215. Aldershot: Ashgate Press.

Goulart, Simon. 1607. *Admirable and memorable histories containing the wonders of our time . . .*, trans. Edward Grimeston. London.

Gramsci, Antonio. 1971. *Selections from the Prison Notebooks of Antonio Gramsci*, ed. and trans. Quitin Hoare and Geoffrey Nowell Smith. London: Lawrence and Wishart.

Granda, Germán de. 1969. 'El Gran Duque de Gandía: comedia de Don Pedro Calderón de la Barca publiée d'après le manuscrit de Mladá Vožice . . .' *Thesaurus* XXIV.3: 530–532.

Grant, Teresa. 2011. 'White bears in "Mucedorus", "The Winter's Tale", and "Oberon, the Fairy Prince"'. *Notes and Queries* 48 (3) (Sept.): 311–313.

Gray, Ann, and Jim McGuigan, eds. 1993. *Studying Culture: An Introductory Reader*. London: E. Arnold.

Graves, R. B. 2009. 'Lighting'. In *The Oxford Handbook of Early Modern Theatre*, ed. Richard Dutton, 528–542. Oxford: Oxford University Press.

Grazia, Margreta de, Maureen Quilligan, and Peter Stallybrass, eds. 1996. *Subject and Object in Renaissance Culture*. Cambridge: Cambridge University Press.

Green, Anna. 2008. *Cultural History*. New York: Palgrave Macmillan.

Greenberg, Marissa. 2015a. *Metropolitan Tragedy Genre, Justice, and the City in Early Modern England*. Toronto: University of Toronto Press.

Greenberg, Marissa. 2015b. 'Processions and History in Shakespeare and Fletcher's *Henry VIII*'. *English Literary Renaissance* 45 (2): 275–302.

Greenblatt, Stephen. 1991. *Marvelous Possessions: The Wonder of the New World*. Chicago, IL: University of Chicago Press.

Greenblatt, Stephen, Ines G. Županov, Reinhard Meyer-Kalkus, Heike Paul, Pál Nyíri, and Friederike Pannewick. 2009. *Cultural Mobility: A Manifesto*. Cambridge: Cambridge University Press.

Greene, Thomas M. 1994 'The King's One Body in the *Balet Comique de la Royne*'. *Yale French Studies* (86): 75–93.

Greene, Thomas M. 2001. 'Labyrinth Dances in the French and English Renaissance'. *Renaissance Quarterly* 54: 1403–1466.

Greer, Margaret. 1997. 'Embodying the Faith: The *Auto* Program of 1670'. In *The Calderonian Stage: Body and Soul*, ed. Manuel Delgado Morales, 133–153. Lewisburg, PA: Bucknell University Press.

Greer, Margaret. 2000. 'A Tale of Three Cities: The Place of the Theatre in Early Modern Madrid, Paris and London'. *Bulletin of Hispanic Studies* 77: 391–419.

Greer, Margaret. 2012. 'Authority and Theatrical Community: Early Modern Spanish Theater Manuscripts'. *Renaissance Drama* 40: 101–112.

Groves, Beatrice. 2015. *The Destruction of Jerusalem in Early Modern English Literature*. Cambridge: Cambridge University Press.

Gurr, Andrew. 2004. *Playgoing in Shakespeare's London*. 3rd edn. Cambridge: Cambridge University Press.

BIBLIOGRAPHY 231

Gurr, Andrew. 2009. *The Shakespearean Stage 1574–1642*. 4th edn. Cambridge: Cambridge University Press.

Hairston, Julia, ed. and trans. 2014. *Poems and Letters of Tullia D'Aragona and Others*. Toronto: ITER.

Harris, Jonathan Gil. 2002. 'Properties of Skill: Product Placement in Early English Artisanal Drama'. In *Staged Properties in Early English Drama*, ed. Jonathan Gil Harris and Natasha Korda, 35–66. Cambridge: Cambridge University Press.

Harris, Max. 2000. *Aztecs, Moors, and Christians: Festivals of Reconquest in Mexico and Spain*. Austin, TX: University of Texas Press.

Harvey, Howard Graham. 1941. *The Theatre of the Basoche*. Cambridge, MA: Harvard University Press.

Havlíčková, Margita. 2014. 'Zu den Beziehungen zwischen barockem Schul- und Berufstheater am Beispiel der *Representation Von S. Bonifacii wunderbarlichen Kampff und Lobwürdigen Sieg* (Nikolsburg 1639)'. In *Johann Georg Gettner und das barocke Theater zwischen Nikolsburg und Krumau*, eds. Margita Havlíčková and Christian Neuhuber, 205–216. Brno: Masaryk University Press.

Havlíčková, Margita, and Christian Neuhuber, eds. 2014. *Johann Georg Gettner und das barocke Theater zwischen Nikolsburg und Krumau*. Brno: Masaryk University Press.

Heijden, C. J. van der, and F. C. van Boheemen. 2006. 'Accommodation and Possessions of Chambers of Rhetoric in the Province of Holland'. In *Urban Theatre in the Low Countries: 1400–1625*, ed. Elsa Streitman and Peter Happé, 253–281. Turnhout, Belgium: Brepols.

Heise, Ursula K. 1992. 'Transvestism and the Stage Controversy in Spain and England: 1580–1680'. *Theatre Journal* 44.3: 357–374.

Helgerson, Richard. 1992. *Forms of Nationhood: The Elizabethan Writing of England*. Chicago: University of Chicago Press.

Henke, Robert. 1997a. 'Toward Reconstructing the Audiences of the *Commedia dell'Arte*'. *Essays in Theatre / Études Théâtrales* 15: 207–222. Rpt. in *European Theatre Performance Practice, 1580–1750*, ed. Robert Henke and M. A. Katritzky, 479–492. Burlington, VT: Ashgate Press.

Henke, Robert. 1997b. *Pastoral Transformations: Italian Tragicomedy and Shakespeare's Late Plays*. Newark, DE: University of Delaware Press.

Henke, Robert. 2002. *Performance and Literature in the Commedia dell'Arte*. Cambridge: Cambridge University Press.

Henke, Robert. 2008. 'Border-Crossing in the *Commedia dell'Arte*'. In *Transnational Exchange in Early Modern Theater*, ed. Robert Henke and Eric Nicholson, 19–34. Aldershot: Ashgate Press.

Henke, Robert. 2013. 'Poor'. In *Early Modern Theatricality*, ed. Henry S. Turner, 460–477. Oxford: Oxford University Press.

Henke, Robert. 2015. *Poverty and Charity in Early Modern Theater and Performance*. Iowa City, IA: University of Iowa Press.

Henke, Robert, and M. A. Katritzky, eds. 2014. *European Theatre Performance Practice, 1580–1750*. Burlington, VT: Ashgate Press.

Henke, Robert, and Eric Nicholson, eds. 2008. *Transnational Exchange in Early Modern Theater*. Burlington, VT: Ashgate Press.

Henke, Robert, and Eric Nicholson, eds. 2014. *Transnational Mobilities in Early Modern Theater*. Farnham, UK: Ashgate.

Herford, C. H., Percy Simpson, and Evelyn Simpson, eds. 1925–52. *Ben Jonson: The Man and his Work*. 8 vols. Oxford: Oxford University Press.

Herrick, Marvin T. 1946. *The Fusion of Horatian and Aristotelian Literary Criticism, 1531–1555*. Urbana, IL: University of Illinois Press.

Herrick, Marvin T. 1947. 'Some Neglected Sources of *Admiratio*'. *Modern Language Notes* 62 (4): 222–226.

Hewitt, Barnard, ed. 1958. *The Renaissance Stage: Documents of Serlio, Sabbattini and Furttenbach*. Coral Gables, FL: University of Miami Press.

Heywood, Thomas. 1612/1978. *An Apology for Actors*, ed. Richard H. Perkinson. Delmar, NY: Scholar's Facsimiles & Reprints.

Hibbard, Howard. 1965. *Bernini*. London: Penguin.

Hillman, David, and Carla Mazzio, eds. 1997. *The Body in Parts: Fantasies of Corporeality in Early Modern Europe*. New York: Routledge.

Hirsch, Brett D. 2013. 'Hornpipes and Disordered Dancing in *The Late Lancashire Witches*: A Reel Crux?' *Early Theatre* 16 (1): 139–149.

Holinshed, Raphael. 1808. *Holinshed's Chronicales of England, Scotland and Ireland*, ed. Sir Henry Ellis. 6 vols. London.

Holsboer, S. Wilma. 1933. *Histoire de la mise en scène dans le théâtre français de 1600 à 1657*. Paris: E. Droz.

Honigmann, E. A. J. 1982. *Shakespeare's Impact on His Contemporaries*. London: Macmillan Press.

Honigmann, E. A. J., and Susan Brock. 1993. *Playhouse Wills, 1558–1642*. Manchester: Manchester University Press.

Horace. 1929. *Satires, Epistles, and Ars Poetica*, trans. H. Rushton Fairclough. Loeb Classical Library. Cambridge, MA: Harvard University Press.

Howard, Jean. 1994. *The Stage and Social Struggle in Early Modern England*. London: Routledge.

Howard, Jean. 1998. 'Women as Spectators, Spectacles, and Paying Customers'. In *Readings in Renaissance Women's Drama: Criticism, History, and Performance*, eds. S. P. Ceresano and Marion Wynne-Davies, 81–86. London: Routledge.

Howard, Jean. 2007. *Theatre of a City. The Places of London Comedy, 1598–1642*. Philadelphia: University of Pennsylvania Press.

Howarth, William D., ed. and trans. 1997. *French Theatre in the Neo-classical Era, 1550–1789*. Cambridge: Cambridge University Press.

Hoxby, Blair. 2007a. '"All Passion Spent": The Means and Ends of a Tragédie en Musique'. *Comparative Literature* 59: 33–62.

Hoxby, Blair. 2007b. 'The Wisdom of Their Feet: Meaningful Dance in Milton and the Stuart Masque'. *English Literary Renaissance* 37: 74–99.

Hoxby, Blair. 2010. 'Allegorical Drama'. In *The Cambridge Companion to Allegory*, ed. Rita Copeland and Peter T. Struck, 191–208. Cambridge: Cambridge University Press.

Hoxby, Blair. 2015. *What Was Tragedy? Theory and the Early Modern Canon*. Oxford: Oxford University Press.

Hoy, Cyrus 1996. *The Laws of Candy*. In *The Dramatic Works in the Beaumont and Fletcher Canon*, ed. Fredson Bowers, 661–662. 10 vols. Cambridge: Cambridge University Press.

Hughes, Charles. 1903. *Shakespeare's Europe: Unpublished Chapters of Fynes Moryson's 'Itinerary'*. London: Sherrat & Hughes.

Hunt, Arnold. 2010. *The Art of Hearing: English Preachers and Their Audiences, 1590–1640*. Cambridge: Cambridge University Press.

Hutton, Ronald. 1996. *The Stations of the Sun: A History of the Ritual Year in Britain*. Oxford: Oxford University Press.

BIBLIOGRAPHY

Huxley, Aldous. 1941. *Grey Eminence: The Biography of Father Joseph, the Paradoxical Mystic Who Inspired the Power Politics of Cardinal Richelieu.* London: Chatto & Windus.

Huygens, Lodewijck. 1982. *The English Journal 1651–1652,* ed. and trans. A. G. H. Bachrach and R. G. Collmer. Leiden: Brill / Leiden University Press.

Hyman, Wendy Beth, ed. 2011. *The Automaton in English Renaissance Literature.* Farnham, UK: Ashgate Press.

Hýzrle z Chodů Jindřich. 1979. *Příběhy Jindřicha Hýzrla z Chodů* [The Stories of Jindřich Hýzrle of the Chods]. Praha: Odeon.

Ingegneri, Angelo. 1989. *Della poesia rappresentativa e del modo di rappresentare le favole sceniche,* ed. Maria Luisa Doglio. Modena: Edizioni Panini.

Ingram, Martin. 1988. 'Ridings, Rough Music and Mocking Rhymes in Early Modern England'. In *Popular Culture in Early Modern England,* ed. Barry Reay, 166–97. London: Routledge.

Ingram, William. 1992. *The Business of Playing: The Beginnings of the Adult Professional Theater in London.* Ithaca, NY: Cornell University Press.

Ingram, William. 1999. 'The Economics of Playing'. In *A Companion to Shakespeare,* ed. David Scott Kastan, 313–27. Oxford: Blackwell.

Jones, Ann Rosalind, and Peter Stallybrass. 2001. *Renaissance Clothing and the Materials of Memory.* Cambridge: Cambridge University Press.

Jones, Gwilym. 2013. 'Storm Effects in Shakespeare'. In *Shakespeare's Theatres and the Effects of Performance,* ed. Farah Karim-Cooper and Tiffany Stern, 33–50. Arden Shakespeare Library. London: Bloomsbury.

Jonson, Ben. 1623. 'To the Memory of My Beloved the AUTHOR, Mr. William Shakespeare'. In *Mr. William Shakespeare's Comedies, Histories, & Tragedies.* London.

Jonson, Ben. 1925–53. *Works,* ed. C. H. Herford and Percy and Evelyn Simpson. 11 vols. Oxford: Clarendon Press.

Jonson, Ben. 1969. *The Complete Masques,* ed. Stephen Orgel. New Haven, CT: Yale University Press.

Jordan, Peter. 2014. *The Venetian Origins of the Commedia dell'Arte.* London: Routledge.

Jowett, John, ed. 2011. *Sir Thomas More.* Arden Shakespeare. London: Methuen.

Kallendorf, Hilaire. 2007. *Conscience on Stage: the Comedia as Casuistry in Early Modern Spain.* Toronto: University of Toronto Press.

Kathman, David. 2004. 'Grocer, Goldsmiths, and Drapers: Freemen and Apprentices in the Elizabethan Theater'. *Shakespeare Quarterly* 55: 1–49.

Katritzky, M. A. 1998. 'Was *Commedia dell'Arte* Performed by Mountebanks? *Album amicorum* Illustrations and Thomas Platter's Description of 1598'. *Theatre Research International* 23 (2): 104–126.

Katritzky, M. A. 2005a. 'Pickelhering and Hamlet in Dutch Art: The English Comedians of Robert Browne, John Green, and Robert Reynolds'. In *Shakespeare and the Low Countries,* ed. Ton Hoenselaars and Holger Klein, 113–140. Lewiston: Edwin Mellen Press.

Katritzky, M. A. 2005b. 'Reading the Actress in Commedia Imagery'. In *Women Players in England, 1500–1660: Beyond the All-Male Stage,* ed. Pamela Allen Brown and Peter Parolin, 109–143. Aldershot: Ashgate Press.

Katritzky, M. A. 2006. *The Art of Commedia: A Study in the* Commedia dell'Arte *1560–1620 with Special Reference to the Visual Records.* Amsterdam / New York: Rodopi.

Katritzky, M. A. 2007. *Women, Medicine and Theatre, 1500–1750: Literary Mountebanks and Performing Quacks*. Aldershot: Ashgate Press.

Katritzky, M. A. 2008. 'English Troupes in Early Modern Germany: The Women'. In *Transnational Exchange in Early Modern Theater*. ed. Robert Henke and Eric Nicholson, 35–46. Aldershot: Ashgate Press.

Katritzky, M. A. 2012. *Healing, Performance, and Ceremony in the Writings of Three Early Modern Physicians: Hippolytus Guarinonius and the Brothers Felix and Thomas Platter*. Burlington, VT: Ashgate Press.

Katritzky, M. A. 2016. 'The Theatrical Impact of St. Francis Xavier's Canonization: Pietro Della Valle's Account of the 1624 Jesuit Festivities in Goa'. *Ludica: Annali di storia e civiltà del gioco* 19–20: 24–38.

Kennedy, Dennis. 2009. *The Spectator and the Spectacle: Audiences in Modernity and Postmodernity*. Cambridge: Cambridge University Press.

Kernodle, George Riley. 1937. 'Perspective in the Renaissance Theater'. Unpublished PhD Thesis. Yale University.

Kernodle, George Riley. 1944. *From Art to Theatre: Form and Convention in the Renaissance*. Chicago, IL: University of Chicago Press.

Kerr, Rosalind. 2015. *The Rise of the Diva on the Sixteenth-Century Commedia dell'Arte Stage*. Toronto: University of Toronto Press.

Kindermann, Heinz. 1957–74. *Theatergeschichtes Europas*. 10 vols. Salzburg: O. Müller.

Klapisch-Zuber, Christiane. 1981. 'La "Mattinata" medievale d'Italie'. In *Le Charivari*, ed. Jacques Le Goff and Jean-Claude Schmitt, 149–164. Paris: L'École des hautes études.

Korda, Natasha. 2011. *Labors Lost: Women's Work and the Early Modern English Stage*. Philadelphia: University of Pennsylvania Press.

Kumpera, Jan. 1992. *Jan Amos Komenský, poutník na rozhraní věků, Jan Amos Comenius, a Pilgrim on the Borders of Ages*. Ostrava: Amosium Servis.

Lancashire, Anne. 2009. *London Civic Theatre: City Drama and Pageantry from Roman Times to 1558*. Cambridge: Cambridge University Press.

Laqueur, Thomas. 1992. *Making Sex: Body and Gender from the Greeks to Freud*. Cambridge, MA: Harvard University Press.

Laughran, Michelle, and Andrea Vianello. 2011. '"Grandissima Gratia": The Power of Italian Renaissance Shoes as Intimate Wear'. In *Ornamentalism*, ed. Bella Mirabella, 253–289. Ann Arbor, MI: University of Michigan Press.

Lavin, Irving. 1980. *Bernini and the Unity of the Visual Arts*. 2 vols. Oxford: Oxford University Press.

Lawrenson, T. E. 1986. *The French Stage & Playhouse in the XVIIth Century: A Study in the Advent of the Italian Order*. 2nd edn. New York: AMS Press.

Le Goff, Jacques, and Jean-Claude Schmitt, eds. 1981. *Le Charivari*. Paris: L'École des hautes études.

Le Roy Ladurie, Emmanuel. 1980. *Carnival in Romans,* trans. Mary Feeney. New York: Braziller.

Lea, Kathleen Marguerite. 1934. *Italian Popular Comedy: A Study in the Commedia dell'Arte, 1560–1620*. 2 vols. Oxford: Clarendon.

Lenton, Francis. 1631. *Characterisimi*. London.

Lescarbot, Marc. 2006. *Spectacle of Empire: Marc Lescarbot's Theatre of Neptune in New France, 400th Anniversary Edition*, ed. Jerry Wasserman. Vancouver: Talonbooks.

Limon, Jerzy. 1985. *Gentlemen of a Company: English Players in Central and Eastern Europe, 1590–1660*. Cambridge: Cambridge University Press.

Lin, Erika T. 2012. *Shakespeare and the Materiality of Performance*. New York: Palgrave Macmillan.

Lindberg, David C. 1976. *Theories of Vision from Al-Kindi to Kepler*. Chicago, IL: University of Chicago Press.

Lohse, Rolf. 2015. 'Gian Giorgio Trissino, *Sophonisba*'. In *Italienisches Theater: Geschichte und Gattungen von 1480 bis 1890*, ed. Daniel Winkler, Sabine Schrader and Gerhild Fuchs, 53–68. Berlin: Theater der Zeit.

Lovejoy, A. O. 1970. *The Great Chain of Being: A Study of the History of an Idea*. Cambridge, MA: Harvard University Press.

Luca, Antonio de. 1981. *Il Teatro Di Ludovico Ariosto*. Vol. 37. N.p.: Bulzoni. Biblioteca Teatrale.

Machiavelli, Niccolò. 1993. *The Prince*. Ware, UK: Wordsworth.

Machielsen, Jan. 2015. *Martin Delrio: Demonology and Scholarship in the Counter-Reformation*. Oxford: Oxford University Press.

MacLean, Sally-Beth, and Scott McMillin. 1998. *The Queen's Men and Their Plays*. Cambridge: Cambridge University Press.

MacNeil, Anne. 2003. *Music and Women of the Commedia dell'Arte*. Oxford: Oxford University Press.

Malherbe, François de. 1862–69. 'Lettres a Peiresc'. In *Oeuvres*, ed. M. L. Lalanne. Paris: Hachette.

Mamczarz, Irene. 1988. *Le Théâtre Farnese de Parme et le drame musical italien (1618–1732)*. Florence: Leo S. Olschki Editore.

Mamone, Sara. 1981. *Il teatro nella Firenze medicea*. Milan: Gruppo Ugo Mursia Editore.

Mancing, Howard, ed. 2004. *The Cervantes Encyclopedia: L–Z*. Westport, CT: Greenwood.

Marks, Jonathan. 1998. 'The charlatans of the Pont-Neuf'. *Theatre Research International* 23: 133–141.

Marlow, Christopher. 2013. *Performing Masculinity in English University Drama, 1598–1636*. Farnham, UK: Ashgate Press.

Marotti, Ferruccio. 1974. *Storia documentaria del teatro italiano: lo spettacolo dall'Umanesimo al Manierismo: Teoria e tecnica*. Milano: Feltrinelli.

Marotti, Ferruccio and Giovanna Romei, eds. 1994. *La Commedia dell'Arte e la società barocca: La professione del teatro*. Rome: Bulzoni.

Matthews-Grieco, Sara F., ed. 2014. *Cuckoldry, Impotence and Adultery in Europe (15th–17th Century)*. Farnham, UK: Ashgate Press.

Mayor, A. Hyatt. 1945. *The Bibiena Family*. New York: H. Bittner and Company.

McCabe, William H. 1983. *An Introduction to the Jesuit Theater*, ed. Louis J. Oldani, S. J. St Louis: Institute of Jesuit Sources.

McConachie, Bruce A., Tobin Nellhaus, Carol Fisher Sorgenfrei, and Tamara L. Underiner. 2016. *Theatre Histories: An Introduction*. 3rd edn. London: Routledge.

McKendrick, Melveena. 1989. *Theatre in Spain, 1490–1700*. Cambridge: Cambridge University Press.

McManus, Clare. 2002. *Women on the Renaissance Stage: Anna of Denmark and Female Masquing in the Stuart Court (1590–1619)*. Manchester: Manchester University Press.

McManus, Clare, ed. 2012. *The Island Princess*. Arden Early Modern Drama. London: Methuen.

McNeill, William H. 1974. *The Shape of European History*. New York: Oxford University Press.

Melton, John. 1620. *The Astrologaster, or, the Figure-Caster.* London.

Meredith, Peter, and John E. Tailby, eds. 1983. *The Staging of Religious Drama in Europe in the Later Middle Ages: Texts and Documents in English Translation.* Kalamazoo, MI: Medieval Institute Publications.

Milesi, Francesco. 2000. *Giacomo Torelli: L'invenzione scenica nell'Europa barocca.* Fano: Fondazione Cassa di Risparmio di Fano.

Mills, David. 1998. *Recycling the Cycle: The City of Chester and Its Whitsun Plays.* Toronto: University of Toronto Press.

Monroe, Will S. 1900. *Comenius and the Beginnings of Educational Reform.* New York: Charles Scribner's Sons.

Montaigne, Michel de. 1957. 'On the Education of Children'. In *The Complete Essays,* trans. Donald Frame, 1.25. Palo Alto: Stanford University Press.

Montanari, Tomaso. 2004. 'Una nuova fonte per il teatro di Bernini'. In *Estetica Barocca,* ed. Sebastian Schütze, 301–320. Rome: Campisano Editore.

Montrose, Louis Adrian. 1996. *The Purpose of Playing: Shakespeare and the Cultural Politics of Elizabethan Theatre.* Chicago, IL: University of Chicago Press.

Morton, Thomas. 1637. *New English Canaan, or New Canaan Containing an Abstract of New England . . . .* London.

Moryson, Fynes. 1907–8. *An Itinerary Containing His Ten Yeeres Travell.* Glasgow: James MacLehose & Sons.

Moryson, Fynes. 1967. *Shakespeare's Europe: A Survey of the Condition of Europe at the End of the 16th Century: Being Unpublished Chapters of Fynes Moryson's Itinerary (1617),* ed. Charles Hughes. 2nd edn. New York: Benjamin Blom.

Muggli, Mark. 1992. 'Ben Jonson and the Business of News'. *Studies in English Literature, 1500–1900* 32 (2): 323–340.

Muir, Edward. 2007. 'The Eye of the Procession: Ritual Ways of Seeing in the Renaissance'. In *Ceremonial Culture in Pre-Modern Europe,* ed. Nicholas Howe, 129–153. Notre Dame, IN: University of Notre Dame Press.

Mullaney, Steven. 1988. *The Place of the Stage. License, Play and Power in Renaissance England.* Chicago, IL: University of Chicago Press.

Mumford, Lewis. 1961. *The City in History.* New York: Harcourt, Brace & World.

Nagler, Alois Maria. 1964. *Theatre Festivals of the Medici 1539–1637.* New Haven, CT: Yale University Press.

Nashe, Thomas. 1972. *The Unfortunate Traveller and Other Works,* ed. J. B. Steane. Harmondsworth: Penguin Books.

Neill, Michael, ed. 2010. *The Renegado,* by Philip Massinger. Arden Early Modern Drama. London: Methuen.

Nelson, Alan. 1994. *Early Cambridge Theatres: University and Town Stages 1464–1720.* Cambridge: Cambridge University Press.

Nelson, Alan. 2009. 'The Universities and the Inns of Court'. In *The Oxford Handbook of Early Modern Theatre,* ed. Richard Dutton, 280–291. Oxford: Oxford University Press.

Newman, Karen. 1991. *Fashioning Femininity and English Renaissance Drama.* Chicago, IL: University of Chicago Press.

Newman, Karen. 2007. *Cultural Capitals: Early Modern London and Paris.* Princeton, NJ: Princeton University Press.

Nicoll, Allardyce. 1966. *The Development of the Theatre.* 5th edn. London: George G. Harrap & Company.

Niefanger, Dirk. 2012. 'Barock'. In *Handbuch Drama: Theorie, Analyse, Geschichte,* ed. Peter W. Marx, 230–243. Stuttgart: Metzler.

BIBLIOGRAPHY

Ogilby, John. 1671. *America: being the latest, and most accurate description of the New World* . . . . London.

Ojeda Calvo, María del Valle. 2007. *Stefanelo Botarga e Zan Ganassa. Scenari e zibaldoni di comici italiani nella Spagna del Cinquecento*. Roma: Bulzoni.

Okoń, Jan. 1970. *Dramat i teatr szkolny* [School Drama and Theatre], 190. Wrocław: Universytet Jagielloński.

Orgel, Stephen. 1971. '*Florimène* and the Ante-Masques'. *Renaissance Drama* 4: 135–153.

Orgel, Stephen. 1975. *The Illusion of Power: Political Theatre in the English Renaissance*. Berkeley, CA: University of California Press.

Orgel, Stephen. 1996. *Impersonations: The Performance of Gender in Shakespeare's England*. Cambridge: Cambridge University Press.

Orgel, Stephen, and Roy Strong. 1973. *Inigo Jones: The Theatre of the Stuart Court*. 2 vols. Berkeley, CA: University of California Press.

Ortolani, Benito. 1995. *The Japanese Theatre from Shamanistic Ritual to Contemporary Pluralism*. Princeton, NJ: Princeton University Press.

Ottonelli, Giovan Domenico. 1655. *Della Christiana Moderatione del Theatro*. 6 vols. Florence.

Pallen, Thomas A. 1999. *Vasari on the Theatre*. Carbondale, IL: Southern Illinois University Press.

Parente, James A. 1984. 'Andreas Gryphius and Jesuit Theater'. *Daphnis* 13: 525–551.

Parente, James A. 1987. *Religious Drama and the Humanist Tradition: Christian Theater in Germany and in the Netherlands 1500–1680*. Leiden: Brill.

Park, Katharine. 2006. *Secrets of Women: Gender, Generation, and the Origins of Human Dissection*. New York: Zone Books.

Parolin, Peter, ed. 2012. 'Access and Contestation: Women's Performance in Early Modern England, Italy, France, and Spain'. Special issue of *Early Theatre* 15 (1).

Parr, Anthony. 1995. 'Introduction'. In *Three Renaissance Travel Plays*, ed. Anthony Parr, 18. Manchester: Manchester University Press.

Parr, Anthony. 2004. 'Wilkins, George (d. 1618)'. *Oxford Dictionary of National Biography*. Oxford University Press.

Paster, Gail Kern. 2004. *Humoring the Body: Emotions and the Shakespearean Stage*. Chicago, IL: University of Chicago Press.

Peters, Julie Stone. 2003. *The Theatre of the Book 1480–1880: Print, Text and Authority in Europe*. Oxford: Oxford University Press.

Petit de Julleville, Louis. 1886. *Répertoire du théatre comique en France au Moyen-Age*. Paris: Cerf.

Petrarca, Francesco. 1999. *De vita solitaria / La vie solitaire. Édition bilingue latin-français*, trans. Christophe Carraud. Grenoble: Editions Jérôme Millon.

Petrarca, Francesco. 2006. *Petrarch's Ascent of Mount Ventoux: The Familiaris IV, I*, ed. Rodney Lokaj. Roma: Edizioni dell'Ateneo.

Pettegree, Andrew. 2005. *Reformation and the Culture of Persuasion*. Cambridge: Cambridge University Press.

Pfahl, Julia. 2012. 'Französische Klassik'. In *Handbuch Drama: Theorie, Analyse, Geschichte*, ed. Peter W. Marx, 244–250. Stuttgart: Metzler.

Phelan, Peggy. 1993. *Unmarked: The Politics of Performance*. New York and Abingdon: Routledge.

Pico della Mirandola, Giovanni. 1997. *Oratio de hominis dignitate / Rede über die Würde des Menschen: Lateinisch / Deutsch*, hrsg. und übersetzt von Gerd von der Gönna. Stuttgart: Philipp Reclam.

Picot, Emile, and Christophe Nyrop, eds. 1880. *Nouveau recueil de farces françaises des XVe et XVIe siècles*. Paris: Morgand et Fatout.

Pirrotta, Nino, and Elena Povoledo. 1982. *Music and Theatre from Poliziano to Monteverdi*. Cambridge: Cambridge University Press.

Platter, Felix, and Thomas. 1892. *Félix et Thomas Platter à Montpellier*. Montpellier: Société des Bibliophiles de Montpellier.

Platter, Thomas. 1968. *Beschreibung der Reisen durch Frankreich, Spanien, England und die Niederlande 1595–1600*, hrsg. von Rut Keiser. Basel: Schwabe.

Podlaha, Antonín. 1901. 'Ein deutsches Theaterspiel aus dem Jahre 1662'. In *Věstník Královské společnosti nauk*.

Pollux, Julius. 1775. *Extracts concerning the Greek theatre and masks, translated from the Greek of Julius Pollux*. London.

Pörtl, Klaus. 1985. *Das spanische Theater. Von den Anfängen bis zum Ausgang des 19. Jahrhunderts*. Darmstadt: Wiss. Buchgesellschaft.

Powell, John. S. 2000. *Music and Theatre in France, 1600–1680*. Oxford: Oxford University Press.

Prisciani, Pellegrino. 1992. *Spectacula*, a cura di Danilo Aguzzi Barbagli. Modena: Franco Cosimo Panini.

Prynne, William. 1633. *Histrio-mastix*. London.

Ravelhofer, Barbara. 2002. '"Beasts of Recreacion": Henslowe's White Bears'. *English Literary Renaissance* 32 (2) (March): 287–323.

Rayner, Alice. 2006. *Ghosts: Death's Double and the Phenomena of Theatre*. Minneapolis, MN: University of Minnesota Press.

Reyff, Simone de. 1998. *L'église et le théâtre: L'exemple de la France au XVIIe siècle*. Paris: Les éditions du cerf.

Richards, Kenneth, and Laura Richards. 1990. *The Commedia dell'arte: A Documentary History*. Oxford: The Shakespeare Head Press.

Richter, Virginia. 2012. 'Frühe Neuzeit – das englische Drama'. In *Handbuch Drama: Theorie, Analyse, Geschichte*, ed. Peter W. Marx, 215–223. Stuttgart: Metzler.

Rigal, Eugène. 1901. *Le théâtre français avant la période classique*. Paris: Hachette.

Riggs, David. 1975. 'The Artificial Day and the Infinite Universe'. *Journal of Medieval and Renaissance Studies* 5: 155–185.

Rinuccini, Pierfrancesco. 1983. *Il corago: o vero alcune osservazioni per metter bene in scena le composizioni dramatiche*, ed. Paolo Frabbri and Angelo Pompilio. Florence: Leo S. Olschki Editore.

Rioux, Jean-Pierre, and Jean-François Sirinelli. 1997. *Pour une histoire culturelle*. *Editions du Seuil*.

Ripa, Cesare. 1765. *Iconologia*. Perugia.

Roberts, Peter. 1994. 'Elizabethan Players and Minstrels and the Legislation of 1572 Against Retainers and Vagabonds'. In *Religion, Culture and Society in Early Modern Britain: Essays in Honour of Patrick Collinson,* ed. Anthony Fletcher and Peter Roberts, 29–55. Cambridge: Cambridge University Press.

Ronconi, Luca, Marzio dall'Acqua, Pompeo de Angelis, and Claudio Gallico. 1992. *Lo spettacolo e la meraviglia: Il Teatro Farnese di Parma*. Turin: Nuova Eri.

Rubidge, Bradley. 1998. 'Catharsis Through Admiration: Corneille, Le Moyne, and the Social Uses of Emotion'. *Modern Philology* 95 (3): 316–333.

Rubin, Miri. 1991. *Corpus Christi: The Eucharist in Late Medieval Culture*. Cambridge: Cambridge University Press.

Rudin, Bärbel. 1976. 'Das fahrende Volk. Puppenspiel als Metier: Nachrichten und Kommentare aus dem 17. und 18. Jahrhundert'. *Kölner Geschichtsjournal* 1: 2–11.

BIBLIOGRAPHY

Rudin, Bärbel. 1980. 'Fräulein Dorothea und der Blaue Montag'. In *Elemente der Literatur: Beiträge zur Stoff-, Motiv- und Themenforschung*, ed. A. J. Bisanz and Raymond Trousson, 95–113. Vol. 1. Stuttgart: Alfred Kröner.

Ruffini, Franco. 1983. *Teatri prima del teatro: Visioni dell'edifico e della scena tra Umanesimo e Rinascimento*. Roma: Bulzoni.

Ruggiero, Guido. 2006. 'Who's Afraid of Giulia Napolitana? Pleasure, Fear, and Imagining the Arts of the Renaissance Courtesan'. In *The Courtesan's Arts: Cross-Cultural Perspectives*, ed. Martha Feldman and Bonnie Gordon, 280–292. Oxford: Oxford University Press.

Saslow, James. 1996. *The Medici Wedding of 1589: Florentine Festival as Theatrum Mundi*. New Haven, CT: Yale University Press.

Sawday, Jonathan. 1996. *The Body Emblazoned: Dissection and the Human Body in Renaissance Culture*. London: Routledge.

Scala, Flaminio. 2008. *The Commedia dell'Arte of Flaminio Scala: A Translation and Analysis of 30 Scenarios*, ed. and trans. Richard Andrews. Lanham, MD: Scarecrow Press.

Scherl, Adolf, and Bärbel Rudin. 2014. 'Joseph Anton Stranitzky'. In *Theater in Böhmen, Mähren und Schlesien. Von den Anfängen bis zum Ausgang des 18. Jahrhunderts. Ein Lexikon*, ed. Alena Jakubcová and Matthias J. Pernerstorfer, 666–670. Prague: IDU and Verlag der ÖAW.

Schindler, Otto G. 2001. '"Englischer Pickelhering—gen Prag jubilierend." Englische Komödianten als Wegbreiter des deutschen Theaters in Prag'. In *Deutschsprachiges Theater in Prag: Begegnungen der Sprachen und Kulturen*, ed. Alena Jakubcová, Jitka Ludvová, and Václav Maidl. Prague: Divadelni ústav.

Schlueter, June. 2012. 'Samuel Daniel in Italy: New Documentary Evidence'. *Huntington Library Quarterly* 75 (2): 283–290.

Schnarr, Hermann. 2002. 'Frühe Beziehungen des Nikolaus von Kues zu italienischen Humanisten'. In *Nicolaus Cusanus zwischen Deutschland und Italien*, hrsg. von Martin Thurner, 187–213. Berlin: Akademie Verlag.

Schnitzler, Henry. 1952. 'The Jesuit Contribution to the Theater'. *Educational Theatre Journal* 4: 283–292.

Schrickx, Willem. 1986. *Foreign Envoys and Travelling Players in the Age of Shakespeare and Jonson*. Wetteren: Universa.

Scott, Virginia. 2000. *Molière: A Theatrical Life*. Cambridge: Cambridge University Press.

Scott, Virginia. 2010. *Women on the Stage in Early Modern France, 1540–1750*. Cambridge: Cambridge University Press.

Scribner, R. W. 2001. 'Perceptions of the Sacred in Germany at the End of the Middle Ages'. In *Religion and Culture in Germany (1400–1800)*, ed. Lyndal Roper, 85–103. Leiden: Brill.

Searles, Colbert. 1916. 'Les Sentiments de L'Académie Francaise sur Le Cid'. *The University of Minnesota Studies in Language and Literature* 3: 1–112.

Shakespeare, William. 1982. *The Tempest / Der Sturm. Englisch / Deutsch*. Übersetzt und hrsg. von Gerd Stratmann. Stuttgart: Philipp Reclam.

Shapiro, Michael. 1977. *Children of the Revels: The Boy Companies of Shakespeare's Time and their Plays*. New York: Columbia University Press.

Shapiro, Michael. 2009. 'Early (Pre-1590) Boy Companies and their Acting Venues'. In *The Oxford Handbook of Early Modern Theatre*, ed. Richard Dutton, 120–135. Oxford: Oxford University Press.

Shergold, N.D. 1967. *A History of the Spanish Stage: From Medieval Times Until the End of the Seventeenth Century*. Oxford: Clarendon.

Shewring, Margaret, ed. 2013. *European Festival Studies: 1450–1700: Waterborne Pageants and Festivities in the Renaissance: Essays in Honour of J. R. Mulryne.* Aldershot: Ashgate Press.

Simon, Eckehard. 2008. 'German Medieval Theatre: Tenth Century to 1600'. In *A History of German Theatre*, ed. Simon Williams and Maik Hamburger, 8–37. Cambridge: Cambridge University Press.

Simons, Joseph. 1989. *Jesuit Theater Englished: Five Tragedies of Joseph Simons*, trans. Richard E. Arnold; ed. Louis J. Oldani and Philip C. Fischer. St Louis, MO: Institute of Jesuit Sources.

Sisson, C. J. 1936. *Lost Plays of Shakespeare's Age.* Cambridge: Cambridge University Press.

Smith, Bruce R. 1988. *Ancient Scripts and Modern Experience on the English Stage, 1500–1700.* Princeton, NJ: Princeton University Press.

Smith, Bruce R. 1999. *The Acoustic World of Early Modern England: Attending to the O-Factor.* Chicago, IL: University of Chicago Press.

Smuts, R. Malcolm. 1989. 'Public Ceremony and Royal Charisma: The English Royal Entry in London, 1485–1642'. In *The First Modern Society: Essays in English History in Honour of Lawrence Stone,* ed. A. L. Beier, David Cannadine and James M. Rosenheim, 65–94. Cambridge: Cambridge University Press.

Smuts, R. Malcolm. 2007. 'Introduction' to 'The Whole Royal and Magnificent Entertainment'. In *Thomas Middleton: The Complete Works*, ed. Gary Taylor and MacDonald P. Jackson, 219–223. Oxford: Oxford University Press.

Southern, Richard. 1973. *The Staging of Plays Before Shakespeare.* New York: Theatre Arts.

Spelman, Henry. 1613. 'Relation of Virginia'. In *Travels and Works of Captain John Smith,* ed. Edward Arber. 2 vols. Edinburgh: Grant, 1910.

Spohr, Arne. 2009. *'How chances it they travel?': Englische Musiker in Dänemark und Norddeutschland 1579–1630.* Wiesbaden: Harrassowitz Verlag.

Stackelberg, Jürgen von. 1996. *Die französische Klassik.* München: Fink.

Stallybrass, Peter. 1992. 'Transvestism and the "Body Beneath": Speculating on the Boy Actor'. In *Erotic Politics: Desire on the Renaissance Stage,* ed. Susan Zimmerman, 64–83. London / New York: Routledge.

Stammler, Wolfgang. 1967. 'Die Wurzeln des Meistergesangs'. In *Der Deutsche Meistersang,* ed. Bert Nagel, 10–42. Darmstadt: Wissenschaftliche Buchgesellschaft.

Štědroň, Petr. 2002. 'Bemerkungen zum "Büchlein" von Ondřej Klatovský'. *SPFFBU* R.7: 171–189.

Steggle, Matthew. 2015. *Digital Humanities and the Lost Drama of Early Modern England: Ten Case Studies.* Oxford: Routledge.

Stern, Tiffany. 2000. *Rehearsal from Shakespeare to Sheridan.* New York: Oxford University Press.

Stern, Tiffany. 2006. '"On Each Wall and Corner Poast": Playbills, Title-Pages, and Advertising in Early Modern London'. *English Literary Renaissance* 36 (1): 57–89.

Stern, Tiffany. 2009. 'Actors' Parts'. In *The Oxford Handbook of Early Modern Theatre*, ed. Richard Dutton, 496–512. Oxford: Oxford University Press.

Stern, Tiffany. 2013. '"This Wide and Universal Theatre": The Theatre as Prop in Shakespeare's Metadrama'. In *Shakespeare's Theatres and the Effects of Performance*, ed. Farah Karim-Cooper and Tiffany Stern, 11–32. Arden Shakespeare Library. London: Bloomsbury.

Storey, Robert F. 1978. *Pierrot: A Critical History of a Mask.* Princeton, NJ: Princeton University Press.

BIBLIOGRAPHY

Strong, Roy. 1984. *Art and Power: Renaissance Festivals, 1450–1650*. Berkeley, CA: University of California Press.

Struna, Nancy L. 1996. *People of Prowess: Sport, Leisure, and Labor in Early Anglo-America*. Urbana, IL: University of Illinois Press.

Stubbes, Philip. 1583. *The anatomie of abuses contayning a discouerie, or briefe summarie of such notable vices and imperfections . . . .* London.

Szarota, Elida Maria. 1967. *Künstler, Grübler, Rebellen: Studien zum europäischen Märtyrerdrama des 17. Jahrhunderts*. Bern: Francke.

Szönyi, György E. 1989. 'Eastern Europe'. In *A Companion to the Medieval Theatre*, ed. Ronald W. Vince, 99–108. New York: Greenwood Press.

Tallemant des Réaux, Gédéon. 1834–1835. *Les Historiettes de Tallemant des Réaux: mémoires pour servir à l'histoire du XVIIe siècle*. Paris.

Tamburini, Elena. 2012. *Gian Lorenzo Bernini e il teatro dell'arte*. Florence: Le Lettere.

Taviani, Ferdinando. 1969. *La Commedia dell'Arte e la società barocca: La fascinazione del teatro*. Roma: Bulzoni.

Taviani, Ferdinando, and Mirella Schino. 1982. *Il segreto della commedia dell'arte*. Florence: La Casa Usher.

Taylor, Charles. 2007. *A Secular Age*. Cambridge, MA: Belknap Press.

Taylor, Diana. 2003. *The Archive and the Repertoire: Performing Cultural Memory in the Americas*. Durham, NC: Duke University Press.

Taylor, John. 1614. *The True Cause of the Water-Men's Suit Concerning Players*. In *Early Prose and Poetical Works*, 201–212. London: Hamilton, Adams, and Co., 1888.

Taylor, John. 1630. *All the Workes of John Taylor the Water-Poet*. London: Taylor.

Teague, Frances. 2009. 'The Phoenix and the Cockpit-in-the-Court'. In *The Oxford Handbook of Early Modern Theatre*, ed. Richard Dutton, 240–259. Oxford: Oxford University Press.

Teresa of Avila, St. 1988. *The Life of Saint Teresa of Avila by Herself*, trans. J. M. Cohen. Harmondsworth: Penguin Books.

Thomas, Keith. 1971. *Religion and the Decline of Magic: Studies in Popular Beliefs in Sixteenth- and Seventeenth-Century England*. London: Weidenfeld and Nicolson.

Thompson, Peter E. 2009. *The Outrageous Juan Rana Entremeses: A Bilingual and Annotated Selection of Plays Written for This Spanish Golden Age Gracioso*. Toronto: University of Toronto Press.

Thomson, Peter. 1997. 'The True Physiognomy of a Man: Richard Tarlton and his Legend'. *Parergon* 14: 29–50.

Tigner, Amy L. 2012. 'The Spanish Actress's Art: Improvisation, Transvestism, and Disruption in Tirso's *El vergonzoso en palacio*'. *Early Theatre* 15 (1): 169–192.

Traub, Valerie. 2002. *The Renaissance of Lesbianism in Early Modern England*. Cambridge: Cambridge University Press.

Trollope, Henry M. 1905. *The Life of Molière*. London: Archibald Constable.

Turner, Henry S. 2016. *The Corporate Commonwealth: Pluralism and Political Fictions in England, 1516–1651*. Chicago, IL: University of Chicago Press.

Tylus, Jane. 2012. 'The Work of Italian Theater'. *Renaissance Drama* 40: 171–184.

Valentin, Jean-Marie. 2001. *Les jésuites et le théâtre (1554–1680)*. Paris: Éditions Desjanquères.

Valerini, Adriano. *c.* 1570. *Oratione d'Adriano Valerini Veronese, In morte della Divina Signora Vincenza Armani, Comica Eccellentissima*. Rpt. in *La commedia dell'arte e la società barocca: la professione del teatro*, ed. Ferruccio Marotti and Giovanna Romei, 27–41. Rome: Bulzoni, 1991.

Vega Carpio, Lope Félix de. 1914. *The New Art of Writing Plays*, trans. William T. Brewster. New York: Dramatic Museum of Columbia University.

Veltrusky, Jarmila F. 1985. *A Sacred Farce from Medieval Bohemia: Mastičkář*. Ann Arbor, MI: University of Michigan Press.

Victor, Benjamin. 2014. 'The Transmission of Terence'. In *The Oxford Handbook of Greek and Roman Comedy*, ed. Michael Fontaine and Adele C. Scafuro, 699–716. Oxford: Oxford University Press.

Vitkus, Daniel. 2003. *Turning Turk: English Theater and the Multicultural Mediterranean, 1570–1630*. London: Palgrave Macmillan.

Vitruvius. 1486. *Lucii Vitruvii Pollionis De Architectura Libri*, ed. Sulpizio da Veroli. Rome: Eucharius Silben.

Vitruvius. 1914. *The Ten Books on Architecture*, trans. Morris Hicky Morgan. Cambridge, MA: Harvard University Press.

Vitse, Marc. 2003. 'Teoría y géneros dramáticos en el siglo XVII'. In *Historia del teatro español. 1. De la edad media a los siglos de oro*, ed. Javier Huerta Calvo, 717–755. Madrid: Gredos.

Waite, Gary K. 2000. *Reformers on Stage: Popular Drama and Religious Propaganda in the Low Countries*. Toronto: University of Toronto Press.

Waith, Eugene M. 1952. *The Pattern of Tragicomedy in Beaumont and Fletcher*. New Haven, CT: Yale University Press.

Walker, C. E. 1931. 'The History of the Joint-Stock Company'. *Accounting Review* 6 (2): 97–105.

Walz, John A. 1927. 'Fynes Morrison and the Tomb of Till Eulenspiegel'. *Modern Language Notes* 42 (7): 465–466.

Weaver, Elissa. 2002. *Convent Theatre in Early Modern Italy: Spiritual Fun and Learning for Women*. Cambridge: Cambridge University Press.

Webster, John. 1960. *The White Devil*, ed. John Russell Brown. Manchester: Manchester University Press.

Weigert, Laura. 2013. 'Stage'. In *Early Modern Theatricality*, ed. Henry S. Turner, 24–46. Oxford: Oxford University Press.

Weil, M. S. 1974. 'The Devotion of the Forty Hours and Roman Baroque Illusions'. *Journal of the Warburg and Courtauld Institutes* 38: 218–248.

Weimann, Robert. 1996. *Authority and Representation in Early Modern Discourse*. Baltimore, MD: Johns Hopkins University Press.

Weinberg, Bernard. 1963. *A History of Literary Criticism in the Italian Renaissance*. 2 vols. Chicago, IL: University of Chicago Press.

Weiß, Wolfgang. 2000. 'Die dramatische Tradition'. In *Shakespeare-Handbuch: Die Zeit – Der Mensch – Das Werk – Die Nachwelt*, ed. Ina Schabert, 48–71. Stuttgart: Kröner.

Wells Slights, Camille. 1981. *The Casuistical Tradition in Shakespeare, Donne, Herbert, and Milton*. Princeton, NJ: Princeton University Press.

West, William. 2002. *Theatre and Encyclopedias in Early Modern Europe*. Cambridge: Cambridge University Press.

Wetmore, Kevin J., ed. 2010. *Catholic Theatre and Drama: Critical Essays*. Jefferson, NC: McFarland.

White, Paul Whitfield. 1993. *Theatre and Reformation: Protestantism, Patronage and Playing in Tudor England*. Cambridge: Cambridge University Press.

Whitney, Charles. 2006. *Early Responses to Renaissance Drama*. Cambridge: Cambridge University Press.

Wickham, Glynne. 1959. *Early English Stages, 1300–1660*. London: Routledge & Kegan Paul.

Wickham, Glynne, Herbert Berry, and William Ingram, eds. 2000. *English Professional Theatre, 1530–1660*. Cambridge: Cambridge University Press.

Wikland, Erik. 1962. *Elizabethan Players in Sweden 1591–92: Facts and Problems*, trans. Patrick Hort; trans. from the Latin by Carl Erik Holm. Stockholm: Almqvist & Wiksell.

Wiles, David. 2003. *A Short History of Western Performance Space*. Cambridge: Cambridge University Press.

Wiles, David. 2011. *Theatre and Citizenship: The History of Practice*. Cambridge: Cambridge University Press.

Wiley, W. L. 1972. *The Early Public Theatre in France*. Westport, CT: Greenwood Press.

Williams, Raymond. 1977. *Marxism and Literature*. Oxford: Oxford University Press.

Williams, Simon. 1990. *Shakespeare on the German Stage, Volume 1: 1586–1914*. Cambridge: Cambridge University Press.

Wilson, Catherine. 1995. *The Invisible World: Early Modern Philosophy and the Invention of the Microscope*. Princeton, NJ: Princeton University Press.

Wilson, Frank P. 1969. *The Oxford History of English Literature*. Oxford: Clarendon.

Winkler, Daniel. 2015. *Italienisches Theater. Geschichte und Gattungen von 1480 bis 1890*. Berlin: Theater der Zeit.

Wintroub, Michael. 1998. 'Civilizing the Savage and Making a King: The Royal Entry Festival of Henri II (Rouen, 1550)'. *Sixteenth Century Journal* 29 (2): 465–494.

Withington, Phil. 2005. *The Politics of Commonwealth. Citizens and Freemen in Early Modern England*. New York: Cambridge University Press.

Wofford, Susanne L. 2008. 'Foreign Emotions on the Stage of *Twelfth Night*'. In *Transnational Exchange*, eds. Robert Henke and Eric Nicholson, 141–158. Aldershot: Ashgate Press.

Wright, Elizabeth R. 2008. 'A Dramatic Diaspora: Spanish Theater and Mexican Interpretation'. In *Nahuatl Theater: Spanish Golden Age Drama in Mexican Translation*, ed. Barry D. Sell, Louise M. Burkhart and Elizabeth R. Wright, 3–25. Norman, OK: University of Oklahoma Press.

Yates, Frances A. 1967. 'English Actors in Paris During the Lifetime of Shakespeare'. In *Ideas and Ideals in the North European Renaissance*, 83–95. Oxford: Routledge.

Ybarra, Patricia. 2009. *Performing Conquest: Five Centuries of Theater, History, and Identity in Tlaxcala, Mexico*. Ann Arbor, MI: University of Michigan Press.

Zorzi, Elvira Garbero, and Mario Sperenzi, eds. 2001. *Teatro e spettacolo nella Firenze dei Medici: modelli dei luoghi teatrali*. Florence: Leo S. Olschki.

Zorzi, Ludovico. 1977. *Il teatro e la città: Saggi sulla scena italiana*. Turin: Giulio Einaudi Editore.

INDEX

Italics denote illustrations. All works are under the author's name.

Abbaye des Conards (Rouen) 21, *55*
absolutism 16–17
Académie Française 156–7, 183–4
academies 22, 81–4, 137
Accademia degli Intronati, Siena 65, 81,
    137, 153
Accademia Olimpica, Vicenza 22, 81, 116,
    137
Accademia Romana 115, 149
Accademici Pomponiani 165
Acosta, Jose de 45, 47
acrobats 40, 45, *46*, 47
acting techniques 120, 159
actresses 40, 41, 54, 61, 63
    See also individual actresses
Addison, Joseph 181
admiration 47, 48
adolescent actors 21–2, 65, 67, 82, 89,
    133–6
Aelius, Donatus, *Andria* 119, 168
Aeschylus
    Eumenides 172
    Prometheus Bound 172
Alberti, Leon Battista, *De re aedificatoria*
    114–15
Alberto, Jaime 63
Aleotti, Giovanni Battista 171–2, 180, *180*
Alexander VI, pope 111
Alleyn, Edward 30, 101, 133, 144–5, *193*

Alter, Jean 47
Alvarado, Pedro de 202
'A Man of Canada' (antimasque) 47–8
amateur performance societies 137
Americas 48, 200
amphitheatres 31, 148, 173, 178
Amsterdam 137, 138
Anderson, Perry 16
Andreini, Francesco 64, 100, 140, 197
Andreini, Giovan Battista (Giambattista)
    94, 140
Andreini, Isabella 65, 100, 140, 190, 197–8
    Rime 64
Anglicus, Bartholomeus, *De proprietatibus*
    rerum 129
animals, in performance 101
animal spirits 40
Annales school, French 10
Anne of Denmark, queen 54–5, 97, 202
antifeminism 58
antimasques 47, 54–5
antiquity culture 149–50
antitheatricalists 40, 60, 109–25, *114*
Anton, Robert, *Vices Anotimie* 60
Antwerp 100, 137
apprenticeships 30, 133, 135
Aquinas, Thomas, *Summa theologica* 120
architecture 77, 113–14
Arenal, Electa 66

246   INDEX

Aretino, Pietro, *Talanta* 167–8, 168–9, *169*
Ariosto, Ludovico 31–2, 75–6, 139, 167, 180
    I suppositi 75, 150
    La Cassaria 75, 76, 150, 167
    Orlando Furioso 150, 152, *193*
aristocratic courts 75–81, 95–6
    European 53
    patronage 22, 24, 29, 32, 98
Aristotle 47, 113, 172
    Poetics 119, 157, 168, 189
Arlecchino/Harlequin 13, *132*
Armani, Vincenza 41, 63–4
Arteaga, Stefano 181
Aubignac, Abbé d', *La Pratique du théâtre* 157
audience
    behaviour 36–41, 58, 60, 73, 74
    children in 130, 131
    community of production 143–4
    groups 47–8, 84, 85, 128
    participation 38–9, 83, 161, 162, 164, 201
    paying 66, 78, 85, 89, 139, 143, 153, 188
    performer and 48–9
    seating 81, 83, 86, 87
    size 60, 85, 87, 89, 150
Audley, Tobias 57–8
automata 98–9
autos sacramentales (Sacramental Performances)
    and the Americas 199
    background 20, 67
    Easter 136, 142
    staging techniques 165
    See also Corpus Christi, Feast of

Bakhtin, Mikhail 8, 11
Baldassare Peruzzi *167*
Baldracca, Florence 78
Bale, John 25
ballet, burlesque 55
Baltens, Peeter, *Een opvoering van de klucht* 56
Banqueting House, London 79, 81
Barbaro, Daniel 170
Barbieri, Niccolò, *La supplica* 120
Bargagli, Girolamo, *La Pellegrina* 79, 81

Baroque theatre 55, 97, 101, 102–4, 169
Basochiens 55–6, 134
Bastiano da San Gallo 168
Bathe, William of Ireland, *Janua linguarum* 103
Battista Guarini, Giovanni *see* Guarini, Giovanni Battista
Beaujoyeulx, Balthazar de, *Ballet comique de la Royne* 24, 54
Beaumont, Francis, *A King and No King* 154
Beccari, Agostino, *Il sacrificio* 151
beggars 4, 28, 36
Belando, Vincenzo 100
Bel Savage Inn, Ludgate Hill 87
Benedictine monks *200*
Benjamin, Walter 97
Bentley, Eric 38
Beolco, Angelo (Ruzante) 151
Berain, Jean *176–7*
Bergeron, David 43
Bernini, GianLorenzo 169–70
    Ecstasy of St. Teresa, The 51, 52
Bertelli, Pietro 60–1, *61–2*
Beza, Theodore, *Abraham sacrifiant* 131
Biancolelli, Domenico 13
Bibiena, Fernando 181
biblical interpretations 99, 114, *165*
Bidermann, Jakob, *Belisarius* 158
Bjurström, Per 172
Blackfriars theatres 31, 89, 97, 131
Bloch, Marc 10
Boaistuau, Pierre, *Théâtre du monde* 184
Boccaccio, Giovanni, *Decameron* 150, 152
Bodin, Jean, *Universae naturae theatrum* 184
Bodleian Library, Oxford 195
Bodley, Thomas 195
body, human 40–1, 52, 123–4
Borgia, Rodrigo 111
Bosse, Abraham *74*
Botarga, Stefanelo 122
bourgeoisie 21–3, 27, 78, 154
Bracciolini, Poggio 6, 148
Bradford, William 48
Bragetta, Ian 121
Braudel, Fernand 10–11
brothels 60, 78
Browne, Robert 27, 75, 95–6, 98
Brueghel the Elder, Pieter 21
Brunelleschi, Filippo 77, 161, *162*

INDEX

Bruni, Domenico 122
Bruscambille (Jean Gracieux) 122
Buchanan, George 82, 131
Buckingham, Duke of 43–4
building, theatre 71–91
Bull Inn, Ludgate Hill 87
Buontalenti, Bernardo 171, 180
Burbage, James 6, 71, 87, 89, 100, 146
Burckhardt, Jacob 1, 110, 198
   Reflections on History 9
Burke, Peter, *Popular Culture in Early*
    Modern Europe 11
burlesque ballet 55
Butler, Judith 49

Calderón, Pedro 21
   Constant Prince 156
   El Gran duque de Gandía 107
   El gran teatro del mundo 128, 155
   El medico de su honra 156
   La vida es sueno 134, 158
   No hay que creer ni en la verdad 107
Calle de la Cruz, Madrid 137
Calle del Principe, Madrid 137
Calliopius 117–18
Camelli, Antonio, *Pamphila & Philostrato*
   150
Camillo, Giulio, *Ideo del Teatro* 203
Canada 47, 201
capitalism 4, 16, 17, 56
   See also joint-stock companies
Carleton, Sir Dudley 202
Carlson, Marvin 77
carnivalesque 55, *123*, 184
carnival plays 78, 135
carnivals 19–20
Cassirer, Ernst 169
Castelvetro, Lodovico 119, 168, 172
Castiglione, Baldassare 76–7
   Book of the Courtier 53
Castillo, Susan 202
Castle of Perseverance (morality play)
   164–5, *166*
Castro, Guillén de
   La fuerza de la costumbre 102
   Las Mocedades del Cid 63
Catholicism
   arts patronage 164
   convent theatre 66
   false-belief 199

Piarist schools 104
post-Reformation 3
and Protestantism 109
rituals 41–3
See also autos sacramentales
   (Sacramental Performances)
cazuela (gallery) 37, 60
Cecchini, Pier Maria 4, 27, 100
Cellini, Benvenuto 4
ceremonial occasions 53, 151
Certeau, Michel de 194, 198
Cervantes, Miguel de 104, 143, 196
   Don Quijote 107, 148
   Los baños de Argel 102
   Ocho comedias 189, 195
   Pedro de Urdemalas 122
Chambers of Rhetoric (*rederijkerskamer*)
   22–3, 83–4, 137–9, *138*
Chapelain, Jean 184
   Discours sur la poesie representative 157
   Lettre sur la regle des vingt-quatre heures
    157
Chappuzeau, Samuel 142, 145–6
charities 28–9, 86–7, 138
charivari ('rough music') 21, 57
charlatans, street 74, 99–100, 121
Charles I, king of England 106, 155
Charles IX, king of France 95
Chester mystery plays 128, 137
child actors 1, 130–3
choir schools 83, 131
choreography 188, 192
Christian IV, king of Denmark 95–6
Christine of Holstein-Gottorp, Princess 95
Christine of Lorraine 79, 95
churches 19–20, 43, 102–4
Cicero 120
civic authorities (London) 87, 153
civic communities 43–5, 72–3, 128, 140
civil wars 16
classical genres 6, 130, 148, 157, 196
Clercs de la Basoche (literary society) *see*
   Basochiens
clowns *19*, 28, 94, 104, 151
   See also individual names
clubs, all-male 55–6
Cockpit-in-Court (theatre) 81
codices *118*
Cofradía de la Novena 29, 145
College of God's Gift, Dulwich 145

College of Guyenne (Bordeaux) 82–3
colonialism 32, 48, 200, 202
Columbus, Christopher 199, *200*
comedia 93, 102, 155–6
comedians 26–7, 74, 96, 104
Comédie Française 26, 87, 143
Comédiens du roi (troupe) 26, 28, 121, 184
comedies 77–8, 80, 100, 113, 121, 150
Comici Fedeli troupe 94, 140
comic scenes *80*
commedia dell'arte
    audiences 37
    background to 151–2
    characters 76, 121
    commercial skills 99, 100
    contracts 145
    patronage of 23
    performers 27, 40, 41, *134*, 195
    royal performances 95
    in Shakespeare 102
    transnational 13
    troupes 94, 128, 129, 139, 140
    visual records of 191–2
    See also Gelosi troupe
Commedia ovvero tragedia di Santa Teodora
    vergine e martire 66
commedia ridicolosa 123
commedia villanesca 81
commercial networks 16, 30, 98–102, 121
communities, of production
    adults 136–7
    childhood 130–3
    old age 144–6
    youth 133–6
Compagnia della Calze (Venice) 21, 55,
    114, 134
Compagnie de la Mère Folle (Dijon) 21, 55
compagnie laudese 33
Condell, William 146, 197
confradias (religious brotherhoods) 28–9
Confraternité de la Passion 22, 28, 86–7, 138
Congrega dei (Italian academy) 81
Congrega dei Rozzi (artisan-performers) 137
Conquest of Jerusalem (play) 25
Conquest of Rhodes (play) 25
Constantino Magno Victore (tragedy) 94
contemporary plays 102
contracts, company 141–2, 145, 194
Controversias sobre la licitud del teatro en
    España (Cotarelo y Mori) 124

convent theatre 66–7
Corbichon, Jean, *Des proprietes des choses*
    129
Cornaro, Alvise 32
Cornaro Chapel, Rome 51, *52*
Corneille, Pierre 104, 130
    Le Cid 102, 157, 183
    L'Illusion comique 133–4
coronations 94, 95–6
Corpus Christi cycles 5, 20, 29, 67
    See also mystery plays
Corpus Christi, Feast of 125, 155, 165,
    168, 202
corrales
    audiences 38, 60, 87
    background 137, 143
    classical genre 148
    design *29*, 85
    lighting 178
    performers 129, 155
Cortés, Hernán 25, 202
costume 53, 66, *68*, 69, 156
Counter-Reformation 12, 21, 67, 131
country dance 49
court entertainment 23
courtesans 40, 60–3, *61–2*
courtiers, male 53
Coventry Corpus Christi plays 33
Cromwell, Thomas 25
cross-dressing 54–8, 60, 64–7, 69, 121, 191
Cupid, depictions of *61*
Curtain Theatre, Shoreditch 87–8, 121

daily theatre 17
dancers
    country 49
    grotesque 55
    Hispaniolan 45, *46*
    hornpipe 49
    morris *19*, 189
    native *46*, 47–8, 49
    as part of play 192, 194
    Powhatan 49
    rope- 45, *46*, 121
Daniel, Samuel 106
Danti, Egnazio 171
Darnton, Robert 5, 10
Davenant, William 101
Day, John, *Travels of the Three English*
    Brothers 102

INDEX

debauchery 40–1
declamation 117
de Eglantier (Amsterdam) 137
de Goudbloem (Antwerp) 137
Dekker, Thomas
   *If This Be Not a Good Play, The Devil Is
     in It* 40
   *Late Murder of the Son upon the
     Mother . . .* 57, 58
   Old Fortunatus 102
   The Roaring Girle 58, 59, 65
   Virgin Martyr 104
Delrio, Martin 170
demons *176*
Denores, Giason 7, 8, 154, 160
De Sommi, Leone 63–4, 179
*Deux jeunes femmes qui coiferent leurs
   maris* 56
devotional rituals 41–2
diagrams, performance *166*
dialect theatre 13, 151
dissolution of the monasteries 25
docu-dramas 57–8
Domatus 168
Donne, John 145
Don Virginio Orsini 53–4
doorkeepers 38
Dovizi, Bernardo da Bibbiena, *Calandria*
   76–7, 150
dramatic philosophies 47
Du Bellay, Joachim 7
Dubreuil, Jean 178
Ducal Palace, Urbino 77
du Ryer, Isaac 64

economic, and political change 15–16
Edward VI, king of England *42*
Ehrstine, Glenn 116
Eisenbarth, Johann Andreas 99
Eisenbichler, Konrad 201
Elckerlijc (morality play) 84
Eleonore of Gonzaga, queen of Bohemia 94
Elizabethan theatre 4, 98, 152–4, 154
Elizabeth I, queen of England 43, 53, 79,
   83, 84, 96
Elizabeth of Austria, Archduchess 95
Elsdon, Anne 57–8
enchantment trope 63
Encina, Juan del 24, 31
   La pastoral 32

Enders, Jody 56
England 28–31, 152–4
Englische Komödianten (English
   Comedians) 129
English Civil War 97
engravings *24, 61–2, 74, 185–7, 200*
entertainments, unscripted 45–9
Erasmus, Desiderius 6, 105, 123, 191, 203
   Colloquies 111
   Institutio Principis Christiani 111
   Praise of Folly 112
   Stultitiae Laus 111
Ernest of Austria, Archduke 96–7
Este, Ercole I d', Duke of Ferrara 115, 139,
   150
Eucharist 41, 42
Eulenspiegel, Till 198
Euripides 6, 149
Everyman (morality play) 84

fairs, seasonal 74–75
family-run companies 140, 144
farces 22, 55–6, 75, 76, 121, 157
Farnese, Runuccio I 180, *180*
Farnese Theatre (Pilotta Palace) *180*
Fastnachtspiele (Shrovetide plays) 21
feast days, church 23, 72, 99, 135, 161, 184
   See also Corpus Christi, Feast of
Febvre, Lucien 3, 10
femininity 53
Fencing School, Gdansk 100, 128
Ferdinand II, Habsburg 94
Ferdinand III, king of Bohemia 94
Ferdinand, king of Spain 16
festival-based theatre 19–20, 33, 67, 84,
   136, 148
feudalism 16, 19, 28, 30
Field, Nathan, *Queen of Corinth* 105
Fight Between Carnival and Lent (Brueghel
   the Elder) 21
fili (poets) 26
Fiorillo, Tiberio 13
Fletcher, John
   Double Marriage 105
   Fair Maid of the Inn 37
   Faithful Shepherd 154
   Henry VIII 43, 45
   Island Princess 102
   A King and No King 154
   Queen of Corinth 105

250   INDEX

Florence 33, 37, 72, 78, *78*
Florentine Baptistry (Brunelleschi) 77
Florimène (pastoral) 47
Foire St Germain (Paris) 75
folk plays 18–19
fools 190
footwear 62, 191, *191*
Ford, John 57, 58
    Laws of Candy 105
Fortune Theatre, London 173
Forty Hours' Devotion (Chiesa del Gesu)
    161–4, *163*
Foucault, Michel 10, 11
Foxe, John, *Actes and monuments of*
    matters most speciall and memorable,
    happening in the Church . . . 42
Franciscans 25
Franco, Giacomo, *Habiti d'huomeni et*
    donne Venetiane con la processione
    della Serma Signoria et altri
    particolari . . . 44
Frankfurt Book Fair 73, 74, 75, 106
Frederick II, king of Denmark and Norway
    95
Furttenbach the Elder, Joseph 164, 179
    Architectura recreationis 171, *171*

galleries 37, 87
Gallus, Quintus Roscius *see* Quintus Roscius
    Gallus
Galluzzi, Tarquinio 170
Gammer Gurton's Needle (Mr S.) 82,
    152
Garguille, Gautier *187*
Garzoni, Tommaso 40, 63
Gascoigne, George, *Supposes* 150
Gaultier-Garguille 184, *187*
Geertz, Clifford 5, 11
Gelosi troupe 63, 64, 79, 100, 140, 149
gender 40, 53, 54, 64–67
Germany, theatre forms in 158–60, 188
gesticulation 117
Gesù, Church of the 161–4, *163*
Gettner, Johann Georg 104
Gil Vicente 24
Ginzburg, Carlo 1, 11
Giordana, Bernandrino de 79
Gl'ingannati (Intronati play) 65, 81, 153
Globe theatre 31, 39, 97, 121
Goddard, William, *Neaste of Waspes* 60

Gonzaga di Guastalla, Cesare,
    Trasformazione di Callisto e Arcade 94
Gosson, Stephen 189
Goulart, Simon 45, 47
'government' 24–5
Gramsci, Antonio 15, 148
Greek theatres 170
Greenberg, Marissa 45
Greenblatt, Stephen 9–10, 11
    Cultural Mobility: A Manifesto 13
Greene, Robert *193*
Green, John 94
Greer, Margaret 85, 194, 195
Gros Guillaume 184, *185*, 190
grotesque dance 55
Grüninger, Johannes, *Ein kurtzweilig lesen*
    von Dyl Ulenspiegel 198
Gryphius, Andreas 105–6
    Absurda Comica, oder Herr Peter
        Squentz: Schimpf-Spiel 106
    Catharina von Georgien 159
    Ein Nagelneues Spiel, traurig und lustig
        106
    Ermordete Majestat, oder Carolus
        Stuardus 106
    Leo Armenius 103, 158
Guarini, Giovanni Battista 7–8, 149, 160
    Il pastor fido 106, 154
Guastalla, Cesare Gonzaga di 94
guilds 20, 21, 23, 29, 128, 141
Guillot-Gorju 184
Guyenne, Louis duc de *118*

Hall, Edward 95
Hardy, Alexandre 28, 196
Harlequin/Arlecchino 13, *132*
    See also clowns
Harrach, Maria Josepha 107
Harrison, William, *Description of England*
    37
hearing (sense) 40, 42, 49
Heinrich Julius of Brunswick-Lüneburg 95,
    96
Helgerson, Richard 190
Heminges, John 146, 197
Henke, Robert 37
Henrietta Maria of France (later queen of
    England) 47, 54, 90, 173
Henri II, king of France 201
Henry VII, king of England 16

INDEX

Henry VIII, king of England 76, 79, 95
Henslowe, Philip 4, 101, 142, 144–5
Herneysen, Andreas *145*
Heywood, Thomas, *Apology for Actors* 120, 196
Hispaniolan dancers (native) 45, *46*
history genre 153
Hocktide plays (Coventry) 136
Holbein the Younger, Hans *112*
Holy Roman Empire 158
homosexuality 41, 61
Horace, *Ars Poetica* 117, 172, 189
hornpipe dance 49
Hôtel de Bourgogne (Paris) 38, 86–7, 139, 143, 145–6, 165
   See also Basochiens; *Comediens du roi*; *Troupe Royale*
households, private 85
Hulpeau, Charles, *Le Jeu royal de la paume* 86
humanism
   and drama 31–2, 47, 81, 111–15
   and education 25, 28, 105
   in England 152–4
   intellectuals and 6–7, 24, 158
   in Italy 149–2, 168
humourism 58
Hundred Years' War 16
Huret, Gregoire *185–7*
Hýzrle, Jindřich Michal 96–7

iconoclasm 42, *42*, *200*
idolatry 41–2, 48, 194, *200*
illiteracy 39, 90, 106
Illustre Théâtre 26, 142
il Rosso (fool) 190
imitatio (imitation). 149
improvisation 109, 122, 151, 158, 159
indigenous peoples 46, 47–8, 49, 200, 201–2
Ingegneri, Angelo 118
ingegni 161, *162*
Inghirami, Tommaso 149–50
innkeeping 101
Inns of Court (London) 21, 22, 84, 105, 134–5
inn-yards 87
intellectual networks 105–7
Ireland 32
Isabella, queen of Spain 16

Italian Order 164, 165–70, 173
Italy 75–9, 149–52
   academies 22
   amphitheatres 31
   carnivals 19
   theatres 5, 85
   troupes 28, 100
itinerant players 26–7, 78, 127–8
   See also individual troupes

Jacobean theatre 4, 65, 88, 98, 152, 154
James I, king of England 79, 83, 96, 97
Japan 67–9, 85
jesters 190, 198
Jesuit
   education plans 25, 32, 103, 130–1
   patronage 20
   theatre 67–9, 84, 94, 96, 104, 158
jeux de paume hall 85–6, *86*, 121
jigs 37, 57, 189, 192, 194
Johnson, Samuel 149
joint-stock companies 28, 30, 128, 141–2
Jones, Inigo
   and Ben Jonson 173, 201, 202
   theatre designer 47, 81, 106
Jonson, Ben
   on audiences 6–7, 143
   Bartholomew Faire 74
   Chloridia 173
   Hymenaei 201
   and Inigo Jones 201, 202
   Masque of Blackness 54, 202
   Masque of Queens 55
   The New Inn 101
   satirical comedy 154
   on Shakespeare 195, 197
   Staple of News 101
   tradesman 190
   Vision of Delight 55
Juvurra, Filippo 181

Kabuki practices (Japanese) 68
Katritzky, M. A. 191–2
Kemp, Will 74, 144, 188
   Nine Day's Wonder 19
Kerr, Rosalind 63
Kilian, Wolfgang *200*
King's Men 3, 30–1, 89, 97, 102, 197
Kirkman, Francis, *Wits, or Sport upon Sport* 97–8

kluchten farces 56
Komenský, John Amos (Comenius), *Ianua linguarum reserata* 103
   Orbis sensualium pictus: hoc est, omnium fundamentalium in mundo rerum . . . 46
Kyd, Thomas 130
   Spanish Tragedy 154

La farce de celui qui se confesse 56–7
Lanci, Baldassare 77, 78
Landi, Antonio, *Il commodo* 168
Las Casas, Bartolomé de 25
Laurana, Luciano 77
La Veniexiana (anon.) 151
Lawrenson, T. E. 165
le Conte, Valleran 28, 121, 149
Lefebvre, Mathieu 133
legacy, theatre 194–8
legal profession, and acting 21–22, 105, 134, 190
Leicester's Men (acting company) 3, 74, 87, 95–6
Leims, Thomas 67
Lenton, Francis, *Characterisimi* 84
Leo X, pope (Giovanni de' Medici) 77, 190
Lescarbot, Marc, *Theatre of Neptune in New France* 200–2
lighting 178–9
Lily, William 130
Liompardi, Zuan Polo 151
Lisi, Cesare *162*
literacy 39, 90, 106
liturgical drama 20
Locke, John 181
Lodge, Thomas 130
Lohenstein, Daniel Casper von
   Cleopatra 158, 159
   Sophonisbe 158
London playing companies 29–31
London theatre culture 98, 121–2
longue durée 5, 10, 17
Lope de Rueda 9, 28, 139
Lope de Vega, Félix
   Castigo sin venganza 156
   classical genres 119
   education 130
   Lo fingido verdadero 97, 102
   New Art of Making Comedies 148, 189

playwright 66, 104, 155, 196
   tradesman 190
Lord Chamberlain's Men *see* King's Men
Lord Mayor's Pageant 33, 73
Louis XI, king of France 16
Louis XIII, king of France 133
Louis XIV, king of France 83, 129, 157
Lovejoy, Arthur 10
Lucerne Passion Play 165
Lujan, Micaela de 66
Lully, Jean-Baptiste, *tragédie en musique*
   Armide 177, *177*
Lutherans 103
Lyly, John 31, 153

Machiavelli, Niccolò 111
   Clizia 137
   Il Principe 150
   La mandragola 79, 137, 150
McManus, Clare 54
MacNeil, Anne 63
Macropedius, *Hecastus* 5
madrigals 107
Maitre Pierre Pathelin (farce) 22
Malherbe, François de 144
Manningham, John 84
Mantua, Duke of 188
marketplaces 8, 33, 74, 99
Marlowe, Christopher
   Doctor Faustus 101–2, 104, 173
   Tamberlaine 153
marriage celebrations 79, 95, 95–6, 201
marriage, in drama 56–7, 59–60, 154
Marston, John 154
Martinelli, Drusiano 100
Martinelli, Tristano 13, 188
   Compositions de rhetorique de Mr. Don Arlequin 132
Martinez de Mora, Diego 194
martyr plays 97, 156, 158
Marx, Karl 11, 15, 28
masculinity 53
masques 54, 76, 95, 178
Massinger, Philip
   Double Marriage 105
   Queen of Corinth 105
   Renegado 102
   Roman Actor 97
   Virgin Martyr 104
Master of the Revels 22, 30, 101

INDEX

Maximilian I, Holy Roman Emperor 16
maypoles 48
Medici, Catherine de' 201
Medici family 33, 53, 66, 77
Medici, Ferdinando I de' 79, 95
Medici festivals 116
Medwall, Henry 24, 31
Meistersinger (guild) 141
Melanchthon, Philip 130
memorials 194–8
Menghini, Niccolò 161–4, *163*
Merchant Taylors Hall, London 131
Merchant Taylors' School, London 130,
139
Metastasio, Pietro 181–2
Mexico 25
Middleton, Thomas
The Roaring Girle 58, *59*, 65
satirical comedy 154
Midsummer Watch *see* Lord Mayor's
Pageant
Mikhailovich, Alexei, tsar 32
minstrels 26, *26*, 101
mise-en-scène 47
missionary theatre 25, 104
Moderata Fonte (Modesta Pozzo) 67
modernity 127–9
Molière
ambitions 157
childhood 184
commedia dell'arte 75, 76
companies of 26, 87, 130, 140–3
death of 144
humanism 158
Imaginary Invalid 144
Molina, Tirso de 155
*El burlador de Sevilla y convidado de
piedra* 156
El condenado por desconfiado 156
Moll Cutpurse *see Roaring Girle, The*
(Middleton and Dekker)
Mondor (street charlatan) 74
Montaigne, Michel de 83, 131
Monteverdi, Claudio 107
Montrose, Louis 11, 12, 153
morality plays 84, 102, 152, 156, 164–5,
166
More, Thomas 115, 140
morris dancers *19*, 189
Morrison, Fynes 75, 188, 198

Morton, Thomas 48
mosqueteros (spectators) 37, 60
Motolinía, *Historia de los Indios de Nueva
Espana* 202
mountebanks 27, 121, 139, 143
Mucedorus (play) 101
Muir, Edward 43
Mulcaster, Richard 130, 131
Mullaney, Steven 11
multilingual theatre 12–13, 75, 93, 188
Mumford, Lewis 72
mumming plays 18, 23, 95
Munday, Anthony, *Sir Thomas More* 26, 105
Muret, Marc Antoine 131
music 26, *26*, 79, 96, 107
mystery plays 20, 21, 33, 128, 137, 152

Narr, Claus 190
Nashe, Thomas 63
native dancers *46*, 47–8, 49
Nelson, Alan 82
Netherlands 22–3, 84
Nicholas of Cusa 113
Nicolas-Marc Desfontaines, *L'illustre
comedien ou Le martyre de
Saint-Genest* 102
nobility 36
nonverbal performances 49
Norton, Thomas 40
Ferrex and Porrex 152
Gorboduc 152
nueva comedia (Spain) 130

Office of the Revels 24
Ogilby, John, *America: being the latest, and
most accurate description of the New
World . . .* 45, 46
Okoń, Jan 103
Okuni, Izumo No 68–9, *68*
open-air theatres 31, 148, 173, 178, 180
opera 181
Opitz, Martin, *Buch von der Deutschen
Poeterey* 158
Orgel, Stephen 61, 65–6, 83
Impersonations 10
Orsini, Don Virginio *see* Don Virginio
Orsini
Other into Self 48, 49, 65–6
Ottonelli, Giovan Domenico 40
Ovid, *Metamorphoses* 94

254 INDEX

pageants 72, 128, 168, 201
Palais-Royal Théatre 87
Palazzo Medici, Florence *169*
Palladio, Andrea 79, 81, 150, 180–1
Palladio, Vincenzo 116
Pantalone 65, 121
Papal Court 111
Parlement de Paris 55, 87
Parma, Duke of *see* Farnese, Runuccio I
Parnassus plays 135
Pasqualigo, Luise, *Gl'intricati* 153
Passion plays 20, 72, 87, 165
pastoral drama 47, 54, 151, 153–4
patronage
    absolutist 17
    aristocratic courts 24, 29, 32
    church 102–4, 115, 164
    Italian 27, 78, 188
    royal 23–4, 54, 97, 98, 153
    Russian 32
    Spanish 31
Pellesini, Giovanni 144, 145
Pembroke's Men 142–3
performance, and preaching 42–3
performance spaces 60, 71–2, 116
performativity 15, 47, 49–50, 99–100,
    152
periaktoi (side scenes) 170, 171, *171*, 172
perspective, theatrical *167*
Peruzzi, Baldassare 77, 167
Peters, Julie 195
Petrarch 6
    De vita solitaria 110
Philip II, king of Spain 17, 124–5
Philip III, king of Spain 155
Philip IV, king of Spain 155
Piazza del Campidoglio (Rome) 150
piazza theatre 15, 27, 73, 148, 151
Pickelhering (clown) 13, 94
Pico della Mirandola, Giovanni, *De hominis
    dignitate* 110–11
Pieroni, Giovanni 94
Piissimi, Vittoria 63, 65
Pirarist college, Hungary 104
Pitti, Francesco 150
platforms 74, 85–6, 89, 170
Platter, Felix 143
Platter, Thomas 85, 97, 125, 127–8, 143–4
Plautius, Caspar, *Nova Typis Transacta
    Navigatio 200*

Plautus 76, 113–15, 196
    Braggart Soldier 82
    Epidicus 113
    Menaechmi 114, 150, 165
    Miles gloriosus 114
    Poenulus 149–50
playwrights 104, 116, 128, 189–90, 196
plazas and streets 72–5
Pléiade (poets) 7, 157
poetry 17, 64, 74, 202
    See also individual poets
poets 7, 26, 157, 190
political, and economic change 15–16,
    20
politics, and theatre 23, 95, 97–8, 111,
    201
Poliziano, Angelo, *Orfeo* 151
Pollux, Julius 170
Polonius 8, 151, 160
Pomponius Laetus, Julius 115, 130, 149
Pont Neuf 73–4, 184, *185–7*
populations, city 90
Portugal 156
Posset, John 13
poverty 28–9
preaching and performance 42–3
pre-Reformation 42, 93, 199
printing, of works 195–7, 199
Prisciani, Pellegrino, *Spectacula* 115
processions 32, 43, 44, 73
producers 4, 22, 133, 173
professional actors 22, 23, 27–8, 120–5
professional companies 28, 32, 104, 109,
    113, 139–42
proscenium arches 87, 162, 180–1
prostitution 60–3, 122
Protestantism 41–2, 103, 109, 183,
    199
public theatres 23, 37, 43, 60, 87–8
Pulcinella *123*
puppetry 98–9, 100
Puritans 97–8, 153
Puteanus, Erycius 64
Pyk, John 133

Queen's Men 30, 79, 96, 143, 144
Querelle du Cid 130, 160
Quinault, Philippe, *tragédie en musique
    Armide* 177, *177*
Quintus Roscius Gallus 120

INDEX

Rabelais, François 8, 10, 11
Racine, Jean
  Athalie 83
  Esther 157
Rana, Juan ('Gracioso') 122
Rastell, John 140
Ratio studiorum (Jesuit education plan)
  103, 130–1
Red Bull Theatre (Clerkenwell) 57
rederijkerskamer (Chambers of Rhetoric)
  22–3, 56, 83–4, 137–9
Red Lion Theatre, Whitechapel 87, 100
Reformation plays 116–17
Reformation 12, 20, 87, 164, 199
religious
  brotherhoods 28–9
  institutions 19–20
  plays 5, 19–20, 104, 202
  rituals 12, 41–3, 199
  statues 52
Renaissance theatre 113–19
  academies 81
  and Baroque era 169
  comedies 76
  features of 89
  knowledge of 184, 188
  performance environments 72
Renata (Renée) of Lorraine, Princess 95
repertoires 148–9
Representation Von S. Bonifacii
  wunderbarlichen Kampff und
  Lobwurdigen Sieg (Piarist play) 104
resources, theatrical 15–33, *18*, *18*
Reynolds, Robert 94
rhetorical texts 105
Riario, Cardinal Raffaele 115, 165
Richelieu, Cardinal 87, 156–7, 165
Riggs, David 168
Rinascimento (Italian Renaissance)
  149–51
Rinuccini, Pierfrancesco 173
Ripa, Cesare, *Iconologia* 191
Riss, Francois Nicholas 26
Rist, Johann, *Friedenswunschendes*
  Teutschland 158
rituals 12, 41–3, 43–5, 72–3, 199
Robortello, Francesco 119
Rogationtide 43
role-playing 57, 61, 134–5
role reversal 54, 55–6, 57, 58

Roman theatres 81, 85, 170
romantic comedy 153
rope-dancers 45, *46*, 121
Rotrou, Jean de, *Le Véritable Saint Genest*
  102
Rousseau, Jean-Jacques 115
Rowley, William 57, 58
  Travels of the Three English Brothers 102
royal courts
  entertainment in 47, 54, 95–6, 155, 190
  European 53, 55
  households of 75–81
  Italian 115, 139, 150, 151, 179
  patronage 23
royal entries 23, 201
Ruggiero, Guido 64
Russian patronage 32

Sabbat(t)ini, Nicola 178, 179, 189
  Pratica di fabricar scene e machine ne'
  teatri 171
Sachs, Hans 21, 102, 139, 144, *145*, 190
Sackville, Thomas
  Ferrex and Porrex 152
  Gorboduc 152
sacra rappresentazione 161, *162*, 170
St Paul's Cathedral choir, London 131
St Paul's School, London 130
San Felix, Marcela de 66
San Gallo, Bastiano da 171
Sansaburo, Nagoya 69
Santa Annunziata 161, *161*
satirical comedy 154
scaena ductilis (screen) 170
scaffolds, use of 84, 164, 165
Scala, Flaminio
  and audiences 130, 135, 148
  Il teatro delle favole rappresentative 65,
  100, 152, 195–6
Scaliger, Joseph 83
Scaliger, Julius Caesar 119, 157
Scamozzi, Vincenzo 79, 81, 85
scandal, in drama 57
scenography *80*, 169, 172–5, *174–7*, 178–9,
  181
Schepelius, Bartholomeo
  Ein Nagelneues Spiel, traurig und lustig
  106
scherzo carnevalesco 123
school drama 81–4, 94, 103–4, 130–1

Scola di Pulcinelli 123
Scott, Virginia 63
screen paintings *68*
scripts 28, 192, *193*
seating 81, 83, 86, 87, 181
Sebillot, Thomas, *Art poétique française* 139
secular plays 22, 23, 87
self-displays 43
Seneca the Younger 31, 152–3, 196
   Controversiae 105
   Hippolytus 130
   Phaedra 150
sensory perception, audience 40–1
Serlio, Sebastiano 79, *80*, 178, 180, 189
sermons, hearing 42
set design 164–70
   influences 79, 150
   machinery 94, 161, *162*, 170–8
set designers 77, *80*, 81, 85
Seven Ages of Life *129*
sexuality 40–1, 51–69
Shakespeare's Globe, Bankside 89, 165
Shakespeare, William
   As You Like It 35, 153, 158
   childhood 33, 154
   career 98, 103, 194
   Comedy of Errors 134–5
   Cymbeline 93
   First Folio 194, 197–8
   First Part of Henry VI 33
   Hamlet 26, 40, 79, 89, 134, 149, 165
   Henry VIII 43, 45
   Julius Caesar 121, 143
   Macbeth 178
   A Midsummer Night's Dream 106, 190, 203
   Othello 40, 178
   retirement 144
   Richard II 3
   Taming of the Shrew 78–9, 101, 150
   The Tempest 102, 178
   Titus Andronicus 165
   Twelfth Night 22, 84
   will of 146
   Winter's Tale 99
shamanism 69
Shepherd's Paradise (pastoral) 54
Shirley, James 90
Shoreditch theatres 71, 87–8
Siege of Jerusalem (poem) 202

sight (sense) 40, 49, 116, 165
Siglo de Oro (Golden Age) 155–6, 195
Silesian drama 159
Simons, Joseph
   Leo Armenus 103, 106
   Tragoedia quinque 103
sirens, classical 63
Sixtus IV, pope 149
Skelton, John 31
skits 37
skomorokhi (minstrels) 26, *26*
Smithfield fairs 74
Smuts, Malcolm 73
social hierarchy 28–9, 35, 36–7, 94
social relationships, portraying 123–4
Society of Jesus (Catholic Church) 109
Sommers, Will 190
Sophocles, *Oedipus Rex* 81, 85, 118, 148
Southwark theatres 60, 62
Spain 28–9, 31–2, 37, 45, 67, 142
Spanish Armada 153
Spanish Golden Age 155–6, 195
spectacles 25, 87, 95, 114, 201
spectatorship *see* audiences
Spelman, Henry 49
stage, fixed 78, 140
stage machinery 94, 161, *162*, 164–5, 170–8
stage reconstruction *162*, *169*
staging techniques 165
Stallybrass, Peter 65
stanze performances 37
statues, religious *52*
Steel, Michael 57
Steen, Jan, *Rhetoricians, The 138*
Stern, Tiffany 165, 194
Strafford, Lord Deputy of Ireland 32
Stranitzky, Joseph Anton 99
street performers 5, 15, 26, 148, 184, *185–6*
streets and plazas 72–5
Stubbes, Philip 40–1, 42–3, 189, 191
Sulpizio da Veroli, Giovanni 31
Sulpizio, Giovanni 115–16
Sun King *see* Louis XIV, king of France
sun machines *169*
Swetnam, Joseph 58
Swetnam the Woman-Hater Arraigned by Women (anon.) 58

INDEX

Tabarin (street charlatan) 74
tableaux vivants 23
Tallemant des Réaux, Gédéon 38
Tarlton, Richard 28, 144, 190, 191
Tasso, Torquato, *Aminta* 64, 151
Taylor, Charles 127
Taylor, Diana 199–200
Taylor, John, 'A Common Whore' 61–2
Teatro all'antiqua (Sabbioneta) 79
Teatro di Baldracca (Florence) 23, 27, 37
Teatro Farnese (Parma) 171–2, 180
Teatro Olimpico (Vicenza)
    background 22, 85
    design of 79, 81, 116, 118
    interior *82*, 148, 180–1
technologies, of performance 94, 161, *162*,
    164
tennis courts 85
Terence 6, 81, 115, 196
    Térence des ducs (illuminated
        manuscript) 113, 117, *118*, 167
Théâtre De Tabarin *74*
theatre districts 71–2
Théatre du Marais (Paris) 87, 143
theatre forms 158–60, 188, 200
Théatre Guénégaud 87
theatre, remembering 194–8
theatre, teaching 188–94
theatre, teaching and remembering with
    199–203
theatrical devices *171, 175*
theatrum 115, 116, 117
theatrum mundi 35, 93, 106, 111
'The Battle of Saint Pensard' (play) 21
'The Theatre' (Shoreditch) 6, 71, 87–8,
    180
Thirty Years War 75, 97, 102, 158
Thomas, Keith, *Religion and the Decline of
    Magic: Studies in Popular Beliefs in
    Sixteenth- and Seventeenth-Century
    England* 12
Torelli, Giacomo 172
Torres Naharro, Bartolomé de, *Comedia
    Soldadesca* 93, 94
tradesmen-actors 21, 98–101, 133, 184,
    190
tragedies 47, 84, 94, 151
tragicomedies 102, 149, 154
tragic scenes *80*
transvestism 56, 61, 65, 69

travelling players 127–8, 149, 159, 195
    See also itinerant players
Treatise on Architecture, Book II *80*
Trissino, Giangiorgio, *Sophonisba* 150–1
Troupe Royale 141, *185–7*
troupes 74–5, 120–1
    See also *individual companies*
Tullia d'Aragona 63
tumblers 40, *46*
Turlupin 184, *186*
Twelfth Night 76, 95
Two Ages (anon.) *134*

Udall, Nicholas, *Ralph Roister Doister* 82,
    152
Udine, Pellegrino da 167
Uffizi Theatre of the Medici 180
universities 81–4
University of Cambridge 82, 135, 152,
    153
University of Oxford 83
unscripted entertainments 45–9
urbanization 71–91, 89–91
utopianism 114–16

Vagrancy Act (1572) 101
Valerini, Adriano 64
Vasari, Giorgio 167, 168, 180
Venetians *44, 61–2*
Venice 13, *44*, 134, 151–2
Veroli, Sulpizio da 165
View of an Ideal City (attrib. Laurana) 77
village plays 19–20
violence 83
Virginia, America 49
Visscher, Claes Jansz, *View of London 88*
visual images 28, 41–2
Vitruvius, *De architettura* 6, 71, 77,
    113–15, 170

Wars of the Roses 16, 153
Weaver, Elissa 66
Webster, John 6–7, 22, 57, 58
    White Devil, The 189
Weelkes, Thomas, *Thule, the Period of
    Cosmographie* 107
Weimann, Robert 128
West End, London 88
Whitehall Palace, Westminster 79, 81, 84
Wilhelm of Bavaria, Crown Prince 95

Wilkins, George 101
    Travels of the Three English Brothers 102
Williams, Raymond 2–3
    on culture 8, 15–16, 147–8, 160
    on Marx 9, 11
wills, actors and 146
Withington, Phil 79
women
    behaviour of 37, 58, 64
    and convent theatre 66–7
    and families 140
    and fashion 191
    and illiteracy 39
    performers 40, 53–5, 61, 63, 69

    theatrical participation 37, 47, 135–6
    See also actresses
woodcuts *19*
Word of God 42

Ybarra, Patricia 202
York mystery plays 20
youth companies 21–2

Zabaleta, Juan de, *Día de fiesta por la tarde* 38
Zan Ganassa 28, 149
zanni 28
Zorzi, Ludovico 168